T0021004

GUILTY OF JOURNALISM
The Political Case Against Julian Assange

GUILTY OF JOURNALISM

The Political Case Against Julian Assange

KEVIN GOSZTOLA

Foreword by Abby Martin

Illustrations by Mr. Fish

THE CENSORED
PRESS

SEVEN STORIES

Fair Oaks, CA • New York

A JOINT PRODUCTION OF THE CENSORED PRESS
AND SEVEN STORIES PRESS

The Censored Press
PO Box 1177
Fair Oaks, CA 95628
censoredpress.org

Seven Stories Press
140 Watts Street
New York, NY 10013
sevenstories.com

LIBRARY OF CONGRESS CATALOGING-IN-PUBLICATION DATA IS ON FILE.

College professors and high school and middle school teachers may order free examination copies of Seven Stories Press titles. Visit https://www.sevenstories.com/pg/resources-academics or email academics@sevenstories.com.

9 8 7 6 5 4 3 2 1

Printed in the USA

Book design by Jon Gilbert

To journalists around the world, my colleagues,
who every day take risks—often without institutional support—
to inform the public about abuses of power:

Your independence inspires us
to confront difficult realities
and to engage in the constant struggle
for a more just and humane world.

CONTENTS

Foreword

ABBY MARTIN

When I first became aware of Julian Assange, it was a time of great hope. It was also a time of great horror.

The 9/11 attacks created a climate of dutiful stenographers and imperial apologia that allowed the Bush administration to wage war on the planet under the auspices of a never-ending "War on Terrorism." But war *is* terrorism, and the United States was committing unspeakable amounts of it under the cover of darkness.

As a freshman in college, I remember the sinking feeling in the pit of my stomach, surrounded by cheering students when the US bombed Baghdad like a video game. I remember the debilitating confusion when so-called opposition leader Nancy Pelosi said impeachment was off the table for the criminals that lied a nation into war, tortured with impunity, and shamelessly profited from their heinous acts. I felt utterly defeated, awash in a sea of propaganda and unquestioning patriotism.

The nation was on the brink at the end of George W. Bush's presidency, and President Barack Obama came in to placate the anti-war agitation. Yet the wars raged on, and the war criminals walked free. They wanted Obama to rehabilitate the empire, but WikiLeaks helped cement its true legacy.

The Iraq War Logs, heroically divulged by Chelsea Manning, dropped during this crucial time, when Americans were forced to confront the truth of what the United States government was doing in our names. The Collateral Murder video, which showed an Apache helicopter indiscriminately mowing down journalists and civilians, then firing on a rescue vehicle while soldiers laughed, changed everything. Suddenly, questioning the legality and morality of the US was mainstream.

The Logs gave proof to Iraqi society of the extent to which US forces had been killing civilians. Just as Washington, through Secretary of Defense Robert Gates, was in Baghdad trying to extend the US military presence in the country, WikiLeaks made this untenable. Who knows what turn the war could have taken were it not for these revelations?

Julian Assange boosted the potential for accountability. As an aspiring journalist, I was moved by his conviction and willingness to make great personal sacrifices to represent this powerful truth-telling effort. The overwhelming sense of despair I felt turned to hope in the potential for great change.

Authoritarian governments shook. The US Empire was unmasked, and the imperial project was in danger of unraveling. It was a time of incredible optimism and inspiring mass movements, with the Arab Spring, Occupy Wall Street, and organizations such as Anonymous and WikiLeaks using technology to take huge risks to expose the seemingly impenetrable elite.

It was during this transformative era that I moved to Washington, DC, to work at Russia Today, and came to know and appreciate the work of journalist Kevin Gosztola. I was immediately impressed with Kevin's intellect and meticulousness through his coverage of WikiLeaks.

He was one of the only journalists to report on Manning's court-martial, tirelessly documenting every detail while being one of the leading advocates for her freedom. I spoke to him frequently on my show *Breaking the Set,* about the injustices of her case as well as the plight of whistleblowers and revelations of

WikiLeaks. Ever since then, he has been my primary source for these pivotal subjects.

Kevin's coverage of Assange is built on his coverage of Manning's court-martial. Weaving in what he recalls from the Manning case adds an extra level of credibility to his journalism on Assange.

Years after the liberal establishment—who once heaped praise upon Assange—abandoned him in droves, Kevin has not relented in his dedication to the case. He is one of the only journalists to provide ongoing and consistent coverage of the intricacies of Assange's trial, which Kevin reports with impressive depth and honesty.

He warned us years ago of the profound implications that indicting Assange would have, and the story he tells here should serve as a beacon for us.

For years, the US government has prosecuted whistleblowers with extreme prejudice. No one embarrasses the Empire without paying dearly in prison. But Assange was only publishing the leaks. He never committed any crime. He only published evidence of the crimes. WikiLeaks released more classified information than the rest of the world's media combined, which is a testament to the utter failure of the world's media to fulfill their primary function—hold power to account.

After being told he was a Russian agent since 2016, the indictment and extradition against Assange today has nothing to do with the 2016 election or Russia. It has everything to do with the Iraq and Afghanistan War logs. Exposing war crimes and war criminals. Tainting the image of the United States. Showing the world this is how the US imposes its world order under the hypocritical banner of "human rights" and "democracy."

They've come at Assange with the full brunt of their power because they have to set fear in the rest of us. They have to instill a chilling effect that will reverberate for generations: this is what can happen to you if you try to replicate Assange's work. This can be your fate, if you dare to challenge us.

Today, the model they used to discredit Assange is now deployed against anyone in the media who contradicts official war narratives.

The burgeoning hope of transparency and accountability of the WikiLeaks era has been extinguished. The internet is now carefully curated and crafted for us by tech overlords, who work hand in hand with state forces.

Assange's story is of major historical importance—both for exposing the crimes of the past and setting a precedent for the future. Against a wall of coverage that aims to attack and discredit him, works such as this book, which accurately document his case, are essential for today and for tomorrow.

We need to organize the resistance to the Empire with eyes wide open, and that cannot happen without this story being properly told. The ramifications of his case for journalists everywhere will keep imperial crimes in the shadows, and if we simply give up and allow Assange to wither away in that black box, this country is beyond saving. Prosecuting Assange will be its death knell.

Introduction

Behind these prison walls there's a man who's won awards
For the work that he has done and all that it affords
Such as the knowledge of the horrors committed in our name
They can't stop the message, so the messenger gets blamed
—DAVID ROVICS, "Behind These Prison Walls" (2021)

During the first months of Donald Trump's presidency, he was furious over what he described as "criminal" leaks from within his administration.[1] He took to Twitter and exclaimed, "Leaking, and even illegal classified leaking, has been a big problem in Washington for years."

The "failing" *New York Times* "must apologize!" Trump demanded. He added, "The spotlight has finally been put on the low-life leakers!"[2]

News sources faced an increase in the number of investigations and prosecutions by the Justice Department (DOJ). Yet as Margaret Sullivan wrote for the *Washington Post*, this was largely the "fault of the Obama administration," which "created a blueprint" that was "easy to follow."

President Barack Obama shared Trump's zeal for identifying leakers. According to journalist Jonathan Alter, Obama had "one pet peeve that could make him lose his cool." He despised leaks.[3]

In Obama's first year, he complained that disagreements about the war in Afghanistan were publicized in newspapers. Alter recalled, "Naturally in Washington nearly every time he got upset about leaks it leaked."

"Leaks offended Obama's sense of discipline and reminded him of everything he disliked about the capital," Alter noted. "He was fearsome on the subject, which seemed to bring out his controlling nature to an even greater degree than usual."

The Obama administration cast itself as the "most transparent administration ever" while refining a system of secrecy that aided officials in concealing military matters and national security programs. It stymied reform of the Freedom of Information Act (FOIA) and censored or withheld a record number of files from disclosure. It pursued federal lawsuits to block the release of photos showing alleged torture and abuse, documents related to kill lists and drone warfare, and videos of force-feedings of prisoners at Guantánamo Bay.

While wielding the Espionage Act of 1917 to prosecute more individuals for unauthorized disclosures than all previous presidential administrations combined, the Obama administration instituted an "insider threat" program that further discouraged whistleblowers from risking their livelihoods to expose corruption.

This secrecy regime aided the Obama administration in entrenching policies of perpetual war, pioneering an assassination program for executing terrorism suspects away from the battlefield, preserving powers of indefinite military detention, and shielding military officers, security agents, and former government officials from prosecution for their role in torture and war crimes.

When the DOJ recommitted itself to prosecuting WikiLeaks founder Julian Assange, officials revived a massive grand jury investigation that had been undertaken by Obama and never publicly shut down by Attorney General Eric Holder. That made it easy for the government to take the unprecedented step of charging a publisher with violating the Espionage Act.

Thanks to Obama, Trump did not have to engage in a power

grab to amass the authority to undermine civil liberties and trample over human rights.

From Manning to Assange

This book is the culmination of more than a decade of journalism that goes back to the time when the "Collateral Murder" video and more than 700,000 documents from Chelsea Manning were published by WikiLeaks.

In May 2010, I graduated from Columbia College Chicago with a bachelor's degree in film and video, and moved into a studio apartment with my wife, Julie. My plan after college was to make documentary films. I understood that would not produce income immediately. However, my father gave me a digital video camera for a graduation gift. The camera made it possible to accept gigs where I recorded weddings, graduations, birthday parties, bar mitzvahs, and the like. I also planned to produce videos for nonprofit organizations.

I must have known this would go nowhere because I spent more of my time writing articles at a website founded by Rob Kall called OpEdNews. In fact, rather than engage in the lifestyle typical of college, I stayed in my dorm and wrote about the war in Iraq and the final years of President George W. Bush's administration. After Obama's election, my focus turned to his administration's continuation of policies in the "Global War on Terrorism." I republished my articles to various communities in the blogosphere and developed an audience.

Throughout college, I met several longtime antiwar activists in Chicago and attended meetings where marches against the Iraq and Afghanistan wars were planned. During the fall of 2010, a scholar named Michael Busch, who writes for *Foreign Policy in Focus*, encouraged me to apply for an internship at *The Nation* magazine. I was granted an internship and traveled cross-country to gain experience in a New York newsroom.

The magazine assigned me to journalist Greg Mitchell, who joined *The Nation* after running *Editor & Publisher,* a trade publication focused on the newspaper industry. From January to June 2011, I helped Greg maintain a live blog that tracked the latest developments with WikiLeaks. I took advantage of my position at *The Nation* and produced my own coverage of the US embassy cables that WikiLeaks published. Greg also invited me to collaborate with him on his self-published books, *The Age of WikiLeaks* (2011) and *Private Manning: Truth and Consequences* (2011).

The Nation launched VideoNation after I convinced them to allow me to produce short interviews with my video camera. One clip featured Ethan McCord, a US soldier who appeared in the "Collateral Murder" video.

I did not act like I was an intern. Multiple times, I published posts critical of *Nation* contributors. While completing tasks that I was assigned, I drafted daily articles at my cubicle in the *Nation* office, because Greg linked to anything related to WikiLeaks that I published. When I launched a weekly podcast called *This Week in WikiLeaks*, Greg linked to my interviews with journalists, lawyers, and advocates in his live blog.

In May 2011, I received an invitation from Alyona Minkovski's RT show after they read my scathing review of the PBS's WikiLeaks documentary called *WikiSecrets*. I was invited to come to RT's New York studio for an interview and left the office early to appear on television—a rare opportunity for a magazine intern.

The internship ended in June, and I left the magazine without any plan for the future. However, I had a scholarship through a progressive group called Democracy For America to attend the Netroots Nation conference in Minneapolis, June 16-19. I received a call while I was in Minneapolis from a staff member of the collaborative news site Firedoglake (FDL). They were familiar with my work because FDL had a community section where I regularly republished my articles while I was at the *Nation.*

FDL editor-in-chief Jane Hamsher invited me to lunch. Jane, a former movie producer, founded the website in 2004. It garnered praise for its coverage of the CIA scandal in which Valerie Plame, a covert officer, had her identity leaked to the press. *The New York Times* lauded Jane, Marcy Wheeler, and her team for their reporting on the Scooter Libby trial.

"With no audio or video feed permitted, the Firedoglake 'live blog' has offered the fullest, fastest public report available. Many mainstream journalists use it to check on the trial," *Times* journalist Scott Shane wrote.

FDL needed someone to replace Marcy, who blogged about national security and civil liberties issues. I was offered a salaried position, and I immediately accepted. We developed The Dissenter, which turned into a vibrant online space that not only picked up where Marcy left off but also covered grassroots protests such as the Occupy Movement.

In January 2011, Jane had driven David House, the founder of the Chelsea Manning Support Network, to visit Manning while she was detained at the Quantico Marine brig. Jane used FDL to create a record of each interview given by FBI informant Adrian Lamo, who helped agents obtain a confession from Manning during online chats. FDL was one of the best places to continue my work on all things related to WikiLeaks.

When an unfortunate set of circumstances led WikiLeaks to suddenly publish more than 130,000 cables on August 29, 2011, I dug through the cables with various journalists and activists throughout the world and used the hashtag #wlfind to amplify what I uncovered. One document I stumbled across was a communications log on a United Nations special rapporteur's inquiry into the executions of ten Iraqis. The WikiLeaks Twitter account shared it with their million-plus followers, and then journalist Glenn Greenwald, academic Norman Finkelstein, and others called attention to the log.

John Glaser of Antiwar.com was the first to write a report on it.[4] McClatchy Newspapers reporter Matthew Schofield had initially reported on the massacre in 2006, and the media organization published a follow-up.[5] *Democracy Now!* resurfaced an interview with Schofield from 2006 on the incident.[6] By October, the communications log played a role in the Iraqi government's decision to deny US soldiers immunity from prosecution if the occupation continued beyond 2011. President Obama refused to expose soldiers to potential liability and withdrew "virtually all troops," which effectively ended the Iraq War.[7]

Manning had a hearing in December 2011 at Fort Meade, where a military judge reviewed the charges against her before sending them to a court-martial. I carried on FDL's tradition of live blogging and attended the proceedings. (When Pentagon Papers whistleblower Daniel Ellsberg attended the fourth day of the hearing, I gave him a ride back to DC.)

Jane committed FDL's funds and resources to covering every phase of Manning's court-martial. I flew from Chicago to DC regularly and lived with Jane during the summer of 2013 as the trial unfolded.

Part of the story became the lack of interest among prestige media outlets. I was one of a handful of journalists who attended proceedings during each phase of Manning's court-martial. That caught the attention of Arun Rath, who was following the case for PBS *Frontline.*

"One reporter had the scoop on the day after the 2012 election, when the lawyer for [Chelsea] Manning, the young Army private accused of leaking more than 500,000 classified documents to WikiLeaks, stood up in the courtroom and announced that Manning would be taking responsibility for [disclosing] some of the documents," Rath wrote. "With no mainstream reporter in attendance, suddenly, Gosztola was being called upon and linked to by news organizations all over the world, including Frontline."[8]

Even when prestige media sent reporters or producers to help them track developments, they found the court-martial to be either too dull or too complex. One *Washington Post* reporter turned to me multiple times with questions because they were not certain of what was said in court. A CNN producer gained notoriety for constantly sleeping in the Fort Meade media center while proceedings were broadcast.

The Center for Constitutional Rights asked me before Manning's trial to join journalists Glenn Greenwald, Amy Goodman, Jeremy Scahill, Chase Madar, and Assange in challenging the US Army's restrictions on access to basic court filings in Manning's case. CCR argued the restrictions violated the First Amendment and undermined the legitimacy of the court-martial.

Often, I had only one opportunity to write or transcribe something read in court accurately so that it could then be shared with my readers. This was not easy because I had to scramble to keep up with a military judge, who read each court filing into the record to make up for the fact that the Army thought sunlight was the best poison rather than the best disinfectant.

Fellow reporters frequently came together to compare notes since the Army would not provide us with actual copies of the documents. The scene was similar to a high school classroom with students whispering to each other to make sure they had all the details necessary to pass a semester exam.

We did not win our lawsuit for transparency, but a week into the trial the Army posted thousands of pages online in a FOIA reading room. I believe our lawsuit played a part in pressuring the Army to come up with a system during this major trial that would help reporters and somewhat promote open justice.

I joined several people in taking the *New York Times* to task for not sending a reporter to cover the court-martial, including the hearing where Manning took the stand to testify about abusive treatment she endured at Quantico. The criticism led Margaret Sullivan, who was the *Times* public editor, to write, "In failing to send its own reporter to cover the fascinating and important pretrial testimony of [Chelsea] Manning, The New York Times missed the boat."[9]

"Giving so little coverage to the hearing is simply weird. This is a compelling story, and an important one," Sullivan added.[10]

On one of the few occasions when the *Times* did have a journalist in the courtroom, I noticed they did not grasp what had happened and incorrectly reported, "The judge, Col. Denise Lind, said the government had provided sufficient evidence to prove beyond a reasonable doubt that Private Manning knowingly gave information to certain enemy groups, [such] as al Qaeda, when [she] passed hundreds of thousands of documents to WikiLeaks in 2009."

I convinced the *Times* to print two corrections. "An earlier version of this article stated incorrectly the year Pfc. [Chelsea] Manning passed hundreds of thousands of documents to WikiLeaks. It was 2010, not 2009," the *Times* acknowledged.

Four days later, the newspaper of record conceded that it had "incorrectly characterized the ruling of the military judge at the trial." Judge Lind had denied a defense request to dismiss the "aiding the enemy" charge, but as the *Times* now acknowledged, Lind had not determined "beyond a reasonable doubt" that Manning "knowingly gave information" to terrorists.

Several times I appeared on the independent news program *Democracy Now!*. "You're speaking to us from your car in the Fort Meade parking lot. That is where the court-martial is taking place, right next to the parking lot," Goodman said. "It also is the headquarters of the National Security Agency. And, Kevin, we can't stress enough how significant it is that you're one of the few reporters that have been there from the beginning."[11]

Manning was found guilty on July 30, 2013, of committing nearly every offense, but crucially, the military judge acquitted her of "aiding the enemy."

While covering the Manning case, Jesselyn Radack, a whistleblower advocate, introduced me to NSA whistleblower Thomas Drake and CIA whistleblower John Kiriakou. Both were indicted under the Espionage Act. I expanded my journalism to include regular coverage of the wider war on whistleblowers and increased efforts in government to crack down on leaks.

John accepted a plea agreement in October 2012, and in February 2013, he reported to prison to serve a thirty-month sentence. At Federal Correctional Institution Loretto in Pennsylvania, he penned several "Letters from Loretto" that were sent to me and published at FDL. John and his family were supported by FDL throughout his incarceration.

FDL shut down in 2015, and I co-founded Shadowproof with Brian Nam-Sonenstein, who had worked on action campaigns for the website. We inherited the FDL archive, and I chose to continue the work of The Dissenter. At one point, Jesselyn connected me with Holly Sterling, the wife of CIA whistleblower Jeffrey Sterling, and asked me to write a story about the fact that the federal prison where Jeffrey was completing a sentence denied him health care for a heart condition.

In 2017, I covered NSA whistleblower Reality Winner, who was charged with violating the Espionage Act. I traveled to Augusta,

Georgia, to report on multiple hearings. Again, I was one of a few reporters to cover every phase of the case.

On April 11, 2019, when Assange was arrested and an indictment against him was unveiled by the DOJ, I renewed my focus on a story that I had already covered extensively. In February 2020, right before the COVID-19 pandemic, I traveled to London to report on an extradition hearing where lawyers from the Crown Prosecution Service and Assange's legal team argued over whether the US–UK extradition treaty gave the UK government the authority to hand Assange over to the US government.

I launched the *Dissenter Newsletter* in July 2020 to expand my coverage of this as well as stories of whistleblowers and the obstacles they face. It was designed to make up for the lack of consistent reporting in the news media.

The pandemic dramatically altered a four-week extradition trial that was held in September 2020. Instead of traveling to London, I woke up every day at 3:30 a.m. for a month to cover the proceedings remotely from my Chicago apartment. Yet again, I was one of the few reporters in the United States to produce daily reports so the public could follow all the testimony from witnesses.

A Guidebook for Following the US Trial

In this book, you will find things that cannot be said in a United States courtroom. Much as whistleblowers are barred from describing their motives at Espionage Act trials, Assange and his legal team will likely be barred from sharing their motives and speaking to the rot at the core of this case.

The political case against Assange is complex. It has many layers, like an onion, and to fully grasp what is at the core, one must peel away each of the layers.

I organized the book thematically. Each chapter methodically unravels each layer of the US government's unprecedented and political case against a journalist. This way, anyone unfamiliar with the Assange saga can follow the various threads.

The chapters form a guide that will live on as a resource before, during, and after Assange's US trial, should it occur. They also collectively illustrate why it is hard to believe that Assange will have access to fair justice.

Chapter One consists of the charges and allegations against Assange. It outlines the government's main arguments for prosecution and the initial reaction of journalists, media organizations, and press freedom groups to each indictment.

Chapter Two and Chapter Three draw from my reporting on the Chelsea Manning court-martial. I recount evidence from Manning's court-martial that was presented by military prosecutors, which contradicts the US government's theory of events in the Assange case. I also explore how military prosecutors and the US military agencies viewed WikiLeaks at the time.

Chapter Four provides an overview of Espionage Act prosecutions from Obama to Trump. The chapter specifically shows how each case informed the next and brought prosecutors to the point where they charged a publisher.

Chapter Five focuses on the Central Intelligence Agency's war on WikiLeaks, which became a driving force for charging Assange, and Chapter Six documents the actions of Undercover Global, the private security company that spied on Assange while he was living in the Ecuador embassy in London. The CIA received access to audio and video collected by the company contracted by the government of Ecuador to provide security.

Chapter Seven offers an overview of the role the FBI played in targeting Assange and WikiLeaks, including the bureau's decision to enlist a criminal sociopath and disenchanted WikiLeaks volunteer named Sigurdur Thordarson as their informant.

Chapter Eight details the federal grand jury investigation against WikiLeaks, which was empaneled by Attorney General Eric Holder in 2010. The DOJ's efforts culminated in an attempt by a grand jury to coerce two WikiLeaks sources—Manning and activist Jeremy Hammond—into testifying against the media organization. Both refused to testify until the grand jury was dissolved. They were jailed.

Chapter Nine goes through revelations from the documents Assange and WikiLeaks published to illustrate the extent to which torture, rendition, and war crimes by the US government were exposed. US officials went to great lengths to hide this information. A body of evidence suggests Assange was charged in retaliation.

Chapter Ten highlights several whistleblowers who were imprisoned after they were convicted of violating the Espionage Act. Despite the sanitized descriptions of confinement from prosecutors, this is the reality of what Assange will endure in a US jail or prison.

Chapter Eleven features testimony submitted in the extradition trial from journalists who partnered with Assange. Along with press freedom advocates, each journalist makes it clear that Assange engaged in standard news-gathering practices.

Chapter Twelve lays out instances of media organizations such as the *New York Times*, CNN, and the *Guardian* aiding and abetting the US prosecution against Assange. The examples come from prosecutors and the Westminster Magistrates' Court judgment in the United Kingdom, which paved the way for Assange's extradition (even though the extradition request was initially denied).

Chapter Thirteen deals with the US media and political establishment's belief that Assange and WikiLeaks helped Russia interfere in the 2016 election. Democrats and Republicans fueled a climate for prosecutors that made it harder to oppose the prosecution of a journalist. In 2020, Russia's invasion of Ukraine only helped those hostile to WikiLeaks and calls to President Joe Biden and Attorney General Merrick Garland to drop the charges went ignored.

The Appendix lists thirty significant WikiLeaks publications from 2009-2020, which further illustrate WikiLeaks' vast contribution to the world's knowledge.

Throughout the book, I use the term "prestige media" when referring generally to mass media such as the *New York Times*, CNN, and *Politico*. Jules Boykoff used the term in his book *Beyond Bullets: The Suppression of Dissent in the United States*, and it captures how these media organizations tend to look down on those who engage in "oppositional activities" that go "beyond sanctioned forms of action."[12]

A US Client State Secures Assange's Extradition

The extradition request against Assange slowly wound its way through the British courts from June 2019 to June 17, 2022, when Home Secretary Priti Patel approved the request.[13] It was another dark day for press freedom. Assange's legal team appealed the decision, but they had little faith in the process. Assange and his legal team believed he would most likely be brought to the US for trial by 2023.

All along, the possibility that the British judiciary would stand up for human rights and challenge the power of the United States was slim. District Judge Vanessa Baraitser accepted the argument put forward by the Crown Prosecution Service that WikiLeaks was a criminal enterprise.

Crown prosecutors maintained that WikiLeaks was an ideologically motivated entity in the "business of encouraging individuals to hack into computers." Further, they charged,

"WikiLeaks' very purpose and design was to recruit persons to break the law—by circumventing classification restrictions and computer and access restrictions."

Baraitser wrote, "[Assange] was acting to further the overall objective of WikiLeaks to obtain protected information, by hacking if necessary. Notwithstanding the vital role played by the press in a democratic society, journalists have the same duty as everyone else to obey the ordinary criminal law. In this case Mr. Assange's alleged acts were unlawful and he does not become immune from criminal liability merely because he claims he was acting as a journalist."[14]

Yet, in spite of this conclusion, Baraitser spared Assange's life and denied the extradition request on January 4, 2021. She was persuaded that Assange would likely be imprisoned in ADX Florence Colorado, a supermax prison, where he would be held under harsh confinement conditions with "special administrative measures," or SAMs, authorized by the US attorney general.

"I am satisfied that, in these harsh conditions, Mr. Assange's mental health would deteriorate causing him to commit suicide with the 'single minded determination' of his autism spectrum disorder," Baraitser declared. "I find that the mental condition of Mr. Assange is such that it would be oppressive to extradite him to the United States of America."

"We are immensely relieved that Julian Assange will not be extradited to the US," stated Rebecca Vincent, the director of international campaigns for Reporters Without Borders (RSF). "At the same time, we are extremely disappointed that the court failed to take a stand for press freedom and journalistic protections, and we disagree with the judge's assessment that the case was not politically motivated and was not centered on journalism and free speech."

Nils Muižnieks, Europe Director for the global human rights

organization Amnesty International, similarly responded, "The fact that the ruling is correct and saves Assange from extradition does not absolve the UK from having engaged in this politically-motivated process at the behest of the USA . . . It has set a terrible precedent for which the US [government] is responsible, and the UK government is complicit."

Although Baraitser determined extraditing Assange would be oppressive for mental health reasons, two days later she sided with the US government and kept the WikiLeaks founder detained at Her Majesty's Prison Belmarsh while the US pursued an appeal. This ensured that he would not emerge from nearly a decade of arbitrary detention and speak to the press. And, most of all, it meant that Assange still could not live with his new family— Stella, whom he married at Belmarsh in March 2022, and their two children, Gabriel and Max.

US officials such as Secretary of State Antony Blinken refused to answer questions about the Assange case because there was an "ongoing legal process," and they needed to "let the legal system work." However, the US State Department did intervene, sending a letter to the UK's Foreign Office with "diplomatic assurances" to salvage the extradition case. A second letter reminded the UK government of the two nations' "long history of cooperation" on "extradition matters."[15]

Amnesty International recognized that the assurances barely diminished the risk of inhumane treatment. For example, the US government promised the UK government that Assange would not be confined at ADX Florence or subject to SAMs. But these pledges gave the US the "discretion" to place Assange in a maximum-security facility and impose SAMs (which include solitary confinement) if he did "something subsequent to the offering of these assurances that meets the tests for the imposition of SAMs or designation to ADX."[16]

"Such latitude to alter the terms of the core assurances after Assange's transfer to the US renders them irrelevant from the start," Amnesty International stated. "The prohibition on torture and other ill-treatment—including prolonged solitary confinement—is absolute and cannot be conditioned on a person's conduct."

On International Human Rights Day, the UK High Court of Justice granted the US government's appeal and overturned the lower court decision that had blocked extradition.

"The United Kingdom and the USA have a long history of cooperation in extradition matters, and the USA has in the past frequently provided, and invariably fulfilled, assurances," the High Court ruled. "There is no reason why this court should not accept the assurances as meaning what they say. There is no basis for assuming that the USA has not given the assurances in good faith."[17]

Lord Chief Justice Ian Burnett, who authored the decision, was a "close friend of Sir Alan Duncan, the former foreign minister who called Assange a 'miserable little worm' in parliament." They had known each other "since their student days at Oxford in the 1970s," according to the media organization Declassified UK.[18]

Duncan was a "key official in the UK government campaign to force Assange from the embassy." Through a feed in an "operations room" in the UK Foreign Office, Duncan watched the British police drag Assange from the Ecuador embassy to a van on April 11.

"I do millions of interviews trying to keep the smirk off my face," Duncan wrote in his diary. He later traveled to Ecuador to thank President Lenín Moreno for expelling Assange.[19]

The UK Supreme Court refused to consider Assange's appeal on March 14, 2022. When the Westminster Magistrates' Court ordered Assange's extradition on April 20 and sent it to Home Secretary Priti Patel for her stamp of approval, a grim reality crystallized.

The British judiciary was captured. Judges were uninterested and unwilling to act contrary to US power. They put close relations between the US and UK governments ahead of human rights.

Or worse, the judges were entirely supportive of the US effort to extradite a journalist for trial because in their minds he was not a journalist who deserved protection.

"This is the outcome that we have been concerned about for the last decade. This decision is a grave threat to freedom of speech, not just for Julian but for every journalist and editor and media worker in [the UK]," declared Jennifer Robinson, an Assange attorney.

Assange's legal team submitted two appeals in June after the UK government authorized extradition. One specifically challenged Patel's decision and the other challenged Judge Baraitser's decision.[20]

On human rights grounds, his attorneys maintained the district judge was wrong to determine extradition would not deny his right to fair trial, his right to be free from inhuman and degrading treatment, his right to freedom of expression, and his right to be free from a novel and unforeseeable extension of the law.

Further grounds of appeal included a claim that Baraitser failed to recognize that the US government "misrepresented" facts in the case and that the case was "pursued for ulterior political motives." They also argued she had not properly factored in the manner in which the "passage of time" had compounded the unjust prosecution.

As the UK High Court of Justice considered whether to grant Assange a hearing on his appeals, the government mourned the death of Queen Elizabeth II and police cracked down on numerous citizens who dared to speak ill of the monarchy. Prime Minister Boris Johnson resigned, and Liz Truss took over as prime minister after the Conservative Party held a vote in which less than 0.3 percent of the population were allowed to participate.[21]

CHAPTER 1

Charges and Allegations

I was a patsy
In a world gone wrong
Because I revealed
That the truth was a lie.
—LEO SAYER, "The Wrong Man" (2014)

Julian Assange is a journalist.

As defined by the Committee to Protect Journalists (CPJ), a press freedom organization based in the United States, journalists are "people who cover news or comment on public affairs through any media—including in print, in photographs, on radio, on television, and online."[1]

Assange is a member of the International Federation of Journalists, which is the world's largest federation of journalists. Since 2010, he has also been a member of the Media Entertainment and Arts Alliance, a trade union in Australia.

Between 2010 and 2017, Assange appeared numerous times on news networks such as CNN and Al Jazeera English to comment on WikiLeaks publications as well as public affairs, such as National Security Agency (NSA) whistleblower Edward Snowden, NSA surveillance, and internet freedom. He frequently appeared on the independent news program *Democracy Now!* to discuss Google, corruption within US security agencies, and even the Catalonia independence movement in Spain.

James Goodale was the general counsel for the *New York Times*.

In 1971, Goodale argued the *Times* had a First Amendment right to publish the Pentagon Papers. According to Goodale, "Assange sought out secret information by setting up a private website for the anonymous transmission of information to him. Journalists asking sources to reveal secrets is the essence of journalism."[2]

WikiLeaks, a media organization, accepted documents voluntarily provided by sources, which is a standard news-gathering practice. Assange and other WikiLeaks staff verified the documents' authenticity, then prepared the documents for publication on the WikiLeaks website.

Assange has no US ties. He has never lived in the US. He has no allegiance to the country, which has officials hell-bent on prosecuting him. The WikiLeaks founder is an Australian citizen.

Each of the charges against Assange represents an extraterritorial application of US laws. They are the product of a superpower run by elites, who believe they have the legitimate and moral authority to enforce US laws against anyone deemed a threat to America's agenda.

Unlike government employees or contractors accused of violating the Espionage Act of 1917, Assange never applied to work for a US military branch or security agency. He never signed a nondisclosure agreement that required him to keep classified information from that branch or agency secret. He never received training on how to protect state secrets, nor did any supervisors advise him that if he shared sensitive documents with the press he would face serious consequences.

In the US, there is no law against publishing classified information. That is largely due to the First Amendment, which historically discouraged officials from following through on threats to prosecute journalists. On the other hand, in the United Kingdom, where Assange was detained at Her Majesty's Prison Belmarsh, journalists are subject to the Official Secrets Acts, which criminalizes anyone who disseminates information "deemed to be damaging to national security."[3]

"Computer Hacking Conspiracy"

The first charge against Assange was drafted on March 6, 2018, and alleged that the WikiLeaks founder engaged in conspiracy to commit computer intrusion. The charge fell under the Computer Fraud and Abuse Act and a general section of the US criminal code used against individuals who "conspire to defraud" the US government.[4]

While prosecutors referred to it as a "computer hacking conspiracy," language in the indictment from the Justice Department (DOJ) was similar to language prosecutors typically include in Espionage Act charges against government employees or contractors accused of leaks to the news media.[5] Prosecutors singled out Assange as an "aider" and "abettor" of espionage for publishing unauthorized disclosures of classified information.

"The WikiLeaks website publicly solicited submissions of classified, censored, and other restricted information," the indictment stated. "Assange, who did not possess a security clearance or need to know, was not authorized to receive classified information of the United States."

On March 8, 2010, according to the indictment, Assange agreed to "assist" US Army intelligence analyst Chelsea Manning in "cracking a password" that was stored on Defense Department computers connected to the Secret Internet Protocol Network, a network the government uses to share and store information databases.

"At the time he entered into this agreement, Assange knew that Manning was providing WikiLeaks with classified records containing national defense information of the United States. Assange was knowingly receiving such classified records from Manning for the purpose of publicly disclosing them on the WikiLeaks website."

The DOJ maintained, "Cracking the password would have allowed Manning to log on to the computers under a username that did not belong to her. Such a deceptive measure would have made it more difficult for investigators to determine the source of the illegal disclosures."

By this point, Manning had already provided WikiLeaks with copies of two databases on the wars in Afghanistan and Iraq, which contained hundreds of thousands of military incident reports. These were released as the "Afghanistan War Logs" and "Iraq War Logs."

Referring to alleged chat messages between Manning and a username that prosecutors claim was associated with Assange, the indictment further accused the WikiLeaks founder of "actively encouraging Manning to provide more information." It highlighted an exchange in which Manning said, "After this upload, that's all I really have got left." Assange allegedly replied, "Curious eyes never run dry in my experience."

Manning possessed a "top secret" security clearance. The DOJ acknowledged she was authorized to access all of the classified documents she submitted to WikiLeaks, but it accused her of "attempting to bypass or circumvent security mechanisms on government-provided information systems."

Journalists who publish classified information are not required to have security clearances. Nonetheless, prosecutors emphasized that Assange did not possess a security clearance and maintained he was never authorized to receive classified information.

Along with criminalizing Assange for publishing classified documents on the WikiLeaks website, prosecutors described the use of a "special folder on a cloud dropbox of WikiLeaks" as a part of the alleged conspiracy.

Many of the headlines from establishment news media spread the DOJ's accusations of a "hacking conspiracy" without acknowledging the implications that the charge could have on freedom of the press. Several outlets defended, or even cheered, the indictment.

Charlie Savage of the *New York Times* wrote of the potential threat to press freedom, "For now, the case significantly reduces such concerns because it is outside traditional investigative journalism to help sources try to break passcodes so they can illegally hack into government computers."[6] He had previously reported on the Manning court-martial for the *Times* but failed to incorporate key details from the proceedings in his coverage of the Assange indictment.

The Economist endorsed the extradition. "The central charge— computer hacking—is an indefensible violation of the law. Neither journalists nor activists, like Mr Assange, have carte blanche to break the law in exercising their First Amendment rights. They are entitled to publish freely; not to break and enter, physically or digitally, to do so."[7]

"If you look at the indictment, on a very narrow charge of computer hacking conspiracy, it's evident that the government stayed well clear of the dangerous notion of prosecuting a publisher for publishing. And, if anything, Assange might get exactly the fight he's looking for, served up to him by the government he purports to loathe," Jack Shafer wrote in *Politico*. He additionally insisted the indictment was a "long way from anything that would scare off journalists from changing the way they do their jobs."[8]

For the *Atlantic*, neoconservative columnist Michael Weiss advocated for Assange's prosecution: "The U.S. accuses him of instructing [Manning] to hack the Pentagon, and offering to help. This is not an undertaking any working journalist should attempt without knowing that the immediate consequence will be the loss of his job, his reputation, and his freedom at the hands of the FBI."[9]

Weiss continued, "If he is innocent of hacking U.S. government systems—or can offer a valid public interest defense for the hacking—then let him have his day in court, first in Britain and then in America. But don't continue to fall for his phony pleas for sympathy, his megalomania, and his promiscuity with the facts. Julian Assange got what he deserved."

An affidavit from FBI special agent Megan Brown attached to the conspiracy charge laid bare the indifference and naïveté of US pundits. It showed prosecutors were targeting Assange for publishing war logs from Iraq and Afghanistan.

Brown, who was assigned to the "counterespionage squad" at the FBI's Washington Field Office in the District of Columbia, was tasked with sifting through information to compile the "basis" for a case against Assange.

"Documents included in the Afghanistan War reports contained information the disclosure of which potentially endangered U.S. troops and Afghan civilians, and aided enemies of the United States," Brown declared. "Numerous ['Secret'] reports, for example, related to the identity and significance of local supporters of United States and coalition forces in Iraq and Afghanistan."[10]

On July 30, 2010, the *Times* published a blog post by Robert Mackey with the headline "Taliban Study WikiLeaks to Hunt Informants."[11] The post was incorporated into Brown's summary of "probable cause" for prosecuting Assange.

"After the release of the Afghanistan War reports, a member of the Taliban contacted the New York Times and stated, 'We are studying the report. We knew about the spies and people who collaborate with U.S. forces. We will investigate through our own secret service whether the people mentioned are really spies working for the U.S. If they are U.S. spies, then we will know how to punish them,'" Brown recalled.

If Assange is Guilty of Aiding Al Qaeda, the *New York Times* is Guilty as Well

The FBI's Megan Brown referenced the raid of al Qaeda leader Osama bin Laden's compound in Abbottabad, Pakistan, on May 2, 2011. This raid was invoked in the US military's court-martial against Manning but failed to convince a military judge that Manning was guilty of "aiding the enemy."

"During the raid," SEAL Team Six "collected a number of items of digital media, which included, among other things, (1) a letter from bin Laden to another member of the terrorist organization al Qaeda in which bin Laden requested that the member gather the DoD material posted to WikiLeaks, and (2) a letter from that member of al Qaeda to bin Laden with information from the Afghanistan War reports released by WikiLeaks."

Brown further asserted the reports were detailed enough that the "enemy" could use the reports to plan future improvised explosive device (IED) attacks because "they described IED techniques, devices, and explosives, and revealed the countermeasures used by United States and coalition forces against IED attacks and potential limitations to those countermeasures."

Yet between November 1, 2009, and March 30, 2010, the time period central to the charge, the *Times* published multiple articles on IED attacks and the US military's response to them.[12]

If Assange is guilty of aiding or abetting the "enemy" through the publication of reports from the Afghanistan War, then so are journalists and editors at the *New York Times*.

Along with the documents that exposed US wars in Iraq and Afghanistan, Brown described classified diplomatic cables from Iceland, particularly a cable marked "confidential" that was sent by a US diplomat on January 13, 2010.

The cable described bullying by the United Kingdom and the

Netherlands over the Icesave referendum that came up for a vote during the country's economic crisis. Icelandic officials claimed that if it failed to pass, Iceland would default on several loans in 2011, and that "could set Iceland back 30 years." They asked US officials for assistance and support, but the officials refused to help Iceland.[13]

"WikiLeaks received and published the classified documents, despite the clear markings indicating that they were classified," Brown stated.

All the frivolous and misguided discussion about the supposed restraint of prosecutors at the DOJ came to an end when an unprecedented seventeen charges under the Espionage Act were unveiled on May 23, 2019.

"At no point was Assange a citizen of the United States nor did he hold a United States security clearance or otherwise have authorization to receive, possess, or communicate classified information," the indictment stated.[14]

Prosecutors explicitly accused Assange of aiding, abetting, counseling, inducing, procuring, and willfully causing Manning, "who had lawful possession of, access to, and control over documents relating to the national defense" to "communicate, deliver, and transmit the documents" to WikiLeaks.

"Assange personally and publicly promoted WikiLeaks to encourage those with access to protected information, including classified information, to provide it to WikiLeaks for public disclosure," prosecutors maintained. "WikiLeaks' website explicitly solicited censored, otherwise restricted, and until September 2010, 'classified' materials."[15]

US journalists frequently publish reporting based on classified documents from various sources. They do not have security clearances, but through the alarming charges, the US government invoked domestic secrecy law and claimed jurisdiction over a non-US publisher.

During a briefing, the DOJ attempted to persuade reporters that the Espionage Act charges were not a dangerous escalation of a war against freedom of the press.

"Some say that Assange is a journalist and that he should be immune from prosecution for these actions," said John Demers, the head of the Justice Department's National Security Division. Julian Assange was "no journalist," Demers asserted.[16]

"No responsible actor, journalist or otherwise, would purposefully publish the names of individuals he or she knew to be confidential human sources in a war zone, exposing them to the gravest of dangers," Demers insisted.

Zach Terwilliger, who was the US attorney in the Eastern District of Virginia where Assange was charged, argued the WikiLeaks founder was charged for publishing a "narrow set of classified documents" in which "innocent people who risked their safety" while helping the US were named, exposing them to potential harm. "Assange is not charged simply because he is a publisher."[17]

The Society of Professional Journalists (SPJ), one of the oldest organizations representing journalists in the US, rejected the DOJ's defense of the Espionage Act charges. "WikiLeaks is clearly a publisher. If this dangerous precedent were applied more broadly, it could have a chilling effect on the publication of newsworthy classified information," stated SPJ national president J. Alex Tarquinio.[18]

In its coverage of the Espionage Act charges, the *New York Times* mentioned that a "Justice Department official" agreed to answer questions "on the condition that he would not be named" and was asked how Assange's actions "differed in a legally meaningful way from ordinary national security investigative journalism—encouraging sources to provide secret information of news value, obtaining it without the government's permission, and then publishing portions of it." However, the unnamed official refused to address this crucial question.[19]

"The *New York Times*, among many other news organizations, obtained precisely the same archives of documents from WikiLeaks, without authorization from the government—the act that most of the charges addressed," the *Times* acknowledged.

Dean Bacquet, who was the executive editor for the *Times*, responded, "Obtaining and publishing information that the government would prefer to keep secret is vital to journalism and democracy. The new indictment is a deeply troubling step toward giving the government greater control over what Americans are allowed to know."[20]

"Dating as far back as the Pentagon Papers case and beyond, journalists have been receiving and reporting on information that the government deemed classified. Wrongdoing and abuse of power were exposed," Marty Baron, who was the *Washington Post*'s editor-in-chief, asserted. "With the new indictment of Julian Assange, the government is advancing a legal argument that places such important work in jeopardy and undermines the very purpose of the First Amendment.

"The administration has gone from denigrating journalists as 'enemies of the people' to now criminalizing common practices in journalism that have long served the public interest. Meantime, government officials continue to engage in a decades-long process of over-classifying information, often for reasons that have nothing to do with national security and a lot to do with shielding themselves from the constitutionally protected scrutiny of the press," Baron concluded.[21]

Barton Gellman, who worked on classified documents from Snowden for the *Post*, reacted, "Assange's motives or membership in an undefinable 'journalist' club are irrelevant to the very dangerous step that the Trump DOJ took today. We'll now find out whether *publishing* information (as well as seeking and obtaining it) may constitutionally be charged as espionage."[22]

Civil liberties and press freedom organizations were even more resolute in their opposition.

"Any government use of the Espionage Act to criminalize the receipt and publication of classified information poses a dire threat to journalists seeking to publish such information in the public interest, irrespective of the Justice Department's assertion that Assange is not a journalist," declared Bruce Brown, executive director of Reporters Committee for Freedom of the Press.[23]

Ben Wizner, the director of the American Civil Liberties Union's Speech, Privacy, and Technology Project, condemned the charges: "For the first time in the history of our country, the government has brought criminal charges against a publisher for the publication of truthful information. This is an extraordinary escalation of the Trump administration's attacks on journalism and a direct assault on the First Amendment."[24]

"Put simply, these unprecedented charges against Julian Assange and WikiLeaks are the most significant and terrifying threat to the First Amendment in the 21st Century," stated Trevor Timm, executive director of the Freedom of the Press Foundation. "The Trump administration is moving to explicitly criminalize national security journalism, and if this prosecution proceeds, dozens of reporters at the New York Times, Washington Post and elsewhere would also be in danger."[25]

Timm added, "This decision by the Justice Department is a massive and unprecedented escalation in Trump's war on journalism, and it's no exaggeration to say the First Amendment itself is at risk. Anyone who cares about press freedom should immediately and wholeheartedly condemn these charges."

Altogether, the reaction of journalists, newspaper editors, press freedom advocates, and civil liberties organizations was very similar to the response of Assange's attorneys. Assange's American attorney Barry Pollack said, "These unprecedented charges demonstrate the gravity of the threat the criminal prosecution of Julian Assange poses to all journalists in their endeavor to inform the public about actions that have been taken by the US government."[26]

Had the Trump administration stopped with the "password-cracking" charge, it would have been much harder to build opposition to the prosecution. Prosecutors were overzealous and crossed a line that the previous DOJ under President Barack Obama went right up to, but ultimately chose not to cross.

A Third Indictment Blindsides Assange's Legal Team

On June 24, 2020, a little more than two months before a major extradition hearing in September, the DOJ blindsided Assange's legal team.

Prosecutors expanded the scope of the computer conspiracy charge to cover the time period from 2009 to 2015. They accused Assange of conspiring with "hackers" organized under the banner of names like "Anonymous." They additionally alleged that "Assange and others at WikiLeaks recruited and agreed with hackers to commit computer intrusions to benefit WikiLeaks."[27]

"Since the early days of WikiLeaks, Assange has spoken at hacking conferences to tout his own history as a 'famous teenage hacker in Australia' and to encourage others to hack to obtain information for WikiLeaks," the Justice Department's press release stated. "In 2009, for instance, Assange told the Hacking At Random conference that WikiLeaks had obtained nonpublic documents from the Congressional Research Service by exploiting 'a small vulnerability' inside the document distribution system of the United States Congress, and then asserted that '[t]his is what any one of you would find if you were actually looking.'"

The press release continued:

In 2010, Assange gained unauthorized access to a government computer system of a NATO country. In 2012, Assange communicated directly with a leader of the hacking group LulzSec (who by then was cooperating with the FBI), and provided a list of targets for LulzSec to hack. With respect to one target, Assange asked the LulzSec leader to look for (and provide to WikiLeaks) mail and documents, databases, and PDFs. In another communication, Assange told the LulzSec leader that the most impactful release of hacked materials would be from the CIA, NSA, or the *New York Times*. WikiLeaks obtained and published emails from a data breach committed against an American intelligence consulting company by an "Anonymous" and LulzSec-affiliated hacker. According to that hacker, Assange indirectly asked him to spam that victim company again.[28]

The fresh allegations were inserted into the computer conspiracy charge to help prosecutors persuade a British court, and later a US jury, that Assange was much more a hacker than a journalist.

Remarkably, the DOJ chose not to call attention to the allegations it added, which criminalized WikiLeaks' support for Snowden.

"To encourage leakers and hackers to provide stolen materials to WikiLeaks in the future, Assange and others at WikiLeaks openly displayed their attempts to assist Snowden in evading arrest," the indictment proclaimed.[29]

It noted that Sarah Harrison ("WLA-4"), who was an investigative editor for WikiLeaks, traveled with Snowden to Moscow from Hong Kong, and it drew attention to a statement from Assange in which he recalled attempts to help Snowden travel to Ecuador.

"We had engaged in a number of these distraction operations in the asylum maneuver from Hong Kong, for example, booking [Snowden] on flights to India through Beijing and other forms of distraction, like Iceland, for example," Assange said, according to the indictment.

Prosecutors additionally targeted Assange's speech in support of Snowden and any future whistleblowers. They included his words from a video that was shown at the annual Chaos Computer Club Conference in Germany on December 31, 2013. But the DOJ cherry-picked fragments to make it seem more nefarious than an endorsement of radical transparency.

This is what appeared in the indictment:

> Assange told the audience that "the famous leaks that WikiLeaks has done or the recent Edward Snowden revelations" showed that "it was possible now for even a single system administrator to . . . not merely wreck[] or disabl[e] [organizations] . . . but rather shift[] information from an information apartheid system . . . into the knowledge common."

But here is the full quote from the video (with the fragments from the indictment in bold):

> And we can see that in the cases of the **famous leaks that WikiLeaks has done or the recent Edward Snowden revelations**, that **it's possible now for even a single system administrator to** have a very significant change to the—or rather, apply a very significant constraint, a constructive constraint, to the behavior of these organizations, **not merely wrecking or disabling them**, not merely going out on strikes to change policy, **but rather**

shifting information from an information apartheid system, which we're developing, from those with extraordinary power and extraordinary information, **into the knowledge commons**, where it can be used to—not only as a disciplining force, but it can be used to construct and understand the new world that we're entering into.

Remarkably, several of the allegations linking Assange to hackers came from a "Teenager," whom Assange met in Iceland. The unnamed individual from Iceland was Sigurdur "Siggi" Thordarson, who embezzled funds from WikiLeaks. Icelandic authorities diagnosed Thordarson as a "sociopath" due to his history of criminal acts. Still, the FBI made an arrangement with Thordarson in which he provided testimony against Assange in return for immunity from US prosecution.

The same section also refers to "Sabu," the moniker for Hector Xavier Monsegur ("Sabu"), who is the FBI informant in LulzSec mentioned in the DOJ's press release.

As journalist Dell Cameron reported, Monsegur was instrumental in targeting and carrying out a cyberattack on the private intelligence firm Stratfor in 2011. The FBI allowed several individuals to submit stolen information from the firm to WikiLeaks, a tactic that ultimately led to the prosecution of hacktivist Jeremy Hammond, who was sentenced to ten years in federal prison in 2013.[30]

This third indictment marked the first mention of staff or individuals linked to WikiLeaks as participants in the alleged conspiracy: Harrison; Daniel Domscheit-Berg, a former spokesperson for WikiLeaks; and Jacob Appelbaum, a computer expert and journalist who spoke on behalf of WikiLeaks at the Hackers on Planet Earth (HOPE) conference in New York in 2010.

Since the indictment did not add any charges, there was a collective shrug from much of the establishment news media.

Coverage of the broadened indictment largely amplified the message in the headline for the Justice Department's press release, "New Allegations Assert Assange Conspired With 'Anonymous' Affiliated Hackers, Among Others."[31]

Assange attorney Barry Pollack declared, "Today's superseding indictment is yet another chapter in the U.S. government's effort to persuade the public that its pursuit of Julian Assange is based on something other than his publication of newsworthy truthful information.

"The indictment continues to charge him with violating the Espionage Act based on WikiLeaks publications exposing war crimes committed by the U.S. government."

On August 21, 2020, the additional allegations were included in an expanded extradition request just a little more than a week before a major hearing where the Assange legal team called witnesses to challenge the US government's case for extradition.

When the extradition trial kicked off on September 7, Mark Summers QC, a lawyer for Assange, called the new request "fundamentally unfair and unjust." He said Assange was in custody and had been without access to visits from his legal team for the last five to six months. Assange's legal team moved to remove alleged misconduct from the new request, because they had no witnesses or testimony prepared to rebut the fresh allegations.[32]

The UK's Crown Prosecution Service maintained there was nothing inappropriate about the fresh extradition request, and District Judge Vanessa Baraitser would be making an error if the court removed the alleged misconduct.

Baraitser sided with prosecutors. Insisting that Assange's defense should have asked for an adjournment in August and that the request was now too late, she rejected their protest against the abuse of process.

CHAPTER 2

Chelsea Manning's Court-Martial

I used to be silent. Now I am ready to let it out, let it all out.
—JOHNNY HOSTILE & JEHNNY BETH, "Let It Out"
(from *XY Chelsea*, 2019)

Private First Class Chelsea Manning received the harshest punishment any United States military officer or federal government employee has ever received for leaking classified information to the press. Colonel Denise Lind, the military judge presiding over her court-martial, sentenced Manning to thirty-five years at Fort Leavenworth prison in Kansas.

She was found guilty of six charges under the Espionage Act, five stealing charges, one charge involving the "wanton publication" of "intelligence," multiple charges of "failure to obey an order or regulation," and one charge under the Computer Fraud and Abuse Act. Notably, Manning was acquitted of an "aiding the enemy" offense that carried a potential sentence of life in prison.[1]

Manning was never charged with any conspiracy offenses, and, unlike the charges against Assange, military prosecutors did not accuse her of attempting to crack a password hash. Even with logs from alleged chats between Manning and Assange, there was scant evidence that Assange or any WikiLeaks staff attempted to enlist her to leak. Prosecutors only expressed disgust that she had independently chosen to become a source and shared more than 700,000 documents.

When Manning's trial occurred in 2013, WikiLeaks was not yet designated a "hostile intelligence agency" by the CIA. However, by 2019, there was no longer division in the government over whether to treat WikiLeaks as a journalistic entity or not.[2] The indictment plainly claimed, "To obtain information to release on the WikiLeaks website, Assange recruited sources and predicated the success of WikiLeaks in part upon the recruitment of sources" in order to "illegally circumvent legal safeguards on information."

Prosecutors at the Justice Department (DOJ) would like the public to believe that Assange posted a "Most Wanted Leaks" list to the WikiLeaks website in 2009 to solicit leaks from "insiders" like Manning, and Manning used it to determine which documents to provide to WikiLeaks.[3]

Yet, this conspiracy theory, which forms the basis of criminal allegations against Assange, was promoted by military prosecutors during Manning's trial, and it was discredited by Manning's own statement to the court and David Coombs, her defense attorney.

Sparking a Debate

In February 2013, prior to her trial, Manning pleaded guilty to some elements of the charges. It was the first time the press and the public heard her speak about her deployment to Baghdad, Iraq, as an all-source military intelligence analyst.[4]

Manning told the court she shared the military incident report databases on Iraq and Afghanistan, which WikiLeaks published as the "Iraq War Logs" and "Afghanistan War Logs," because they showed what troops saw on the ground in great detail. She believed if the public had access to this information it would "spark a domestic debate on the role of the military and [US] foreign policy in general." It might even call into question the doctrine of counterinsurgency popularized by General David Petraeus, as well as the obsession with "capturing and killing human targets on lists."⁵

Probably the best known disclosure is footage of a 2007 Apache helicopter attack published by WikiLeaks as the "Collateral Murder" video. It showed two Reuters employees as they were killed in Baghdad. A "Good Samaritan" with two children drives up in a van to help wounded individuals, and the aerial weapons team opens fire on the vehicle.

Manning was appalled by the way soldiers disregarded the value of human life. As they watched a wounded person crawl away from the wrecked van, one crew member said they wished the person would pick up a weapon so they could fire on survivors. She likened this to children torturing ants with a magnifying class and described the video as "war porn." In fact, once the crew learned the van had children inside, a crew member replied, "Well, it's their fault for bringing their kids into a battle."⁶

"Light 'em all up," commanded one officer.

This particular video was also significant to Manning because Reuters submitted a Freedom of Information Act (FOIA) request for it, but the Pentagon denied the request. Manning and WikiLeaks exposed a shameful cover-up, which may be why none of the specific charges against Assange relate to the publication of the video.

On the detainee assessments from Joint Task Force Guantánamo that WikiLeaks published as the "Gitmo Files," Manning said it seemed the US military was "holding an increasing number of individuals indefinitely that we believed or knew to be innocent, low level foot soldiers that did not have useful intelligence and would be released if they were still held in theater." She also recalled President Barack Obama said in early 2009 that he would close Guantánamo.⁷

The more Manning read cables from the US State Department,

the more she came to believe that "this was the type of information that should become public."

"I once read and used a quote on open diplomacy written after the First World War and how the world would be a better place if states would avoid making secret pacts and deals with and against each other," Manning added. "I thought these cables were a prime example of a need for a more open diplomacy."[8]

Manning became aware of the portal with US diplomatic cables after Captain Steven Lim, one of her superior officers, sent a section-wide email in late December 2009 that contained instructions to look at the cables and incorporate them in intelligence work products. She read many of the cables from Iraq as well as "other random cables" that "piqued" her "insatiable curiosity."[9]

WikiLeaks had an instant relay chat for messaging and conferencing that Manning followed in January 2010. She observed discussions about Icesave, which related to the collapse of banks in Iceland, and searched for cables that mentioned the issue. On February 14, after finding one cable—10Reykjavik13—she submitted it to WikiLeaks.[10]

Army training introduced Manning to the military incident reports from Iraq and Afghanistan. According to Manning, Master Sergeant David Adkins assigned her to develop an incident tracker. She used reports from Afghanistan because she was initially scheduled to deploy to the Logar and Wardak provinces in Afghanistan, then switched to tracking reports from Iraq when she was reassigned to Baghdad.[11]

Rules of engagement documents related to the Iraq War were submitted to WikiLeaks with the "Collateral Murder" video on February 21. This enabled the public to watch the Apache helicopter attack and see that the soldiers did not follow certain rules they were trained to follow.

After the Iraqi federal police detained fifteen individuals who were accused of "printing anti-Iraqi literature," on March 2 a section officer instructed Manning to "investigate the matter." None of the detainees had any apparent "ties to anti-Iraqi actions or suspected terrorist militia groups." The literature was essentially a "scholarly critique" of Iraqi prime minister Nouri al-Maliki, corruption in the Iraqi government, and the "financial impact" on Iraqis.

Manning shared this information with multiple superior officers, who instructed her to "drop" the issue and assist the Iraqi federal police in finding the rest of the print shops producing this literature. She became concerned that she was helping the police arrest Iraqis who would be tortured, and submitted evidence she collected to WikiLeaks on March 4.[12]

To Manning's disappointment, WikiLeaks chose not to publish the information. However, the incident involving the Iraqi federal police led her to the Guantánamo detainee assessments. Many of the files involved prisoners who were already released, and she shared the documents with WikiLeaks on March 8, 2010.

The 'Most Wanted Leaks' List

Despite Manning's statement, DOJ prosecutors concocted their own conspiracy theory to further their political case. Central to this theory is the "Most Wanted Leaks" list.

On May 14, 2009, WikiLeaks requested nominations from human rights groups, lawyers, historians, journalists, and activists for documents as well as databases from around the world that the media organization would work to expose.[13]

The list, according to prosecutors, was "organized by country and stated that documents or materials nominated to the list must 'be likely to have political, diplomatic, ethical, or historical impact on release.'" WikiLeaks suggested the information should be "plausibly obtainable to a well-motivated insider or outsider."

With little to no evidence, military prosecutors called the list Manning's "guiding light," a characterization Manning's defense attorney David Coombs directly challenged during his closing argument.[14]

"It was WikiLeaks saying, look, tell us, humanitarians, activists, NGOs, fellow reporters, what do you want to know in your country? What in your country is being hidden from the public that you believe the public should know? Give us a list," Coombs said.

"We are going to compile that list, and we are going to work to obtain that list. What does this sound like? Any journalistic organization that has like a hotline or anything else says, call us. You got a story. Call us. We'll investigate."

There were seventy-eight items on the list. As Coombs noted, military prosecutors were only able to "remotely" tie Manning to "four of the things on the list." She could have used Intelink, which is a US intelligence network of top secret, secret, and unclassified databases, to search for specific items on the list. She did not.[15]

DOJ prosecutors emphasized in their indictment that the list requested "bulk databases," including Intellipedia, a classified Wikipedia for US intelligence analysts. Yet Manning never released this database to WikiLeaks, nor did she release the complete CIA Open Source Center database or PACER database containing US federal court records, which were listed as "important bulk databases."[16]

Chat logs show Manning brought up the CIA Open Source Center on March 8, 2010, and a user, whom the government claims was Assange, replied, "That's something we want to mine entirely." But Manning never engaged in any attempts to download and transfer this database to WikiLeaks.

Manning released four sets that could be labeled "bulk databases." She released the Afghanistan and Iraq War Logs, the US State embassy cables in the Net-Centric Diplomacy database, and the database containing detainee assessments from Joint Task

Force Guantánamo. None of those documents were on the "Most Wanted Leaks" list.

DOJ prosecutors contended Manning's searches on November 28, 2009, for "retention+of+interrogation+videos" and "detainee+abuse" matched up with the "Most Wanted Leaks" list. However, at the time, WikiLeaks was interested in obtaining copies of any of the ninety-two CIA torture tapes that were destroyed as well as "detainee abuse photos withheld by the Obama administration." It is far more plausible that Manning searched for abuse photos or torture videos.[17]

Contrary to Manning's version of events, DOJ prosecutors insisted that Assange convinced Manning to find the detainee assessment briefs and release them. FBI special agent Megan Brown, of the "counterespionage squad" at the Washington Field Office in the District of Columbia, wrote, "Manning asked Assange, 'how valuable are JTF GTMO detention memos containing summaries, background info, capture info, etc?' Assange replied, 'Time period?' Manning answered, '2007–2008.'"[18]

Assange allegedly responded, "Quite valuable to the lawyers of these guys who are trying to get them out, where those memos suggest their innocence/bad procedure," and added, "also valuable to merge into the general history. Politically, Gitmo is mostly over though."

Yet in the messages Brown referenced, Assange never specifically asked Manning to provide the reports to WikiLeaks. He did not say whether WikiLeaks would publish the documents. He certainly did not solicit Manning to leak the detainee assessments. All Assange allegedly did was state his opinion that the documents were in the public interest.

Prosecutors attempted to link Manning's disclosure of rules of engagement for US military forces in Iraq to the supposed "Most Wanted Leaks" list because it included "Iraq and Afghanistan U.S. Army Rules of Engagement 2007–2009." They suggested Manning provided the files to WikiLeaks on March 22, 2010, after Assange allegedly wrote on March 8, "Curious eyes never run dry."[19]

Manning said she uploaded the rules of engagement with the "Collateral Murder" video on February 21, weeks before the alleged exchange with Assange.[20]

One lesser-known Espionage Act charge against Manning involved the alleged disclosure of video showing the Garani massacre by US military forces in the Farah province of Afghanistan. An air strike killed at least eighty-six Afghan civilians on May 4, 2009. She was acquitted, a fact that poses a problem for the DOJ's theory.

According to evidence presented during the trial, Jason Katz, an employee at Brookhaven National Laboratory from February 2009 to March 2010, tried to help WikiLeaks and downloaded an encrypted file with the air strike video onto his work computer on December 15. Katz was unable to use a password-cracking tool to open the file.

WikiLeaks indicated on Twitter on January 8, "We need super-computer time." The media organization apparently had an encrypted file of the attack, but they were never able to decrypt the file.

Military prosecutors attempted to connect Manning to Katz. They claimed during their case that Manning's earliest violations began on November 1, and Manning had provided the video to Katz to decrypt with a supercomputer. Although Manning searched and downloaded "Farah" files, the video Katz had did not match any of Manning's files.

"Let's go along with the government and its logic. Pfc. Manning hits the ground in Iraq in mid-November," Coombs argued. "For whatever reason, [her] motive, I'm now going to use the 2009 'Most Wanted [Leaks]' List as my guiding light. And I'm going to give something to WikiLeaks. I'm going to do it because I'm now a traitor. I'm now an activist.

"So what is the first thing I'm going to choose? What is the very first thing I'm going to give to WikiLeaks and say look, WikiLeaks, I'm for you? Well, I'm going to give you an encrypted video I can't see. You can't see. Guess what? We don't have a password for it. By the way, you never asked for it. That's not on your 2009 'Most Wanted [Leaks]' list."

Coombs suggested, "This is kind of like someone showing up to a wedding and giving you something that's not on the list that you registered for. What do you think Pfc. Manning is doing at this point? According to the government, [she] is like, hey, you know what, I can go to the seventy-eight things that you want, but I don't want to give you that stuff."

Military prosecutors seem to have failed to persuade the military judge that Manning used the "Most Wanted Leaks" list as her guide. Lind's "special findings" show she accepted evidence that Manning viewed a tweet from WikiLeaks on May 7, 2010, which requested a list of as many military email addresses as possible. This led Manning to compile a list of over 74,000 addresses for WikiLeaks. Except Lind did not find that WikiLeaks had solicited Manning to leak any of the more than 700,000 documents that were published.

Password-Cracking Was Not Possible, According to US Military Forensic Expert

When the first indictment against Assange was disclosed by the Justice Department on April 11, 2019, the response from some attorneys and advocates was mixed. It was widely viewed as "narrowly tailored" to avoid "broader legal and policy implications."[21]

The DOJ did not accuse Assange of hacking into a US military computer. He was accused of "conspiracy to commit computer intrusion" when he allegedly "agreed" to assist Manning in "cracking a password hash" to help her browse information databases anonymously.

DOJ prosecutors were already presented with evidence related to these allegations during Manning's trial. Patrick Eller, a command digital forensic examiner responsible for a team of more than eighty examiners at US Army Criminal Investigation Command headquarters, reviewed court-martial records for Assange's defense. He testified during the evidentiary hearing in the extradition case in September 2020.[22]

Eller found testimony from the US military's own forensic expert that contradicted presumptions at the core of the computer crime charge. Password hashes are generally used to help authenticate users and passwords on a computer. Manning never provided the two files necessary to "reconstruct the decryption key" for the password hash. According to Eller, at the time it was not "possible to crack an encrypted password hash, such as the one Manning obtained."

James Lewis QC, a prosecutor for the Crown Prosecution Service, asked Eller if he agreed that Manning and Assange "thought they could crack a password and agreed to attempt to crack a password." Eller told Lewis a hash was provided and that the account user that the US government associated with Assange said they had "rainbow tables for it." (Using "rainbow tables" is one decryption method for cracking the hash by guessing different password values.)

However, Manning never shared where she obtained the hash.

"The government's own expert witness in the court-martial stated that was not enough for them to actually [crack the password]," Eller added. A user must also have a system file to complete an attempt at password-cracking.

During the Manning trial, David Shaver, a special agent for the Army Computer Crimes Investigating Unit, testified that the "hash value" was included in the chat, but it was not the "full hash value."[23]

Major Thomas Hurley, who was on Manning's defense team, asked if Manning would have needed more of the hash value to crack the password. Shaver replied, "I mentioned the system file, you would need that part as well." (This was one of the two files Eller said were necessary for decryption.)

"So the hash value included in the chat wouldn't be enough to actually gain any passwords or user information?" Hurley asked.

Shaver replied, "Correct."

Eller's statement submitted to the Westminster Magistrates' Court in London was even more explicit.[24]

> Upon reading the indictment, it became clear that the technical explanation of the password hashing allegations is deficient in a number of ways which cast doubt upon the assertion that the purpose of the Jabber chat was for Manning to be able to download documents anonymously.

Jabber is the software Manning used to chat with the account allegedly associated with Assange.

Manning had already downloaded the Reykjavík cable, Guantánamo Files, Iraq War Logs, and Afghanistan War Logs before the alleged exchange on password-cracking occurred. "Routinely in the course of work," according to Eller, she downloaded military incident reports to have "offline backups" in the event of "connectivity issues" with the Secret Internet Protocol Router Network that hosted the information.

"The only set of documents named in the indictment that Manning sent after the alleged password-cracking attempt were the State Department cables," he said. However, Eller acknowledged, "Manning had authorized access to these documents."

Eller showed that soldiers at Forward Operating Base Hammer in Iraq, where Manning was stationed, constantly tried to crack administrative passwords to install programs that were not authorized for their computers.

Jason Milliman, a computer engineer contracted to manage laptops at the base, testified during Manning's court-martial that "soldiers cracked his password in order to install a program and then deleted his administrator account."

As Eller asserted, Manning never would have tried to use a password hash to exfiltrate files for submission to WikiLeaks because she already had a way to anonymously access the files: a Linux CD that allowed her to bypass Windows security features.

Sgt. David Sadtler, a soldier in Manning's battalion, testified that Manning proposed starting "some sort of hash cracking business." The idea had already been done in the "open source world." So "reimplementing it" made sense to Sadtler.

Eller concluded, "While she was discussing rainbow tables and password hashes in the Jabber chat, she was also discussing the same topics with her colleagues. This, and the other factors previously highlighted, may indicate that the hash cracking topic was unrelated to leaking documents."

During the court-martial, military prosecutors underscored the fact that Manning exchanged messages with a user identified as "Nathaniel Frank," a name the government believed was associated with Assange.

Assange attorney Mark Summers QC asked Eller multiple times if he found evidence that linked Assange to this account. "No, I did not," Eller replied.

Summers asked if Eller was aware of the person who sat at the other end of whatever computer terminal "Nathaniel Frank" used. "Of course not. I could not have that personal knowledge," Eller added.

Major Ashden Fein, a military prosecutor, said during the closing argument, "[Manning] was a determined soldier with a knowledge, ability, and desire to harm the United States in its war effort. And, Your Honor, [she] was not a whistleblower. [She] was a traitor—a traitor who understood the value of compromised information in the hands of the enemy and took deliberate steps to ensure they, along with the world, received all of it."[25]

The attacks on Manning's character were nasty. In addition to questioning her loyalty to the United States, military prosecutors pejoratively labeled Manning an "anarchist" and a "hacker."[26] But missing from the prosecutors' narrative of her acts was any explicit claim that she collaborated with WikiLeaks founder Julian Assange or that she engaged in a password-cracking conspiracy.

As Captain Joe Morrow, one of the military prosecutors, declared during her sentencing. "Pfc. Manning is solely responsible for [her] crimes. Pfc. Manning is solely responsible for the impact."[27]

Manning was not an insider or spy who worked for WikiLeaks to steal US government documents. She had whistleblower motives that inspired her to take action. That is an inconvenient truth for prosecutors, who are compelled to deny her agency to bolster their arguments.

In fact, submitting documents to WikiLeaks was not Manning's first choice. As she recounted in her 2022 memoir, *README.txt*, "While I shared WikiLeaks' stated commitment to transparency, I thought that for my purposes, it was too limited a platform. Most people back then had never heard of it. I worried that information on the site wouldn't be taken seriously."

Manning used landlines, mostly at Starbucks, to reach out to "traditional publications." She contacted the *Washington Post* in January 2010. During her court-martial she testified that a reporter she spoke to at the *Post* had not taken her seriously. Next, she called the *New York Times*. No one responded to the message she left for the *Times'* public editor. She considered going to Politico, but weather conditions hampered plans to travel to its offices in Arlington, Virginia.

WikiLeaks, as she put it in her memoir, was "the publication of last resort."[28]

CHAPTER 3

How the US Government Viewed WikiLeaks

They're calling me a terrorist
Like they don't know who the terror is
—LOWKEY, "Terrorist?" (2011)

The United States defense budget for the 2020 fiscal year, passed by Congress and signed into law by President Donald Trump on December 20, 2019, contained an incendiary provision adopting the Central Intelligence Agency's stance against WikiLeaks.

"It is the sense of Congress that WikiLeaks and the senior leadership of WikiLeaks resemble a non-state hostile intelligence service often abetted by state actors and should be treated as such a service by the United States."[1]

Although there was always animosity toward WikiLeaks, the so-called "sense of Congress" was not consensus in 2010 when WikiLeaks published documents from Pfc. Chelsea Manning.

US agencies were abstractly focused on the potential threat that leak submission sites posed. They viewed the WikiLeaks website as a central location adversaries could visit to read previously classified information. Yet they did not accuse WikiLeaks of being an anti-US organization, as US government officials regularly did in 2019.

Moreover, the charges against Manning did not describe WikiLeaks as a "hostile entity," and the US military was unable to persuade a military judge that WikiLeaks existed for the purpose of publishing secret documents for America's so-called enemies.

What if *New York Times* Were Substituted for WikiLeaks?

The US Army charged Manning with knowingly giving "intelligence" to "the enemy, through indirect means," or what was more commonly known as an "aiding the enemy" offense. WikiLeaks was viewed as the "indirect means." If found guilty, Manning faced a potential life sentence at Fort Leavenworth's military prison in Kansas.

During a key hearing in December 2011, Captain Ashden Fein, lead military prosecutor, argued that Manning knew the documents published by WikiLeaks would end up in the hands of al Qaeda, al Qaeda in the Arabian Peninsula (AQAP), and similar enemies. The government even played an al Qaeda propaganda video featuring Adam Gadahn, an American who was a spokesperson for the terrorist group.[2]

Gadahn referred to the US State Department cables, and said they revealed "foreign dependencies." He urged jihadists to rely on the "wide range of resources on the internet," which Fein contended was a call to followers of AQAP to "collect and archive WikiLeaks information."[3]

Fein also contended the material was helpful not only to "declared enemies" of the US but also to "all other enemies with internet access."

More than a year later, in January 2013, the theory of how Manning aided terrorists grew more tortuous. Military prosecutors informed the judge, Colonel Denise Lind, that "digital media" were uncovered during the May 2011 raid in Abottabad, Pakistan, against al Qaeda leader Osama bin Laden. The media allegedly contained a letter from bin Laden to al Qaeda "requesting a member gather [Defense Department] information." A response to that letter allegedly had war logs from Iraq and Afghanistan and State Department cables attached.[4]

David Coombs, Manning's civilian defense attorney, called attention during the trial to the "very, very unique position" taken by the government. "No case has ever been prosecuted under this type of theory, that an individual by the nature of giving information to a journalistic organization would then be subject to [aiding the enemy].

"To avoid the slippery slope of basically punishing people for getting information out to the press," which included bringing the hammer down on whistleblowers, Coombs contended, the government should have to prove intent. If a person had the intent to use an organization to communicate "intelligence" to the "enemy," that could make a person guilty. But to Coombs, what military prosecutors advanced was the criminalization of anyone who gave sensitive information to a media organization for publication because the "enemy" might eventually see that information.

Judge Lind asked the government at a pretrial hearing if they would present any evidence involving the nature of WikiLeaks. She asked if the government had a theory that WikiLeaks was somehow different from the *New York Times*. Military prosecutors informed her they would have a witness testify during the trial, who would "characterize" WikiLeaks.

"If we substituted the New York Times for WikiLeaks, would you still charge [Chelsea] Manning in the way that you have?" Lind asked, insisting on a clear answer. Without hesitation, prosecutors said yes.[5]

The issue came up during the second month of Manning's trial. Lind again asked the government if it made any difference whether Manning provided documents to "WikiLeaks or any other news organization—any news organization, New York Times, Washington Post, or Wall Street Journal?"[6]

Captain Angel Overgaard answered, "No, it would not. It would not potentially make a difference," an acknowledgment that the government believed it had the authority to criminalize information published by prestige media.

WikiLeaks' Role in the Networked Fourth Estate

In March 2013, Harvard professor Yochai Benkler, a scholar who wrote a widely cited paper that examined how WikiLeaks was part of the networked fourth estate, co-authored a column for the *Times* that condemned the "aiding the enemy" charge. He described it as a "severe threat to future whistle-blowers, even when their revelations are crystal-clear instances of whistle-blowing."[7]

"We cannot allow our concerns about terrorism to turn us into a country where communicating with the press can be prosecuted as a capital offense," the editorial added.

Benkler testified as a defense witness at Manning's trial. Lind permitted Benkler to share his views on WikiLeaks and what made it a legitimate media organization.[8]

The government objected to the judge qualifying Benkler as an expert on technology and how WikiLeaks fit into developing forms of communication. They did not want Benkler to testify about the way the US government viewed WikiLeaks.[9]

It was important that the military court allowed Benkler's testimony. According to defense attorney David Coombs, bin Laden requested documents after hearing the US government's "rhetoric against WikiLeaks," which made the organization seem like an "enemy." This was what drove bin Laden to take an interest in WikiLeaks.

As Coombs put it, this showed how the US government could

recast a journalistic organization as a "terrorist organization based upon the response of the government."[10]

"I see WikiLeaks as an organization that fulfilled a discrete role in network journalism of providing a network solution to leak-based investigative journalism that in the past was done only by relatively large and unified organizations," Benkler told the court.

WikiLeaks, according to Benkler, performed the gathering, authentication, and selection for dissemination of information that was later analyzed by partnering media organizations. It fit in with the "idea of a journalistic organization."[11]

In 2008, Julius Baer Bank and Trust, a Swiss bank branch in the Cayman Islands, sued WikiLeaks for posting company documents. A federal judge ordered the domain name registrar to disable WikiLeaks' web address, and WikiLeaks was prohibited from distributing the bank documents. Benkler said this was the moment when WikiLeaks was first widely recognized as a journalistic organization.

The New York Times published an editorial in support of WikiLeaks, described it as a muckraking website, and stated, "The free speech burdens of closing down a website are just as serious as closing down a print publication."[12]

A collection of Congressional Research Service reports were posted by WikiLeaks in February 2009.[13] Senator Joe Lieberman used the moment to urge Senator Chuck Schumer and other senators to develop a system for regularly making reports public. (The reports are designed to inform members of Congress and their staff on issues and policy questions.)

Federal Times, a publication for US government employees, also published favorable coverage and described WikiLeaks as "a site maintained by investigative journalists and Freedom of Information Act fans, who promote a free and transparent government."[14]

"Beholden to Nobody"

After WikiLeaks released the war logs from Afghanistan in July 2010, the attitude of US officials soured. Admiral Mike Mullen, chairman of the Joint Chiefs of Staff, accused WikiLeaks of having blood on its hands. General James Jones, a national security advisor, said the publication could put American lives and US "partners at risk."

The Iraq War Logs were released in the last week of October 2010. US deputy defense secretary William Lynn "told a small group of reporters during a brief visit to Baghdad" that groups had said they were "mining the data to turn around and use" against the US military occupation.

As WikiLeaks released diplomatic cables, US officials grew even more bellicose. Vice President Joe Biden labeled Assange a "high-tech terrorist." Secretary of State Hillary Clinton referred to the publication not only as an attack on "America's foreign policy interests" but also as an attack on the "international community." Senator Lieberman opposed forced transparency on US wars and foreign policy and encouraged numerous companies to deny WikiLeaks access to their services.

"WikiLeaks and people that disseminate information to people like this are criminals, first and foremost. And I think that needs to be clear," proclaimed Robert Gibbs, press secretary for President Barack Obama's White House.

P.J. Crowley, the assistant secretary of state for public affairs, foreshadowed the case against Assange. "Under our laws, the transfer of classified information to those who aren't authorized to receive it is a crime. And the fact that we still have our classified information in the possession of WikiLeaks is a continuation of that crime.

"What's crucial here is that Assange is not a journalist. He's an anarchist, and he is not worthy of the protections of a journalist," Crowley also asserted. The indictment would later criminalize Assange for the "unauthorized possession" of classified war documents.

Asked how the State Department would distinguish between the publication of cables by WikiLeaks and by prestige media organizations, Crowley dodged the question and repeated, "In our view, Mr. Assange is not a journalist."

Yet beneath the bitter responses to WikiLeaks was a deep sense of anxiety over the government's lack of influence over the media organization. Marine Corps colonel Dave Lapan, a Pentagon spokesperson, grumbled, "The concern is that WikiLeaks as an organization should not be made more credible by having credible news organizations facilitate what they're doing."

Geoff Morrell, another Pentagon spokesperson, told CNN host Howard Kurtz that WikiLeaks represented a "frightening new development," because he could not "negotiate with it like American news outlets." The group, Morell said, was "beholden to nobody" and had a "'damn the consequences' approach to publishing."

"Individuals who are not involved in this kind of warfare and expose this kind of information" cannot appreciate and "understand the impact," Mullen suggested. He was troubled by the existence of a media organization that might not fall in line when reminded of US military doctrine.[15]

Military officials demanded WikiLeaks remove the Iraq and Afghanistan war documents from their site and "return" them to the US government. WikiLeaks ignored their far-fetched and authoritarian request.[16]

Army Intelligence Center Recognizes WikiLeaks' Responsible Journalism

Military prosecutors attempted to block Benkler from testifying as a qualified expert on WikiLeaks. When the military judge allowed his testimony, prosecutors were caught unprepared. They scrambled to arrange testimony from a "forensic investigator" who could testify about WikiLeaks. But Judge Lind stopped them from calling this witness to challenge Benkler.[17]

"You knew Professor Benkler was testifying for months," Lind told them. They knew what he was testifying about; however, they had no cross-examination or witness ready for a rebuttal.[18]

"The government did not know how much testimony the court would allow from Professor Benkler," Fein complained.[19]

Lind replied, "You do no preparation and wait for the relevance ruling and then you start?" She was bothered by the laziness of the government.

The testimony from this "forensic investigator" would have been helpful to understanding what drove the Justice Department to charge Assange with committing crimes. Although, as Lind pointed out, the evidence on WikiLeaks was not relevant. "Whether Pfc. Manning thought WikiLeaks was a legitimate journalistic organization" is what mattered.[20]

To show Manning should have known WikiLeaks was not a legitimate journalistic organization, military prosecutors referred to a March 2008 report, "WikiLeaks.org—An Online Reference to Foreign Intelligence Services, Insurgents, or Terrorist Groups?" It was produced by the Army Counterintelligence Center (ACIC), and Manning shared it with WikiLeaks.

The report examined the potential threat WikiLeaks posed to the US Army as a "publicly accessible internet website," but not as a media organization. It stated:

> The intentional or unintentional leaking and posting of US Army sensitive or classified information to Wikileaks. org could result in increased threats to [Defense Department] personnel, equipment, facilities, or installations.

The leakage of sensitive and classified [Defense Department] information also calls attention to the insider threat, when a person or persons motivated by a particular cause or issue wittingly provides information to domestic or foreign personnel or organizations to be published by the news media or on the Internet. Such information could be of value to foreign intelligence and security services (FISS), foreign military forces, foreign insurgents, and foreign terrorist groups for collecting information or for planning attacks against US forces, both within the United States and abroad.

Captain Joe Morrow, a military prosecutor, maintained during opening argument that the report "alerted readers that WikiLeaks was a source of intelligence for adversaries." Yet over the government's objection, the judge allowed Benkler to share his analysis of the ACIC report. Benkler said it consisted of "theoretical statements" about how enemies could use WikiLeaks but contained no evidence "that any enemy had, in fact, used WikiLeaks."[21]

As Benkler noted, the report referred to Assange as a "foreign staff writer" who "wrote several news articles, coauthored other articles, and developed an interactive database" for accessing documents on military equipment in Iraq and Afghanistan that WikiLeaks published. The intelligence center also concluded, "[WikiLeaks.org's] attempts to verify the information were prudent and show journalist responsibility to the newsworthiness or fair use of the classified document if they are investigated or challenged in court."[22]

Remarkably, the report did not single out the US government as a government that would likely block access to WikiLeaks. It instead focused on China, Israel, North Korea, Russia, Thailand, Zimbabwe, and other countries that clamped down on "WikiLeaks-type websites." Those governments apparently claimed the "right to investigate and prosecute WikiLeaks.org and associated whistleblowers or insisted they remove false, sensitive, or classified information, propaganda, or malicious content from the internet."[23]

It additionally acknowledged that "diverse views exist among private persons, legal experts, advocates for open government accountability, law enforcement, and government officials in the United States and other countries on the stated goals of WikiLeaks.org."

"Anyone looking at WikiLeaks prior to the charged releases, including the 2008 document produced by the Army Counter-intelligence Center, would have viewed WikiLeaks as a legitimate news organization," Coombs stated.

The government's own witnesses undermined their characterization of WikiLeaks. Mark Mander, a computer crimes investigator for the Army, said WikiLeaks was "an uncensorable Wikipedia for untraceable mass document leaking and analysis."[24] Sheila Glenn, who worked for ACIC, put it more plainly. "WikiLeaks is an organization that exposes illegal activity."[25]

Manning was found not guilty of "aiding the enemy" partly because WikiLeaks was seen as a new media organization that took advantage of a digital renaissance in journalism. It was not a "non-state hostile intelligence service." Perhaps the most crucial part of the ACIC report was the section that foretold how the US would seek to expand its ability to disrupt WikiLeaks' means to publish documents. The easiest way to undermine WikiLeaks was to destroy trust in the organization.

"Websites such as Wikileaks.org have trust as their most important center of gravity by protecting the anonymity and identity of the insider, leaker, or whistleblower," the ACIC report concluded.[26] "Successful identification, prosecution, termination of employment, and exposure of persons leaking the information by the governments and businesses affected by information posted to WikiLeaks.org would damage and potentially destroy this center of gravity and deter others from taking similar actions."

CHAPTER 4

The Espionage Act

Every time the curtain falls on some forgotten life
It is because we all stood by, silent and indifferent
It's normal.
—ROGER WATERS, "Is This the Life We Really Want?" (2017)

While the United Kingdom has the Official Secrets Acts, which are used to punish whistleblowers or journalists who publish government secrets, the United States has no such law. In fact, during President Bill Clinton's final months in office, he vetoed legislation on November 4, 2000, that would have given the US government the power to prosecute any person who "revealed official secrets, including whistleblowers or even ambassadors who briefed news reporters."[1]

Under President Barack Obama, the Justice Department (DOJ) claimed a broad authority to target whistleblowers with the Espionage Act in order to defend a regime of secrecy during the "Global War on Terrorism." Obama pursued "more than twice as many [leak] prosecutions as there were in all previous administrations combined."[2]

Director for National Intelligence Dennis Blair and Attorney General Eric Holder believed the government was too "passive" when it came to leaks. "My background is in the Navy, and it is good to hang an admiral once in a while as an example to the others," Blair told the *New York Times.* "We were hoping to get somebody and make people realize that there are consequences to this and it needed to stop."[3]

In contrast, 153 cases of "national security leaks" were referred to the DOJ during President George W. Bush's second term. Only twenty-four resulted in Federal Bureau of Investigation (FBI) cases. No one was charged with any crimes, although two cases led to indictments in 2010.[4]

US Army whistleblower Chelsea Manning, and later National Security Agency (NSA) whistleblower Edward Snowden, drove the Obama administration to develop and expand an "insider threat" program, which had the chilling effect of discouraging government employees and contractors from challenging corruption. Journalists were also increasingly swept up in leak investigations and had to worry that the safety of their confidential sources could be compromised.

The Espionage Act was useful to the Obama administration because it helped officials pioneer a weaponized drone program that involved kill lists, maintain the authority to engage in indefinite military detention, and shield former government officials and military officers from accountability for their role in committing torture and other war crimes. It helped preserve a state of permanent war.

The act was adopted in 1917 to repress antiwar dissent, particularly among left-wing organizations. The most well-known case was brought against Pentagon Papers whistleblower Daniel Ellsberg in 1971 for exposing the fact that the government was lying about the Vietnam War. Nearly a century later, the government could now wield the Espionage Act against anyone who effectively challenged the US military–industrial complex or the post-9/11 security state.

Under Obama, the DOJ perfected the art of Espionage Act prosecutions in order to create a chilling effect and disrupt the flow of information from government sources to news reporters.

"Firm Hand of Stern Repression"

Carey Shenkman, an expert on the Espionage Act, was an associate of Michael Ratner, who was an esteemed human rights attorney and a part of the WikiLeaks legal team until he died of cancer in 2016. For Assange's extradition trial in September 2020, the defense turned to Shenkman to help educate District Judge Vanessa Baraitser on the law and its history.

According to Shenkman, the Espionage Act was a product of "one of the most repressive periods in the history of the United States."[5]

President Woodrow Wilson introduced legislation to prosecute spies after the United States entered World War I, but as Shenkman said the conduct the law could be used to criminalize "went well beyond spying." Wilson went on to call the law a "firm hand of stern repression" against anyone who dissented against US involvement in the war.

Immediately, the Espionage Act "reflected the government's desire to control information and public opinion regarding the war effort. It embraced broad proscriptions against the possession and transmission of information related to national defense; established severe penalties for criticism of the war; contained conspiracy provisions; and established a censorship system for the press." The law's powers were not limited to wartime.

Socialist Party presidential candidate Eugene Debs was prosecuted under the law and sentenced to prison for ten years after he gave a speech in 1918 in Canton, Ohio. The speech was considered the most famous protest speech of its time.

"The master class has always declared the wars; the subject class has always fought the battles. The master class has had all to gain and nothing to lose, while the subject class has had nothing to gain and all to lose—especially their lives," Debs proclaimed.[6]

Debs warned before his sentence, "Free speech, free assemblage, and a free press, three foundations of democracy and self-government, are but a mockery under the espionage law administered and construed by the official representatives of the ruling class."

In 1919, the Supreme Court issued a landmark decision and found the law did not violate the First Amendment. Philadelphia socialist Charles Schenck distributed a pamphlet to conscripted soldiers that encouraged them to oppose the draft. Justice Oliver Wendell Holmes professed, "When a nation is at war, many things that might be said in a time of peace are such a hindrance to its effort that their utterance will not be endured so long as men fight, and that no court could regard them as protected by any constitutional right."[7]

As Shenkman noted, during this period, "nearly 2,500 individuals were prosecuted under the act on account of their dissenting views and opposition."

With the case against Ellsberg, Espionage Act prosecutions began to take on the form that became common under Obama.

"I believed that these 7,000 pages of top secret documents demonstrated that the conduct of the war in Vietnam had, over more than one administration, been started and continued by the US government in the knowledge that it could not be won," Ellsberg recalled. He also thought President Lyndon B. Johnson lied to Congress and the public about the "origins, costs, and prospects" of the Vietnam War.

Twelve charges, including several under the Espionage Act, were filed against Ellsberg. He faced a possible sentence of 115 years in prison, and in 1973, his case went to trial.

Ellsberg did not initially tell the public why he disclosed the Pentagon Papers. He saved that testimony for his trial, but when his lawyer asked him why he copied the Pentagon Papers, prosecutors immediately objected. His lawyer tried to rephrase the question. Each time the court sided with the prosecution and stopped him from speaking.

"The notion of motive or extenuating circumstances is irrelevant," Ellsberg learned. "The meaning of which is I did not get a fair trial, despite a very intelligent and conscientious judge."

Fortunately, revelations related to criminal actions by President Richard Nixon's administration against Ellsberg led Judge William Byrne to dismiss the charges with prejudice.

The case against Samuel Morison was another precedent-setting case. Morison, an intelligence analyst at the Naval Intelligence Support Center from 1974 to 1984, leaked US satellite photographs that showed a Soviet naval vessel at a shipbuilding center.

New York Times columnist Anthony Lewis wrote in 1985 that President Ronald Reagan's administration used the Morison case "to try to turn the Espionage Act into something the United States has never had: a criminal statute against leaks. And by persuading the trial judge and then the jury, it did create something very much like the British Official Secrets Act."[8]

Morison sent the photographs to *Jane's Defence Weekly*, a British military magazine. "He was not paid," Lewis noted. "He did it, he said, because the carrier was a significant new element in the Soviet fleet and publication would alert Americans to the threats."

Despite trying to warn the US government of what he believed was a threat, Morison was convicted of two counts of violating the Espionage Act on October 17, 1985.

In the US District Court of Maryland, Morison's defense attempted to challenge the government's novel use of the Espionage Act by arguing the charges were "unconstitutionally vague and overbroad" and that the law was "intended to punish only 'espionage' in the classic sense of divulging information to agents of a hostile foreign government and not to punish the 'leaking' of classified information to the press."

The DOJ argued the Espionage Act was a strict liability law. If a defendant willfully transmitted photographs "relating to the national defense" to a person known by the defendant "not to be entitled to receive it," then they were guilty of violating the law regardless of any "laudable" motives.

Judge Joseph Young adopted a requirement that the government must prove information released was "national defense information," yet he embraced all other aspects of the prosecution. His comments even foreshadowed the "aiding the enemy" arguments that military prosecutors would make against Manning in 2013.

"The danger to the United States is just as great when this information is released to the press as when it is released to an agent of a foreign government," Young stated. "The fear in releasing this type of information is that it gives other nations information concerning the intelligence gathering capabilities of the United States. That fear is realized whether the information is released to the world at large or whether it is released only to specific spies."

A 2017 report from the Congressional Research Service on leak prosecutions acknowledged the "Morison prosecution involved a leak to the media, with seemingly no obvious intent to transmit sensitive information to hostile intelligence services." But that did not convince a jury or the courts that Morison was not guilty.[9]

"The Justice Department did, however, come under some criticism on the basis that such prosecutions are so rare as to amount to a selective prosecution in his case, raising concerns about the chilling effect such prosecutions could have on would-be whistleblowers, who could provide information embarrassing to the government but vital to public discourse," the report added. "On leaving office, President Clinton pardoned Morison."

Lawrence Franklin was charged with violating the Espionage Act in 2005. He was a Defense Department analyst who worked on US policy toward Iran. Upset that policy under President

George W. Bush was not more supportive of regime change efforts, Franklin leaked classified information to Steven Rosen and Keith Weissman, who were part of the Israeli lobbying group known as the American Israel Public Affairs Committee (AIPAC).

Rosen and Weissman were indicted too. Prosecutors accused the AIPAC lobbyists of cultivating "relationships with government officials with access to sensitive US government information," including "national defense information," obtaining information from the officials, and transmitting the "information to persons not otherwise entitled to receive it, including members of the media, foreign policy analysts, and officials of a foreign government."[10]

Like Assange, Rosen and Weissman were recipients of the information and did not sign a nondisclosure agreement. Neither had a security clearance.

Judge T. S. Ellis in the Eastern District of Virginia issued a ruling in which he made it clear the government needed to prove: "(1) that the information relates to the nation's military activities, intelligence gathering or foreign policy; (2) that the information is closely held by the government, in that it does not exist in the public domain; and (3) that the information is such that its disclosure could cause injury to the nation's security."[11]

In May 2009, prosecutors complained that they would have to meet what they viewed as an "unexpectedly higher evidentiary threshold in order to prevail at trial." It was in the "public interest" to dismiss the charges against Rosen and Weissman.[12]

Burden of Proof Lowered for Prosecutors

The CIA was furious when Fox News published a report in June 2009 that revealed US intelligence was "privy to the private discussions of North Korean leaders" and knew the country planned an "imminent nuclear test." It spurred the Obama administration's hawkish policy against leaks.[13]

On August 19, 2010, the DOJ unsealed an indictment against a State Department employee, Stephen Kim, for violating the Espionage Act. Back in March, FBI agents had raided Kim's condo, confiscated his computers, and looked everywhere for classified documents in his possession. They accused Kim of disclosing information about the US government's knowledge of North Korea's nuclear program and the threat it posed. Kim had communicated with Fox News reporter James Rosen in June 2009.[14]

Kim pled guilty in April 2014 and was sentenced to thirteen months in prison. The government told the court Kim had no motivation to "expose any government misconduct" and was not a whistleblower. They argued that he did not disclose "any government waste, fraud, abuse, or any other kind of government malfeasance" and "acted with knowledge that this disclosure was both unauthorized and unlawful."

If Kim had gone to trial, he never would have had a chance to argue he went to the media to reveal information in the public interest.

Furthermore, Judge Colleen Kollar-Kotelly lowered the burden of proof for prosecutors and ruled that they did not have to show the information could have damaged the United States.

Kim's defense contended the Espionage Act would transform into an Official Secrets Act, "enabling the government to punish disclosure of anything that was designated classified, even if it was improperly classified," if this interpretation were allowed. They referred to the Morison case, but the judge countered, "The Morison approach invites (if not requires) the jury to second guess the classification of the information."[15]

While pursuing Kim, FBI special agent Reginald B. Reyes asserted there was "probable cause to believe" that Rosen—the reporter—committed a violation of the Espionage Act, as "an aider and abettor and/or co-conspirator."[16]

A broad request sought the seizure of records related to Rosen's "communication with any other source or potential source of the information" published by Fox News. Agents wanted records showing Rosen's knowledge of "laws, regulations, and/or procedures prohibiting the unauthorized disclosure of national defense or classified information." And they wanted records related to Rosen's "knowledge of government rules and/or procedures regarding communications with members of the media."[17]

The DOJ compromised Rosen's ability to engage in journalism by sifting through records of his communications, and they were also open to potentially prosecuting him to send a message that could discourage leaks.

During the same period, US Attorney Rod Rosenstein charged FBI linguist Shamai Leibowitz with violating the Espionage Act on December 8, 2009.[18] Prosecutors invoked a provision that criminalizes the transmission of "communications intelligence," and Leibowitz pled guilty less than ten days later.[19]

"I discovered that the FBI was committing what I believed to be illegal acts. After I revealed these to a blogger, the Department of Justice came after me with a vengeance," Leibowitz recalled in 2013.[20]

"When the FBI confronted me, I admitted what I had done," he said. "I tried to negotiate for a reasonable resolution of my case. The documents I disclosed were never explicitly published anywhere, but that didn't matter. The DOJ was adamant that I be charged under the Espionage Act and spend time in jail.

"My family and I pleaded with the DOJ lawyers to avoid a prison term, agree to a lesser punishment, and put this case to rest without any media attention. But the FBI and DOJ were insistent on imprisoning me and splashing it all over the media. The ink was not even dry on my plea bargain before they ran to the media with a press release, announcing to the whole world how the 20-month prison sentence [would] teach me—and any future whistleblowers—a great lesson."[21]

Judge Alexander Williams Jr. said at Leibowitz's sentencing hearing, "I don't know what was divulged other than some documents, and how it compromised things, I have no idea." It was later reported that Leibowitz disclosed "secret transcripts of conversations caught on F.B.I. wiretaps of the Israeli Embassy in Washington."[22]

The Obama DOJ also prosecuted NSA whistleblower Thomas Drake, who was a senior employee opposed to unconstitutional surveillance—a case it had inherited from the Bush administration.

Drake was wrongly suspected by the DOJ of being a source for a major *New York Times* report on Bush's warrantless wiretapping program. Investigators discovered that Drake communicated with a *Baltimore Sun* reporter about waste, fraud, and abuse at the agency.[23]

The FBI raided Drake's home in 2007, yet he was not charged until April 2010. They accused him of "improperly retaining" classified information.

Prosecutors asked the court to bar the introduction of "evidence, examination of witnesses, or argument by counsel" related to Drake's "need" to expose waste and abuse at the NSA. "The defendant's motive for his conduct is irrelevant."

By June 2011, the government's case collapsed. Drake pled guilty to a misdemeanor of "exceeding authorized use of a computer," which is not an Espionage Act offense, and received probation. Judge Richard Bennett in the US District Court for the District of Maryland scolded prosecutors during sentencing for putting Drake through "four years of hell" and refused to incarcerate Drake.[24]

"I don't think that deterrence should include an American citizen waiting two and a half years after their home is searched to find out if they're going to be indicted or not. I find that uncon-scionable," Bennett declared. "It is at the very root of what this country was founded on against general warrants of the British. When it happens, it should be resolved pretty quickly, and it sure as heck shouldn't take two and a half years before someone's charged after that event."

Bennett objected to lead prosecutor William Welch's request to "send a message" and fine Drake $50,000 after he received the Ridenhour Prize for Truth-Telling that included a $10,000 award. He noted that Drake spent more than $80,000 on a lawyer and would never receive his federal pension, even though he was only five years away from eligibility.[25]

"There has been financial devastation wrought upon this defen-dant that far exceeds any fine that can be imposed by me. And I'm not going to add to that in any way," Bennett stated.

Edward Snowden and Chelsea Manning have each said Drake inspired them to become whistleblowers.

Two CIA Whistleblowers Prosecuted

Embarrassment from the Drake case had little impact on the Obama administration's hawkishness.

Jeffrey Sterling, a Black CIA officer, faced several Espionage Act charges in December 2010. The DOJ claimed Sterling leaked information related to a top-secret CIA operation called "Opera-tion Merlin" to James Risen, a *New York Times* reporter.

The government additionally maintained Risen published information from Sterling in his book *State of War*, which was released in January 2006. They accused Sterling of a "scheme to disclose classified information" that began in August 2000 and lasted until Risen's book on the CIA and President George W. Bush's administration went on sale.[26]

In 2001, Sterling sued the CIA for allegedly engaging in racial discrimination. He was one of the first Black officers to challenge the CIA in this manner, and the DOJ responded by arguing the lawsuit would reveal state secrets if it proceeded.[27]

An appeals court blocked his civil rights complaint in 2005. "There is no way for Sterling to prove employment discrimination without exposing at least some classified details of the covert employment that gives context to his claim," the appeals court ruled.[28]

Sterling was a part of Operation Merlin, which he described as "an ostensible effort to hamper Iran's development of a nuclear weapons program."[29]

"The CIA assured me the operation was safe," he said, "and plans we provided were flawed so they would undermine Iran. Yet, I became concerned that safety protocols were not what the agency had promised, and after the invasion of Iraq, I dreaded the operation could be used against US soldiers.

"Following whistleblower procedures, I took my concerns to both the Senate and House intelligence committees. Despite their assurances of confidentiality and initial responses to my concerns, neither committee saw fit to act on my disclosures."

The CIA fired Sterling in 2002. He moved to St. Louis, Missouri, and "could not find a job." In 2006, the FBI raided his home, and for the next several years a cloud of investigation hung over Sterling's head.

Unlike most whistleblowers charged under the Espionage Act, Sterling took his case to trial, making it the first federal leak case to proceed to trial since Samuel Morison's case in 1985. Sterling maintained he was not the source of the leak.

Before trial, prosecutors moved to bar any arguments that "leaks are good or necessary or that [Sterling] was a whistleblower, thereby justifying his conduct or negating his criminal intent."

A jury issued a guilty verdict. The government convinced jurors with largely circumstantial evidence that Sterling leaked information to Risen. Prosecutors argued Sterling leaked information as an act of revenge after he was stopped from pursuing his racial discrimination lawsuit, although no emails showing Sterling sent Risen classified information were ever presented.

Bizarrely, the hairdresser for an FBI investigator was called to testify that they had read Risen's book in order to prove Sterling was charged in the appropriate judicial district. Sterling's defense had argued he should have been charged in Missouri, where he lived, and not the Eastern District of Virginia.

The trial was not held until January 2015—over eight years after the FBI raided Sterling's house—because the DOJ spent seven years trying to force Risen to testify against Sterling.

Risen filed a lawsuit that asserted he had a reporter's privilege under the First Amendment to protect his confidential sources. The Supreme Court refused to hear Risen's appeal in 2014. Only because of an outcry from media organizations did Attorney General Eric Holder relent and pursue the prosecution of Sterling without Risen's testimony.

Sterling received a forty-two-month prison sentence. Arguably, Risen could have helped minimize punishment by definitively saying that Sterling was not his source for *State of War*.

Another CIA whistleblower, John Kiriakou, became the target of an Espionage Act prosecution after he went on ABC News in 2007 and spoke out against the CIA torture program. He confirmed that the CIA had waterboarded prisoners and that waterboarding was part of the agency's official policy.

On January 23, 2012, a criminal complaint was filed against Kiriakou for allegedly violating both the Espionage Act and the Intelligence Identities Protection Act. Prosecutors accused Kiriakou of illegally disclosing the identities of two CIA employees, including one involved in the capture of Abu Zubaydah, which Kiriakou spearheaded.[30]

The Bush administration investigated Kiriakou but apparently concluded he had not committed a crime. When Obama was elected, memos that Kiriakou obtained during discovery showed CIA director John Brennan asked the DOJ to "charge him with espionage." The DOJ replied, "But he hasn't committed espionage."

"The CIA leadership was furious that I blew the whistle on torture and the Justice Department never stopped investigating me from December 2007," Kiriakou claimed.

"In the summer of 2010, a foreign intelligence [agent] offered me cash in exchange for classified information," Kiriakou recounted. "I turned down the pitch, and I immediately reported it to the FBI. So the FBI asked me to take the guy out to lunch and to ask him what information he wanted and how much information he was willing to give me for it. They were going to put two agents at a nearby table.

"They ended up canceling the two agents, but they asked me to go ahead with the lunch. So I did. After the lunch, I wrote a long memo to the FBI—and I did this four or five times."[31]

While he was putting together his defense, Kiriakou learned there was no foreign intelligence officer. An FBI agent pretended to be an intelligence officer to try to set up Kiriakou on an Espionage Act charge. By repeatedly reporting the contact, Kiriakou foiled the effort.[32]

The FBI launched a criminal investigation into the American Civil Liberties Union and attorneys for prisoners at Guantánamo Bay who sought to identify their torturers. That helped the FBI find a pretext for charging him.

Kiriakou recalled, "The FBI asked Guantánamo defense attorneys where they got the names [of the torturers]. They got the names from an investigator for Human Rights Watch by the name of John Sifton. They went to John Sifton and asked where he got the names. Instead of saying no comment, Sifton said I got the names from Matthew Cole."[33]

Cole represented himself as a journalist with ABC News. He sent Kiriakou two lists that each had a dozen names of people allegedly with the CIA. Kiriakou knew none of them. But there was one individual whom Cole asked about who was mentioned in Kiriakou's book, *The Reluctant Spy*. Kiriakou made the mistake of confirming that agent's last name.

"The FBI went to Cole and said, where did you get the name? Cole ratted me out to the FBI, and then later testified against me to the grand jury. As it turned out, Cole was on the Guantánamo defense attorneys' payroll. He was moonlighting from ABC and never told ABC that he was doing this."[34]

In October 2012, Kiriakou came to the realization that the Eastern District of Virginia, which he has called the "Espionage Court," would not allow him a fair trial. His lawyer Plato Cacheris advised him to accept a plea agreement. "In any other district, I'd say let's go for it, we're going to win. But your jury is going to be made up of people with friends, relatives at the CIA, the Pentagon, national security, intelligence contractors. You don't stand a chance. Just take the deal."[35]

The deal allowed Kiriakou to plead guilty to the charge of violating the Intelligence Identities Protection Act. It limited his federal prison sentence to thirty months.

Assange faces the prospect of a trial in this court, and his lawyers are unlikely to obtain the kind of bargain that prosecutors offered to Kiriakou.

US Revokes Snowden's Passport, Stranding Him in Moscow

In May 2013, NSA contractor Edward Snowden released documents to journalists Glenn Greenwald, Ewen MacAskill, and Laura Poitras that exposed the US government's mass surveillance programs to unprecedented scrutiny. He was charged with violating the Espionage Act on June 4, 2013.

Snowden met with Greenwald, MacAskill, and Poitras in Hong Kong. After revealing that he was the whistleblower behind reports in the *Guardian*, Snowden left the country. (WikiLeaks investigative editor Sarah Harrison accompanied Snowden, and the June 2020 indictment against Assange criminalized WikiLeaks staff for helping Snowden.)

Joe Biden, who was vice president, pressured countries to deny Snowden's requests for political asylum.[36] He asked Ecuador president Rafael Correa, who granted political asylum to Assange, not to offer Snowden protection from US prosecution.[37] The State Department revoked Snowden's passport and stranded him in Moscow.

Jen Psaki, a State Department spokesperson, declared, "Persons wanted on felony charges, such as Mr. Snowden, should not be allowed to proceed in any further international travel other than is necessary to return him to the United States."[38]

Russia granted Snowden asylum in 2013, and he offered to come back to the US for a trial if prosecutors would allow him to make a public interest defense and tell a jury why he revealed the documents.[39]

Despite the fact that the DOJ was unable to seize Snowden and bring him back to the US for trial, it did succeed in convincing a judge that the government had a right to confiscate proceeds from his memoir, *Permanent Record*, as well as money he earned from giving speeches.[40]

Snowden and his wife, Lindsay Mills, had two children in Russia. To ensure they would never be separated from their children, in 2020 they applied for Russian citizenship. In September 2022, they were granted Russian citizenship, while maintaining their US citizenship.

As of October 2022, the Espionage Act indictment against Snowden was still pending.

Anyone Could Be Perceived As An "Insider Threat"

While federal prosecutors made an example out of whistleblowers with Espionage Act prosecutions, US government agencies adopted "insider threat" programs that further intensified the climate of fear.

A 2014 file from the National Insider Threat Task Force, which is part of the Office of the Director for National Intelligence (ODNI), held up Chelsea Manning as someone who had all the hallmarks of an "insider threat."[41]

"During Pvt. Manning's service in the US Army, [she] struggled with [her] self image as a man, when [she] wanted to be an openly accepted female in the US Army. Pvt. Manning was also an advocate for homosexuals openly serving" in the Defense Department against the "Don't Ask, Don't Tell" policy, the file stated.

She "obsessively researched websites regarding [Don't Ask, Don't Tell] and politicians who supported or didn't support the lesbian/gay community." She "conducted this activity while being assigned to research and analyze the patterns and threats of IED attacks."

The file additionally claimed, "Pvt. Manning was associated [with] a group of self-proclaimed 'hackers' who deemed all information (government in particular) should be public knowledge.

[She] was accepted in this group and associated [herself] as a 'hacker' and subscribed to the group's ideology." (The "group" referenced was clearly WikiLeaks.)[42]

In addition to the homophobic and transphobic description, several "motives" or "behavior indicators" were listed to help agencies stop the next Manning.

Manning noted, "Agencies implementing the insider threat program could examine anyone who has motives of 'greed,' 'financial difficulties,' is 'disgruntled,' has 'an ideology,' a 'divided loyalty,' an 'ego' or 'self-image,' or 'any family/personal issues' – the words used to describe my motives. Such subjective labeling could easily be applied to virtually every single person currently holding a security clearance."[43]

The following year, ODNI official Patricia Larsen presented training that labeled NSA whistleblower Thomas Drake an "insider threat" and lumped him in with Fort Hood shooter Nidal Hasan and Navy Yard shooter Aaron Alexis, who were both responsible for murdering people.

Larsen asserted, "any employees and contractors who damage an entity's reputation, be it government or business, by exposing inside information should be considered insider threats, as they 'would be in the business world.'" The extremely broad definition upset more than twenty civil society organizations, which wrote to the ODNI's inspector general and complained.

"This kind of wanton misuse of the term 'threat' demonstrates that this program fails to distinguish between those who want to fix problems from those who wish to do harm to our national security."[44]

By all accounts, the insider threat programs cultivated a total surveillance system that was capable of monitoring government employees and contractors' every keystroke.

"End This Culture of Leaks"

President Bush had dealt with national security leaks. Yet as Gabriel Schoenfeld, a conservative, anti-leaks scholar for the Hudson Institute, put it, "Bush would have faced a greater public backlash had he sought to imprison leakers." Bush was not "willing to spend the political capital." Obama, on the other hand, was "very hawkish" against leaks and succeeded in refining a system for enforced secrecy.[45]

Trump cranked this system into overdrive. He immediately struck a vengeful tone when it came to leakers: "Leaking, and even illegal classified leaking, has been a big problem in Washington for years." Well before he was banned from Twitter, Trump cried, "The spotlight has finally been put on the low-life leakers! They will be caught!"[46]

In August 2017, Attorney General Jeff Sessions, who had a track record of aggressive opposition to leaks when he was a US senator, announced that intelligence agencies would refer more cases to the DOJ and investigate more leaks. An FBI "counterintelligence unit" was created.[47]

"This nation must end this culture of leaks. We will investigate and seek to bring criminals to justice. We will not allow rogue anonymous sources with security clearances to sell out our country," Sessions proclaimed.

The first person charged under the Espionage Act while Trump was president was Reality Winner, an NSA contractor who printed and mailed a report to the Intercept on May 9, 2017. She believed the report contained proof that Russian hackers targeted voter registration systems during the 2016 election. Intercept reporter Matthew Cole foolishly aided the investigation by sharing a copy of the document with the NSA's media affairs office.[48]

On June 5, the FBI came to her home in Augusta, Georgia, and interrogated Winner. One FBI agent said, "I think you might've been angry over everything that's going on, politics-wise," and suggested that she had probably made a mistake. The same agent also said they didn't think she was trying to be Snowden.[49]

A second FBI agent asked Winner why she used privacy tools, such as the TOR browser, which the DOJ criminalized in its case against Assange. "There was one day when I was interested in WikiLeaks [and] I opened it up once. I shouldn't have done [that]. I was in between jobs, just had gotten out of the Air Force," Winner replied.

Yet, as Kiriakou learned, "FBI agents will lie, trick, and deceive you. They will twist your words and play on your patriotism to entrap you." The agents acted in a friendly manner toward Winner to obtain a confession. As the grueling experience came to an end, Winner admitted to leaking the document because the agents threatened to charge her with lying to the FBI.

Winner was arrested and detained until she pled guilty in June 2018. In August, she was sentenced to prison for sixty-three months, the longest sentence ever for an unauthorized disclosure of information.[50]

Titus Nichols, who was part of the legal team that represented Winner, said, "From the very beginning, the entire goal was to prevent the worst possible scenario from happening: her being sentenced to ten years in prison."[51]

In Winner's case, the government seized upon the precedent set in Stephen Kim's case and maintained the "plain language" of the Espionage Act did not require prosecutors to "prove harm—whether potential or actual—to the national security occurring as a result of an unauthorized disclosure." They mentioned that the judge in Kim's case had lowered the burden of proof.[52]

"Under the Espionage Act, we can't just come to trial and say, hey, we've got this piece of paper. It's classified, and then discuss it before a jury," Nichols added. "We first have to file a motion explaining what document we're going to be using, what specific lines, and why we're using it.

"The government can then object and say, well, that's not a good enough reason to disclose that, and then the court has to decide whether [it will] allow that piece of classified information."

Intent does not matter in Espionage Act cases. "The fact that you willingly disclosed, that is the only intent that the laws looks at, which is very unfair because the reason why it's classified and the reason why it's prosecuted so heavily [is] because the government says, well, this piece of paper, this book, this picture, this whatever, could cause exceptionally grave injury to the United States of America," Nichols argued.

It does not matter who received the information. It does not matter why the person released the information. It does not matter if damage occurred as a result of the disclosure or publication of the information. It is all the same to DOJ prosecutors.

The next person prosecuted under the Espionage Act was Terry Albury, a Black FBI special agent assigned as an airport liaison to Customs and Border Protection at the Minneapolis–Saint Paul International Airport. Albury disclosed documents on the FBI's racial profiling, surveillance, and informant recruitment practices to the Intercept, and prosecutors charged him on March 27, 2018.

Albury pled guilty less than a month later and was sentenced to forty-eight months in prison on October 18.[53]

His attorneys said his disclosures were an "act of conscience" by a person who was the only Black field agent in the Minneapolis field office.

"It has long been a critique of the FBI that it consists of and reflects a predominantly white male culture, which, as a result, has often treated minority communities with suspicion and disrespect," the statement declared. "[Albury] was required firsthand to implement FBI investigation directives that profiled and intimidated minority communities in Minnesota and other locations."

Albury was profiled by journalist Janet Reitman for a *New York Times Magazine* article published on September 1, 2021. His whistleblower motives were crystal clear.[54]

"There is this mythology surrounding the war on terrorism, and the FBI, that has given agents the power to ruin the lives of completely innocent people based solely on what part of the world they came from, or what religion they practice, or the color of their skin," Albury said. "And I did that. I helped destroy people—for 17 years."

But if Albury had gone to trial, the judge would have prohibited him from telling the jury about the abusive acts he was tasked with carrying out in his daily work for the FBI.

Whistleblower Motives Are "Irrelevant"

Around a month after Julian Assange was jailed, Daniel Hale, a former Air Force intelligence analyst, was arrested and charged with violating the Espionage Act. He disclosed classified information to journalist and Intercept co-founder Jeremy Scahill about the US government's targeted assassination program and drone warfare, which was published as "The Drone Papers" in October 2015.

The information Hale disclosed not only exposed the extent to which drone strikes kill innocent civilians, but also brought attention to the US government's out-of-control watchlisting system. One document on watchlisting, which Hale released, was used by the Council on American-Islamic Relations to convince a court that a number of Muslim Americans were erroneously placed on the No Fly List and should be removed.[55]

Again, as with the indictment against Assange, prosecutors criminalized the Intercept's recommendation that sources use privacy tools, including TOR software and the Tails operating system, which are designed to help users leave no digital footprint.

Hale appeared in the 2016 documentary *National Bird*, directed by Sonia Kennebeck. The FBI raided his home on August 8, 2014, before production was completed. However, the DOJ did not immediately charge Hale, and the reasons were never made clear.

Similar to its actions in previous Espionage Act cases, the government moved to block Hale from presenting evidence related to his "good motives."

"The defense likely will want to argue that, even if the defendant engaged in the conduct alleged, he had good reasons to leak the documents at issue and is being unfairly prosecuted under criminal statutes that carry significant penalties," the government declared. "Any attempt to inject a necessity, whistleblower, or similar motive for the defendant's conduct is irrelevant.[56]

Prosecutors also claimed the Espionage Act did not require the government to prove that Hale "intended to harm the United States."

The defense was alarmed by what the case might mean for Scahill because one of the charges accused Hale of obtaining information with "reason to believe that another person—presumably the reporter with whom he allegedly shared it—would possess or communicate the information in violation of the Espionage Act."

"If that is the government's theory, it will require this court to instruct a jury that a journalist's possession or publication of defense information is a crime," Hale's defense argued.

After consulting with NSA whistleblower Thomas Drake, CIA whistleblower John Kiriakou, and attorney Jesselyn Radack, Hale pled guilty. This made Hale the first whistleblower convicted under the Espionage Act during President Joe Biden's administration. He was sentenced to forty-five months in prison.

On August 8, 2022, FBI agents executed a search warrant against Trump and searched his Mar-a-Lago estate in Florida for classified documents that he claimed as his personal property. He effectively stole the files, some of them marked top secret, and withheld them after the DOJ requested their return. For the first time in US history, the DOJ invoked the Espionage Act to take legal action against a former US president.

The fact that Trump, who was president when Assange was hit with Espionage Act charges, now faced legal jeopardy under the same draconian law was a kind of hole in the space-time continuum event. Rather than allow the moment to bring newfound legitimacy to the antiquated law, it was an opportunity to overhaul the Espionage Act or totally abolish it.

CHAPTER 5

The CIA's War on WikiLeaks

Who can be so overtly covert?
Sometimes even covertly overt.
—THE FUGS, "CIA Man" (1967)

When the Central Intelligence Agency (CIA) joined Twitter in June 2014, WikiLeaks welcomed the agency: "We look forward to sharing great classified info about you." They shared links to documents previously published by the CIA, along with a link to a search for "CIA" documents in their database.[1]

High-ranking CIA officials despised Julian Assange for exposing the agency to unwanted scrutiny; however, agents were largely discouraged from targeting WikiLeaks until the media organization helped National Security Agency (NSA) whistleblower Edward Snowden leave Hong Kong.

On March 7, 2017, WikiLeaks published what they described as the "largest ever publication of confidential documents on the agency."[2] The Vault 7 documents described the agency's cyber warfare and hacking capabilities, and the leak embarrassed CIA Director Mike Pompeo.

The gloves came off at the CIA. As reported by Yahoo News, Pompeo authorized a disruption campaign to further neutralize the media organization.[3] WikiLeaks was labeled a "hostile entity," and Pompeo focused his first speech as CIA director on the "threat" posed by WikiLeaks.

CIA Loses Control of Its Hacking Arsenal

Several United States senators were skeptical of Pompeo's attitude toward WikiLeaks. During his confirmation hearing to be CIA director in January 2017, Maine Democratic senator Angus King confronted Pompeo with a tweet Pompeo had sent during President Donald Trump's 2016 campaign.[4] Pompeo had tweeted, "Need further proof that the fix was in from President Obama on down. Busted, 19252 emails from DNC [Democratic National Committee] leaked by WikiLeaks."

Trump, Pompeo, and various Republicans were enthusiastic about WikiLeaks when the media organization exposed Democratic presidential nominee Hillary Clinton and the Democratic Party to criticism for their actions, which greased the skids for Clinton to secure the nomination against any primary challenger. However, with the power entrusted to him as CIA director, Pompeo inducted himself into what former CIA employee Victor Marchetti and former State Department employee John D. Marks deemed the "cult of intelligence."[5]

"I have never believed that WikiLeaks is a credible source of information," Pompeo replied.

On February 16, 2017, WikiLeaks published "CIA espionage orders" that called attention to how all of the major political parties in France were allegedly "targeted for infiltration" in the run-up to the country's 2012 presidential election.[6]

Next came the publication of Vault 7 materials.

"The CIA lost control of the majority of its hacking arsenal including malware, viruses, trojans, weaponized 'zero day' exploits, malware remote control systems and associated documentation," WikiLeaks declared in its press release.[7] "This extraordinary collection, which amounts to more than several hundred million lines of code, gives its possessor the entire hacking capacity of the CIA."

For the first time, the CIA's "fleet of hackers," who have the capability to target smartphones and computers, were challenged.

WikiLeaks suggested the "archive" was "circulated among former US government hackers and contractors in an unauthorized manner." One of these presumed hackers or contractors allegedly shared a portion of the archive with WikiLeaks.

Nearly 9,000 documents came from "an isolated, high-security network inside the CIA's Center for Cyber Intelligence." (The espionage orders published that February were from this cache of information.)

A program called "Weeping Angel," which made it possible for the CIA to attack Samsung televisions and convert them into spying devices, was exposed.

As CNBC reported, the CIA identified fourteen "zero-day exploits," which were "software vulnerabilities" that had no fix yet.[8] The agency had the ability to use them to "hack Apple's iOS devices, such as iPads and iPhones." Documents showed the exploits were shared with the NSA and Government Communications Headquarters (GCHQ), the British spy agency. "The CIA did not tell Apple about these vulnerabilities."

It was additionally revealed that the CIA could target Microsoft Windows, as well as Signal and WhatsApp users, with malware.[9]

Snowden, who worked for a time as a CIA contractor, said the documents showed the US government developed "vulnerabilities in US products" and intentionally kept "holes open. Reckless beyond words."

Files were curated and shared periodically throughout 2017. They were not dumped on the internet. For example, in November, WikiLeaks revealed "Hive," which the CIA used to control its malware.[10] The CIA could steal data from "target organizations" by impersonating "uninvolved entities," so the targets would likely misattribute the theft to other actors.

"The three examples included in the source code build a fake certificate for the anti-virus company Kaspersky Laboratory, Moscow pretending to be signed by Thawte Premium Server CA, Cape Town," according to WikiLeaks.

The "Marble Framework" was exposed in March 2017.[11] It reflected the CIA's "anti-forensics approach" and was reportedly in use during 2016. With Marble, the CIA could "obfuscate" and prevent forensic investigators and anti-virus investigators from attributing cyber attacks to the CIA.

"By pretending that the spoken language of the malware creator was not American English, but Chinese, but then showing attempts to conceal the use of Chinese," the CIA could steer forensic investigators to the wrong conclusion about who perpetrated an attack, WikiLeaks claimed.

An infuriated CIA responded, "The American public should be deeply troubled by any WikiLeaks disclosure designed to damage the intelligence community's ability to protect America against terrorists and other adversaries. Such disclosures not only jeopardize US personnel and operations but also equip our adversaries with tools and information to do us harm."[12]

"There is an extreme proliferation risk in the development of cyber 'weapons,'" Assange contended. "Comparisons can be drawn between the uncontrolled proliferation of such 'weapons,' which results from the inability to contain them combined with their high market value, and the global arms trade." Their significance may go beyond "cyber war and cyber peace."[13]

Although the debate WikiLeaks attempted to provoke was important, Pompeo and the CIA detested the conversation and responded vindictively.

Pompeo Labels WikiLeaks a "Non-state Hostile Intelligence Service"

On April 13, 2017, Pompeo spoke at an event hosted by the Center for Strategic and International Studies, headquartered in Washington, D.C., in which he displayed his thirst for revenge against WikiLeaks. "It is time to call out WikiLeaks for what it really is—a non-state hostile intelligence service often abetted by state actors like Russia.

"WikiLeaks walks like a hostile intelligence service and talks like a hostile intelligence service and has encouraged its followers to find jobs at the CIA in order to obtain intelligence," Pompeo jeered.[14]

This was when the CIA first introduced the public to the conspiracy theory that would later make up the core of the Justice Department's indictment against Assange in 2019.

"[WikiLeaks] directed Chelsea Manning in her theft of specific secret information. And it overwhelmingly focuses on the United States while seeking support from anti-democratic countries and organizations," Pompeo asserted.

"Julian Assange and his kind are not the slightest bit interested in improving civil liberties or enhancing personal freedom. They have pretended that America's First Amendment freedoms shield them from justice. They may have believed that, but they are wrong."

Pompeo continued, "Assange is a narcissist who has created nothing of value. He relies on the dirty work of others to make himself famous. He is a fraud—a coward hiding behind a screen. And in Kansas [Pompeo had been a congressman from Kansas], we know something about false wizards.

"We've had administrations before that have been squeamish about going after these folks under some concept of this right to publish," Pompeo said. Assange has "no First Amendment freedoms," because "he is not a US citizen."

The speech was emblematic of Pompeo's zealousness, which stemmed from the embarrassing leak of Vault 7 materials. It also foreshadowed the CIA's "secret war plans" to kidnap or kill the WikiLeaks founder.

Yahoo News reporters Zach Dorfman, Sean Naylor, and Michael Isikoff spoke with more than thirty former US government officials in 2020. Their sources included officials who worked in the Trump administration.[15]

According to their reporting, in 2013 the Obama administration permitted US intelligence agencies to spy on WikiLeaks. This occurred after WikiLeaks helped Snowden. Later, the CIA was granted renewed support for targeting WikiLeaks staff and alleged associates following the media organization's publication of emails from Hillary Clinton's 2016 presidential campaign.

The Obama White House was lobbied by US intelligence officials to classify Assange, as well as journalists Glenn Greenwald and Laura Poitras, as "information brokers." This would help the CIA pursue them as "agents of a foreign power." (Greenwald and Poitras obtained NSA documents from Snowden.)

"Is WikiLeaks a journalistic outlet? Are Laura Poitras and Glenn Greenwald truly journalists?" one former official said to Yahoo News. "We tried to change the definition of them, and I preached this to the White House and got rejected."[16]

Another major revelation in the Yahoo News report involved a "carveout" that Pompeo and other CIA officials seized upon to avoid briefing Congress or the need for a presidential finding, which is typically required if the agency plans to "secretly interfere in the activities of any foreign actor." By treating WikiLeaks as a rival spy service, they could mount "offensive counterintelligence" operations free of any oversight.

Pompeo allegedly proposed kidnapping Assange in the summer of 2017. He considered authorizing CIA agents to break into the

Ecuador embassy in London to drag the WikiLeaks founder out and load him onto a rendition flight.

CIA officials allegedly approved a disruption campaign to attack WikiLeaks' "digital infrastructure." Agents had the green light to provoke "internal disputes within the organization by planting damaging information" and even steal the electronic devices of WikiLeaks staff.[17]

"Agency executives requested and received 'sketches' of plans for killing Assange and other Europe-based WikiLeaks members who had access to Vault 7 materials, said a former intelligence official. There were discussions 'on whether killing Assange was possible and whether it was legal,' the former official said," according to Yahoo News.

When Yahoo News sought comment from Pompeo, the former CIA director did not respond to requests. However, during an event at Hillsdale College following publication, a student questioned him. "Don't believe everything you read in Yahoo News," Pompeo replied, as he scratched his forehead nearly the same way Director of National Intelligence James Clapper did when he lied to senators about NSA warrantless surveillance.[18]

Next, Pompeo appeared on conservative radio host Glenn Beck's show and attacked Isikoff, who co-authored the report.[19] He claimed the Yahoo News sources didn't know what the CIA was doing. "I make no apologies," Pompeo added, because there were "bad actors" who stole "really, really sensitive material."

"I came to believe that [WikiLeaks was] one of the first non-state hostile intelligence entities. They weren't engaged in even crappy reporting, like Isikoff does," Pompeo said, which induced a belly laugh from Beck. "They were engaged in active efforts to steal secrets themselves and pay others to do the same."

Days later, Pompeo went on the *Megyn Kelly Show* and contended the report made for "pretty good fiction." This is "classic Isikoff."[20]

"I can't say much about this other than—whoever these thirty people are who allegedly spoke with one of these reporters—they should all be prosecuted for speaking about classified activity inside the Central Intelligence Agency," Pompeo declared. "Maybe they didn't. Maybe Isikoff just made it up. But you should know I take seriously my responsibilities to protect that information." He repeated the agency viewpoint that WikiLeaks was committed to stealing US secrets.

"There's pieces of it that are true," Pompeo later conceded. The CIA believed the DOJ had a "valid claim" to extradite Assange for a US trial. He said US law prohibits assassinations and scoffed at the idea that the CIA might have circumvented DOJ lawyers.

"Well, we know [the CIA] never acted on it because Julian Assange is still alive. The reporting is that there was a plot, you know, plans and sketches," Kelly interjected. Pompeo replied with a non-denial answer, "We never conducted planning to violate U.S. laws, not once in my time."

Pompeo's dog barked loudly through the last minute of the interview. Even his dog could apparently tell he was being dishonest.

"You Don't Get to Love Truth One Day and Seek Its Suppression . . . the Next"

Days after Assange's arrest, Pompeo infamously said during a Q&A session at Texas A&M University, "I was the CIA director. We lied, we cheated, we stole. We had entire training courses."[21] Former CIA director Michael Hayden, not WikiLeaks, also professed in Alex Gibney's 2013 WikiLeaks documentary, "We steal secrets. We steal other nations' secrets."[22]

Following Pompeo's 2017 speech, the *Washington Post* gave Assange a platform to respond to the CIA director's venomous attack on WikiLeaks.[23]

"When the director of the CIA, an unelected public servant, publicly demonizes a publisher such as WikiLeaks as a 'fraud,' 'coward,' and 'enemy,' it puts all journalists on notice, or should. Pompeo's next talking point, unsupported by fact, that WikiLeaks is a 'non-state hostile intelligence service,' is a dagger aimed at Americans' constitutional right to receive honest information about their government. This accusation mirrors attempts throughout history by bureaucrats seeking, and failing, to criminalize speech that reveals their own failings," Assange declared.

"Pompeo liked WikiLeaks when he perceived it was publishing material revealing the shortcomings of his political rivals. It was only when our publications touched Pompeo's rice bowl that WikiLeaks became his target. Pompeo subsequently deleted the tweet, but he is learning that in the digital age, the truth is hard to hide. You don't get to love the truth one day and seek its suppression and the incarceration of its publisher the next."

Assange continued, "The 'Pompeo doctrine' articulated in his speech ensnares all serious news and investigative human rights organizations, from ProPublica to Amnesty International to Human Rights Watch. The logic that WikiLeaks, or these organizations, are somehow 'intelligence agencies' would be as absurd as the suggestion that the CIA is a media outlet.

"Both journalists and intelligence agencies cultivate and protect sources, collect information and write reports, but the similarities end there. The world cannot afford, and the Constitution does not permit, a muzzle placed on the work that transparency organizations do to inform the American and global public," Assange concluded.

In September 2017, Pompeo canceled a speech at the Harvard Kennedy School of Government because the school planned to honor Chelsea Manning as a "visiting fellow." He called Manning an "American traitor." Pompeo's opposition, along with former

CIA deputy director Mike Morell's resignation from the school, pushed the university to rescind the honor.[24]

By this time, Attorney General Jeff Sessions had indicated the Trump DOJ had prioritized Assange's arrest.[25] CNN reported there were criminal charges drafted against Assange.[26]

The Yahoo News report on the CIA's war against WikiLeaks contained revelations related to the improper pressure prosecutors faced.[27]

"Some National Security Council officials" in Trump's administration "worried that the CIA's proposals to kidnap Assange would not only be illegal but also might jeopardize the prosecution of the WikiLeaks founder," according to the report. "Concerned the CIA's plans would derail a potential criminal case, the Justice Department expedited the drafting of charges against Assange to ensure that they were in place if he were brought to the United States."

Discussions about putting Assange on a rendition flight alarmed senior administration officials like John Eisenberg, who was the top lawyer for the National Security Council, and his deputy, Michael Ellis.

"Pompeo [was] advocating things that are not likely to be legal," including "rendition-type activity," one former national security official told Yahoo News.

The DOJ had not indicted Assange, "even under seal." If the CIA kidnapped Assange from the Ecuador embassy, they would be doing so without any "legal basis to try him in the United States."

Eisenberg allegedly "urged Justice Department officials to accelerate their drafting of charges against Assange, in case the CIA's rendition plans moved forward, according to former officials. The White House told Attorney General Jeff Sessions that if prosecutors had grounds to indict Assange they should hurry up and do so, according to a former senior administration official."

Alarming actions by the CIA amounted to improper pressure on prosecutors to charge Assange.

The Yahoo News report was a rare example of journalism in the US press that brought much-needed attention to the political nature of the case against Assange. It also played a key role in rekindling interest among media outlets throughout the world.

More journalists remotely followed the US government's appeal at the United Kingdom High Court of Justice, which took place in October 2021, than had followed most days of the extradition trial in September 2020. Media organizations were eager to hear the court's and the Assange legal team's reactions to allegations against the CIA.

One of the judges argued it was not "controversial" for the CIA to be "intensely interested" in Assange. Mark Summers QC, an attorney for Assange, believed the court failed to grasp the gravity of the issue. The scandal was not that the CIA took interest in someone who published their leaked documents. Rather, it was what agency officials allegedly plotted to do against Assange and the way that undermined the credibility of US diplomatic assurances related to how they would treat him.

The CIA never carried out any of the agency's alleged assassination or kidnapping plans. The agency did, however, collaborate with a private Spanish company called Undercover Global that had been contracted by Ecuador to manage the London embassy's security. The company helped the CIA further a disruption campaign against WikiLeaks, and Assange sued Undercover Global's director in a Spanish criminal court.

CHAPTER 6

The Spying Operation Against Assange

They want to stop the spread of the fire.
But there are some fires that can't be extinguished with water.
—CALLE 13, "Multi_Viral" [featuring Tom Morello,
Kamilya Jubran, and Julian Assange] (2014)

Stella Moris, a lawyer who was part of Julian Assange's legal team, fell in love with him while he was living in Ecuador's London embassy.

"If I had to pinpoint it, it was possibly when his personal trainer broke his arm, and so we were boxing, sparring together," Stella told ARD, a German public broadcaster. She wound up spending a lot of time with Assange.[1]

Stella became attracted to the "private side of him," the side that "cracks jokes all the time and cooks and likes to do nice things."

"We created romantic atmospheres," Stella said. "We got a tent for Julian's room so there's a tent space and put fairy lights inside. If you're in a tent, you could be anywhere. You could be on a beach. You can imagine there is a different environment outside."[2]

Initially, Stella and Julian did not believe the situation permitted them to form a family, even if they wanted children. But a United Nations working group on arbitrary detention concluded Julian had been "arbitrarily detained" on February 5, 2016. The group urged authorities to stop depriving Julian of his liberty.

Later that year, President Barack Obama commuted Chelsea Manning's sentence, and she was released from Fort Leavenworth military prison.

The couple saw these developments as an indication that the "trajectory of the situation" could not possibly last forever. Julian and Stella prepared for life after political asylum. Gabriel was born in 2017. Max was born in 2019. But Stella understood it could not become public knowledge that she was Julian's partner. That would make her a target.[3]

As it turned out, their fears were well founded. The Assange family was targeted by an espionage operation carried out by Undercover Global, the Spanish security company hired by the Ecuador government to provide security for the embassy in London.

The Central Intelligence Agency (CIA) allegedly supported the operation. Whistleblowers from UC Global claimed security personnel were deployed to the embassy to monitor meetings Julian had with his lawyers, "as this was required by our 'US friends.'" The company also targeted doctors and journalists who visited Julian, and company materials show employees documented Stella's regular visits to the embassy in 2017.

Their relationship was eventually forced out into the open by District Judge Vanessa Baraitser.

While fighting prosecution, Stella and Julian defied the harsh circumstances and married during a small ceremony at Her Majesty's Prison Belmarsh on March 23, 2022, nearly a month before the extradition request was sent to the British Home Office for approval.

"Crimes Against Privacy"

Attorneys for Assange filed a criminal complaint against UC Global in Spain on July 29, 2019, a few months after he was expelled from the embassy and jailed at Belmarsh. The complaint accused UC Global director David Morales and the company of "crimes against privacy," including violations of attorney-client privilege. It further alleged that Morales and the company engaged in bribery, money laundering, and "misappropriation" [embezzlement] against Julian Assange.[4]

On September 7, 2019, a Spanish court ordered the arrest of Morales. The company's headquarters and Morales's home were raided. The court agreed to treat the UC whistleblowers as "protected witnesses" and take a statement from Assange. The following month the court charged Morales with several crimes.[5]

Aitor Martínez, an attorney with the law firm representing Assange in the Spanish criminal case, collected witness statements and a "large volume of company material (consisting of emails, video and audio recordings, documents, and files in other formats)," which contained evidence of alleged criminal acts.[6]

In one statement submitted during the extradition hearing in September 2020, Martínez described the "sophisticated espionage operation" that targeted Assange. It involved the "installation of cameras inside the embassy that recorded audio, the installation of hidden microphones to record meetings, the digitization of visitors' documents and electronic devices, and even in some cases physical surveillance, all of which were carried out to feed an FTP server (and later a web repository) that gave remote access, directly through an intermediary, to US intelligence."[7]

The surveillance was not authorized by the Ecuador government. As former Ecuadorian foreign minister Guillaume Long testified in Spanish court, Morales was involved in forging documents. "For example, they used the wrong email endings for Ecuadorian diplomatic officials. In addition to fake email addresses, the documents themselves also bore fake serial numbers," *Jacobin* reported.

Long asserted that UC Global was clearly enlisted by the CIA "to spy on all of us, especially Assange." He described the operation as a "violation of Ecuador's sovereignty, of the human rights of dozens of individuals, including the human rights of Ecuadorian citizens, and of all the rules regarding the sanctity and inviolability of diplomatic missions."[8]

The company materials provided for the Spanish criminal case showed Morales was in "continuous contact" with US authorities, who recommended specific targets for the operation.

Judge Baraitser allowed two UC Global whistleblowers to submit statements for Assange's defense without revealing their identities.

"Witness #1" informed the court that UC Global was contracted to provide security for the embassy because Ecuadorian security personnel had difficulties with the United Kingdom's visa requirements. In contrast, on the basis of their citizenship in the European Union, UC Global staff members of Spanish nationality were permitted to travel to London, live in the UK, and travel to Ecuador if necessary without any restrictions.[9]

Morales traveled to Las Vegas for a "security sector trade fair" in July 2016. Though Witness #1 asked to accompany Morales, they said he insisted on traveling alone.

While in Vegas, Morales allegedly secured a contract with Las Vegas Sands, owned by Sheldon Adelson, a billionaire and a major bankroller of President Donald Trump's campaign.[10]

"The contract did not make sense," Witness #1 asserted. It was for security for Adelson's boat, the *Queen Miri*, whenever it was in the Mediterranean Sea. However, the boat already had a security detail.[11]

Witness #1 learned that Morales "entered into illegal agreements with US authorities to supply them with sensitive information" about Assange and Ecuador president Rafael Correa. Zohar Lahav, the vice president of security for Las Vegas Sands, developed the contract with Morales, and Lahav was suspected of acting as an intermediary for passing information to the CIA. (In fact, after Trump won the 2016 election, Lahav "traveled to Spain and stayed at Morales' home for a week.")[12]

After returning from Vegas, Morales allegedly told employees he "switched to 'the dark side,'" referring to cooperating with US authorities. The collaboration meant "the Americans [would] get us contracts all over the world."

Morales subsequently made regular trips to the United States, particularly New York, Chicago, and Washington, DC. Witness #1 said Morales informed him that he had traveled to talk with UC Global's "American friends." At some point in 2017, Morales asked a "person from the company to supply a secure phone, with secure applications, as well as an encrypted computer" for communications with these "American friends," which Morales admitted were "US intelligence." Yet he would not be more specific about whom he met with on his trips.[13]

A second whistleblower, "Witness #2," was an information technology expert working for UC Global.[14]

"[Once] Donald Trump won the elections, at the end of 2016," Witness #2 recalled, "the collection of information intensified as Morales became more obsessed with obtaining as much information as possible."

Between June and July 2017, Witness #2 was allegedly summoned by Morales to form a task force of workers at the company's headquarters in the southern Spanish city of Jerez de la Frontera.[15]

"I was tasked with executing David Morales's orders, with the technical means that existed in the embassy and additional measures that were installed by order of Morales, in addition to the information gathered by the UC Global employees, who were physically present in the diplomatic mission. This unit also had to travel to London every month to collect information," according to Witness #2.[16]

Morales informed the task force that "the contract with Ecuador required that the cameras had to be changed every three years." The instruction made little sense to Witness #2. At no point had Morales ever taken an interest in fulfilling the clause, even though the contract was more than three years old.

Witness #2 believed the closed-circuit television security cameras, which did not record sound, were "sufficient to provide physical security against intrusion inside the building." However, Morales allegedly asked Witness #2 "explicitly" to find providers who would "sell security cameras with sophisticated audio recording capabilities."[17]

The cameras were not to show they were recording sound—or even appear to be recording sound.

"Around June 2017, while I was sourcing providers for the new camera equipment, David Morales instructed that the cameras should allow streaming capabilities so that 'our friends in the United States,' as Morales explicitly put it, would be able to gain access to the interior of the embassy in real time. This request alarmed me greatly, and in order to impede the request, I claimed that remote access via streaming the camera circuit was not technically achievable."[18]

Morales allegedly insisted the remote access be established "for the Americans" and emailed Witness #2 a slide show in English with instructions on how to install the system, which prompted Witness #2 to inform Morales that Assange would clearly discover the cameras were recording. That argument apparently discouraged Morales.

Nonetheless, security cameras with audio recording capabilities were installed in early December 2017, and Witness #2 was instructed not to share information about the system. If asked, Witness #2 was to deny that the cameras were recording audio.[19]

Assange apparently asked several times if the new cameras

recorded sound. "To which I replied that they did not, as my boss had instructed me to do," Witness #2 recalled.[20]

Going forward, Assange was recorded everywhere in the embassy except in his bedroom and a study room, which did not have cameras.

Bugging the Women's Bathroom

Morales "showed at times a real obsession in relation to monitoring and recording the lawyers who met with the 'guest' [Assange] because 'our American friends' were requesting it," according to Witness #1.[21]

A fire extinguisher in the meeting room of the embassy, where Assange would meet with his legal team, and another in a bathroom were each bugged with microphones. In January 2018, Morales allegedly tried to convince Witness #2, as part of his "dealings with US intelligence," to install microphones in all the fire extinguishers.[22]

"Once again, I challenged Morales on the legality of these measures and I tried to dissuade Morales indicating that, in addition to it being completely illegal, installing microphones at this scale would be discovered for sure," Witness #2 shared.

Witness #2 believed installing this many microphones would be a "crazy act," and he did not think Morales's plan was ever carried out.[23]

Also in January, Morales allegedly urged staff to "place certain stickers on all the external windows of the embassy. Specifically, he requested that I place them in the top left corner of all the windows. The stickers were rather rigid. They indicated that CCTV was in operation," Witness #2 stated.

"I found this strange because there had been a closed-circuit system for several years, and it didn't make sense to now have to advertise this on the windows of the embassy. Nonetheless, during my visit to London I placed the stickers that had been supplied in the upper left hand corner of the windows of the embassy."[24]

"Our American friends," Morales told Witness #2, had laser microphones that were directional and pointed at the windows. They would "capture all conversations." But according to Witness #2, Assange used a white noise machine that "produced a vibration in the window that stopped the sound [from] being extracted via the laser microphone, which US intelligence had installed outside."[25]

By placing a sticker in the upper left-hand side of each window, the vibration was eliminated, allowing the laser microphones to record conversations.

The installation of cameras with audio-recording capabilities had occurred in December 2017, the same month that Assange received a diplomatic passport from Ecuadorian authorities and planned to leave the embassy on Christmas Day.

"I recall that the security personnel of UC Global deployed at the embassy were closely monitoring the then-consul of Ecuador, Fidel Narvaez, who was in charge of the relevant documentation with which he entered and exited the embassy," Witness #2 said.

Gathering intelligence on Baltasar Garzón, a Spanish former judge and member of Assange's legal team, was a priority. "The security guards at the embassy were requested to search for evidence of travels to Argentina and Russia in Garzón's passport pages, which were photographed.

"Security personnel that were physically deployed in the embassy were specifically asked to monitor these meetings of Assange with his lawyers, as this was required by our 'US friends,'" Witness #2 claimed.

During November 2017, Morales allegedly raised the idea of breaking into the office of the law firm headed by Garzón.

"Two weeks after this conversation, the national media reported that men in balaclavas had entered Garzón's law offices," Witness

#2 stated. "I recall that the news was shared amongst the employees in the Jerez office, and we speculated whether this could have to do with what our boss, David Morales, had suggested."

El País reported that Morales suspected a baby "repeatedly brought into the embassy by Stephen Hoo," an actor and friend of Assange, might be Julian's child. According to a company report, in late October Morales became obsessed with Gabriel, Stella and Julian's first child.[26]

Morales allegedly ordered employees to "steal the baby's diapers to analyze the contents for DNA, although the task was never carried out." Witness #2 said Morales instructed him to help "the Americans" find out if Assange was the father. Upon recognizing that DNA could not be obtained from feces, they discussed stealing the baby's pacifier.[27]

Rather than follow any of Morales's instructions, in December 2017, Witness #2 "approached the mother of the infant outside the embassy" and informed Stella that she should no longer bring the baby into the embassy.

"The Americans" supporting UC Global grew increasingly desperate for an end to Assange's "permanence in the embassy" during this time. Morales allegedly proposed that the door to the embassy be left open, as an "accidental mistake," so a team could enter and "kidnap" Julian. Poisoning Julian was also discussed with Morales's "contacts in the United States." (This allegation matches the reporting from Yahoo News on the CIA's "secret war plans" against Julian.[28])

"We employees were shocked at these suggestions and commented amongst ourselves that the course that Morales had embarked on was beginning to become dangerous," Witness #2 concluded. They did not want to collaborate in "an illegal act of this magnitude."

Following the arrest of Julian, Witness #1 said they alerted his lawyers that Morales had "betrayed both the terms of the contract and the trust that had been given to him by the government of Ecuador by systematically handing over information to US intelligence agencies."[29]

The information allegedly included all records on embassy security and security for Correa and his family, which UC Global had been hired to provide.

CIA, FBI Effectively Spy on US Citizens

The intense spying operation primarily occurred between the fall of 2017 and March 2018, when Ecuador president Lenín Moreno suspended Julian Assange's "privilege" to meet with visitors.

While providing access to audio and video from cameras at the Ecuador embassy, UC Global operated a checkpoint near the entrance to the embassy. Visitors, according to *El País*, were instructed to "hand over their bags, computers, electronic devices, and cellphones." Company employees rummaged through visitors' private possessions and compiled reports on attorneys, doctors, and any Russians or Americans.[30]

The reports included the date of the visitor's meeting, a copy of the visitor's passport, the content of conversations, and video from the meeting. Employees allegedly shared the reports with the CIA via a server in Jerez de la Frontera. The FBI allegedly had access, too.

El País had access to testimony and graphic documents similar to the files the whistleblowers shared with Assange's legal team. The files showed that UC Global "took apart and photographed the cellphones of American journalists who visited the founder of WikiLeaks."[31]

Lowell Bergman, an investigative journalist; Ellen Nakashima, a national security reporter for the *Washington Post*; Evgeny Morozov, a writer and scholar who covers the social implications of technology; actress Pamela Anderson; and Timothy Eric Ladbrooke, Assange's doctor, were some of the individuals whom UC Global viewed as "priority targets."[32]

"On some occasions," UC Global employees opened the casing of targets' cellphones in order to photograph the International Mobile Equipment Identity (IMEI) number, which *El País* described as "a unique code that identifies a device and is one of the most valuable pieces of information for anyone looking to hack a phone. When a cellphone connects to a network, this identity number is automatically transmitted."[33]

The company even tried to steal Nakashima's phone battery. Incredibly, an employee put this in writing. "I took her phone, her recorder. I took out the battery. I tried to keep it, but the woman remembered it at the exit."

Glenn Greenwald, who was part of a team awarded a Pulitzer Prize for their work exposing the National Security Agency (NSA) mass surveillance programs, had "photos taken of the Russian visas in his passport, as well as his cellphone." The Russian visas were from visiting NSA whistleblower Edward Snowden, who was stranded in Moscow after Vice President Joe Biden and others in President Barack Obama's administration revoked his passport.[34]

"Affiliates of the US government, including the CIA and FBI, were effectively spying on their own citizens, including me, through an elaborate fraud in which visitors to the Ecuadorian Embassy in London who visited Julian Assange were lied to, told they had to give their passport for identification purposes and their cellphone for security purposes when, in reality, those items were seized so they could be photographed and put on a server, which both the CIA and FBI could access," Greenwald stated.

"It's unclear which parts of my cellphone were surveilled as part of this process," Greenwald added. "But what *El País* has reported constitutes an illegal and unconstitutional search of my property by the US government."

Beginning in 2009, WikiLeaks invited Stefania Maurizi, an Italian journalist who worked for *La Repubblica*, to become a media partner.

"Immediately after Christmas in December 2017, I visited Julian Assange in the embassy, and it was really problematic, as the guards seized all my belongings, even my backpack in which I had important notes and my pens. I was completely upset," Maurizi shared. "How can you protect your sources in these conditions?"[35]

"In March 2018," she reported, "I visited Julian Assange again for an interview, which my newspaper *La Repubblica* published on March 28, 2018," the same day Moreno revoked Assange's visitor privileges.

Maurizi was "very uncomfortable about using the women's toilet." When the report in *El País* revealed the women's bathroom was bugged, it confirmed Maurizi's fear.

"In the embassy, I always tried to drink as little as possible to avoid going to the toilet. I remember one day I asked to go to the toilet, and a diplomatic staffer invited me to use the diplomatic staff's toilet rather than the women's toilet."

According to Maurizi, security agents unscrewed her phone, recorded her conversations, and filmed her. She obtained a video and audio recording of one of her meetings with Assange, and later joined other international journalists in suing UC Global in Spain.

Ecuador's Pressure Campaign

For the final fifteen months that Julian Assange lived under asylum in Ecuador's embassy, he did not see his children. Ecuador's pressure campaign to force him to abandon the embassy greatly intensified. The government reportedly cut off his internet access in March 2018 around the same time that he was blocked from seeing any more visitors.[36]

Assange was assigned a diplomatic passport to Russia against his wishes, according to Aitor Martinez. "Foreign Minister María Fernanda Espinosa's cousin worked at the Ecuadorian Embassy in Moscow, and through this cousin, she concocted a plan to appoint Assange to the one country that was the subject of mass media hysteria."[37]

When Rommy Vallejo, the head of Ecuador intelligence, met with Assange on December 21, 2017, to discuss plans to leave the embassy, he was provided a passport to replace the one for Russia. UC Global reportedly listened through the door and documented their meeting.[38]

The US ambassador showed up to Martinez's office and allegedly said, "We know that Julian Assange is about to leave the embassy using a diplomatic passport, and we will never allow it."[39]

Urged to link Assange to Russia, "UC Global drafted exaggerated and faked reports for the Americans," Martinez added. "The protected [UC Global] witness claimed before a court that they had drafted exaggerated reports just to feed the Americans with information and to show that UC Global is very important for them at the embassy. If you check UC Global reports, it's very funny. They make up everything."[40]

Sondra Crosby, a doctor who works with asylum seekers and refugees who have experienced torture, visited the embassy on February 23, 2019, to conduct a medical evaluation of Assange. At one point, she left the embassy to pick up some food and returned to the room where they were meeting to find her confidential medical notes had been taken. Crosby found her notes "in a space utilized by embassy surveillance staff" and presumed they had been read, in violation of doctor-patient confidentiality.[41]

Ecuador officials ended Assange's asylum on April 11, 2019, and opened the embassy doors for British police to arrest him. They allegedly took Assange's shaving kit months before he was expelled from the embassy to ensure that he would emerge with an unkempt beard that made him look like a hermit hacker rather than a respectable journalist.[42]

President Lenín Moreno referred to Assange as a "spoiled brat" the following day and declared, "From now on we'll be more careful in giving asylum to people who are really worth it, and not miserable hackers whose only goal is to destabilize governments."[43]

Stella Assange fought to protect her family's privacy until March 2020, when Julian faced the spread of COVID-19 in prison. She asked the judge to allow her to make the case for releasing him to home confinement anonymously, and the judge refused. The news of their "secret family" resulted in a number of salacious headlines in the media.

While defending the US extradition request, the Crown Prosecution Service minimized the alleged spying that occurred. "There is no absolute rule against surveillance, which includes privileged communications, as a matter of UK law. English law permits the surveillance of communications and consultations between a lawyer and client." Plus, prosecutors contended Julian Assange's defense failed to "demonstrate any nexus between the alleged surveillance and these proceedings."[44]

Judge Vanessa Baraitser generally agreed with Crown prosecutors. In her ruling, which blocked the extradition, she wrote, "If the US was involved in the surveillance of the embassy, there is no reason to assume this related to these proceedings. The US would be aware that privileged communications and the fruits of any surveillance would not be seen by prosecutors assigned to the case and would be inadmissible at Mr. Assange's trial as a matter of US law.

"A possible alternative explanation for US surveillance (if there was any) is the perception that Mr. Assange remained a risk to their national security."[45]

Baraitser noted that three of the charges involved general allegations claiming he was engaged in the unauthorized possession and disclosure of classified information right up until British police arrested him in 2019.

Leon Panetta, who was CIA director when Assange published the documents, was interviewed by the German broadcaster

ARD. They informed him of the "recordings in the embassy." Panetta grinned and let out a belly laugh. "That doesn't surprise me." Chuckling, he said, "That kind of thing goes on all the time."

"In the intelligence business, the name of the game is to get information any way you can, and I'm sure that's what was involved here," Panetta declared.

However, this kind of spying operation was not always something the US security services could engage in without jeopardizing a case. In June 1971, President Richard Nixon was appalled at the media response to Pentagon Papers whistleblower Daniel Ellsberg's actions. Nixon instructed aides to uncover any "damaging personal information" about Ellsberg that could be used to blackmail him.

"Don't worry about his trial," Nixon told Attorney General John Mitchell and Henry Kissinger, his national security advisor. "Just get everything out. . . . Leak it out. We want to destroy him in the press."[46]

According to Ellsberg, the clandestine unit known as the White House Plumbers broke into his psychiatrist's office in September. A dozen CIA assets, including Cuban-born operative Bernard Barker, were brought from Miami in a plan to attack Ellsberg and break both his legs at a Capitol Hill rally on May 3, 1972. Evidence of unlawful wiretapping was disclosed during his trial, where he faced allegations of violating the Espionage Act.[47]

Judge William Byrne dismissed all charges with prejudice on May 11, 1973, and declared the "totality of the circumstances . . . offend a sense of justice. The bizarre events have incurably infected the prosecution of this case."[48]

Spanish National High Court judge Santiago Pedraz issued an order in 2019 informing UK authorities that the Spanish court required "witness testimony from the British lawyers and Assange's doctors who were spied on at the embassy." UK authorities thwarted the request.

Remarkably, in an unrelated lawsuit filed by Assange attorney Jennifer Robinson in the European Court of Human Rights, the UK government admitted in June 2022 that they violated her privacy rights and right to confidential journalistic material when they shared information about Robinson with the US government.[49]

Judge Pedraz also summoned former CIA director Mike Pompeo and William Evanina, a former chief of the CIA's counterespionage group, days before Home Secretary Priti Patel approved the extradition request. Evanina spoke to Yahoo News for their report on the CIA's "secret war plans" against Assange.[50]

The summons was another sign of the court's commitment to pursuing all avenues in order to uncover information that could bring Assange, his family, and his journalistic colleagues justice. But Evanina and Pompeo's cooperation with the court was as likely as US indictments against former CIA officials for torturing detainees in the "war on terrorism."

Back in the US, in August 2022, Margaret Ratner Kunstler and Deborah Hrbek, two attorneys who had represented Assange, along with journalists Charles Glass and John Goetz, sued both the CIA and Pompeo as a private individual for allegedly violating their privacy rights. Goetz had partnered with WikiLeaks on the Iraq and Afghanistan War Logs while working for *Der Spiegel*.

"The United States Constitution shields American citizens from US government overreach even when the activities take place in a foreign embassy in a foreign country," declared Richard Roth, their attorney. "They had a reasonable expectation that the security guards at the Ecuadorian embassy in London would not be US government spies charged with delivering copies of their electronics to the CIA."

CHAPTER 7

The FBI's Role in the Case

Hands up, hands down
Wake up, snap out
We gon' stand up
When they try to
Control, control
—M.I.A., "Ctrl" (2020)

United States prosecutors did not name Federal Bureau of Investigation (FBI) informant Sigurdur Ingi Thordarson in their updated indictment against the WikiLeaks founder. Instead, Thordarson, a citizen of Iceland, was referred to as "Teenager."

The Justice Department (DOJ) withheld Thordarson's identity, even though Thordarson was well known, and not as some helpless minor but as a known liar and diagnosed sociopath with a criminal record.

No longer a teenager, Thordarson was charged in 2015 with "rape, sex with minors, paying for sex with a minor, and instigating the prostitution of a minor."[1] He engaged in sex with nine underage boys and abused one boy forty times for around two years when the boy was between the ages of fifteen and seventeen, according to the *Iceland Monitor*.

Another Icelandic publication said Thordarson offered the boys money and "valuables" for sex, ranging from $200,000 to "vacations and expensive cars." He "promised to hack the computer network of their schools to change their grades and attendance. When the young men refused to meet him, [Thordarson] harassed them systematically, pressuring them to perform sexual acts with him or to meet him."[2]

While volunteering for WikiLeaks, Thordarson embezzled around $50,000 from the organization's online store and faced a sprawling eighteen-count prosecution in 2014 that Iceland police said involved "pretending to be Julian Assange online" to solicit donations, "tricking three men in Luxembourg into giving him" funds for a bank account in their name that was never opened, and "using the credit card of a company to which he did not even belong to buy goods and services."[3]

There is little reason to believe the DOJ was unaware of their cooperating witness's history of deplorable acts, and yet US prosecutors turned to Thordarson to prop up their claims that Assange engaged in hacking, which were necessary to convince District Judge Vanessa Baraitser that Assange had gone beyond standard news-gathering practices as WikiLeaks editor-in-chief.

It worked. Although Baraitser blocked the extradition on January 4, 2021, her decision upheld every allegation from the Justice Department.

If the allegations from Thordarson were proven by US prosecutors, the judge agreed that it would "take [Assange] outside any role of investigative journalism." She believed Assange conspired with hackers to "further the overall objective of WikiLeaks to obtain protected information.

"Notwithstanding the vital role played by the press in a democratic society, journalists have the same duty as everyone else to obey the ordinary criminal law. In this case, Mr. Assange's alleged acts were unlawful, and he does not become immune from criminal liability merely because he claims he was acting as a journalist," Baraitser declared.

Months after the major decision, Bjartmar Alexandersson, a reporter for the Icelandic biweekly newspaper *Stundin*, interviewed Thordarson. They talked for nine hours in March and April. Thordarson admitted that allegations against Assange were based on lies.

Siggi "The Hacker"

The second superseding indictment, filed on June 24, 2020, alleged that Assange met with Siggi Thordarson in early 2010, and that the seventeen-year-old provided Assange with "data stolen from a bank." It further alleged Assange asked Thordarson to "commit computer intrusions and steal additional information, including audio recordings of phone conversations between high-ranking officials" of Iceland, such as members of parliament.

"On July 21, 2010, after Assange and Teenager failed in their joint attempt to decrypt a file stolen from [an Icelandic] bank, Teenager asked a US person to try to do so. In 2011 and 2012, that individual, who had been an acquaintance of Manning since early 2010, became a paid employee of WikiLeaks and reported to Assange and Teenager," the indictment claimed.

The indictment also claimed that Assange directed Thordarson in September 2010 to "hack into the computer of an individual formerly associated with WikiLeaks and delete chat logs containing statements of Assange."

After a group of hacktivists organized under the banner of LulzSec engaged in a distributed denial of service (DDOS) attack on the CIA website in June 2011, Thordarson contacted the group. The indictment said he posted a video to YouTube that showed he was sitting by Assange to gain LulzSec's trust.

By August 23, 2011, Thordarson no longer wanted to be a part of WikiLeaks. He emailed the US Embassy in Reykjavík at 3:30 a.m. and requested a meeting with embassy officials to become an FBI informant.

"After a quick search on the internet, I have [not yet] been able to find a reliable contact form to establish a meeting with a person regarding an ongoing criminal investigation," Thordarson wrote. "The nature of the intel that can be brought to light in that investigation will not be spoken over email conversation."

The DOJ omitted a key allegation Thordarson made in interviews with journalists. Thordarson, who used the aliases "Q" and "Penguin X" to communicate with LulzSec hacktivists, told journalist Ryan Gallagher that he "suggested" WikiLeaks "wanted assistance to find evidence of anti-WikiLeaks sentiment" within Iceland's Ministry of Finance. The finance ministry stopped an "attempt by DataCell, a company that processes WikiLeaks donations, to purchase a large new data center in Reykjavík."[4]

"That was basically the first assignment WikiLeaks gave to LulzSec, to breach the Icelandic government infrastructure," Thordarson asserted.

Thordarson provided Gallagher "access to a pseudonymous email account," which he contended the FBI created for him. He also shared documents and travel records from his work for the FBI.[5]

Gallagher confirmed through chat logs and emails from 2011 that Thordarson communicated with LulzSec. "By claiming that he effectively solicited LulzSec to break into government computers," Thordarson "implicated himself in a potential international criminal conspiracy, leaving WikiLeaks open to the allegation that it, too, was somehow involved."[6]

While Thordarson claimed Assange approved contact with LulzSec, as well as the "assignment" to "find evidence of anti-WikiLeaks sentiment," WikiLeaks spokesperson Kristinn Hrafnsson told Gallagher if Thordarson contacted LulzSec, it was "highly unlikely" WikiLeaks staff, including Assange, knew what he was doing. Hrafnsson contended that Thordarson inflated the "role he played as a volunteer."[7]

Stundin reporter Bjartmar Alexandersson asked Thordarson if he told the FBI that Assange asked him to hack into an Icelandic government computer to obtain "audio recordings of phone conversations between high-ranking officials." Thordarson said he did not.[8]

"Then why does the indictment claim you said that?" Alexandersson asked.

"I can't answer that," Thordarson replied.

"Is it because you don't want to, or is it because of the FBI you can't answer?" Alexandersson added.

"I can't answer that," Thordarson insisted.

Alexandersson pressed. "Why can't you answer that?"

"Because I'm not allowed to," Thordarson declared.

During conversations with Alexandersson, Thordarson claimed he received "some files from a third party" who claimed to have recorded members of parliament. He offered to share the files with Assange but did not know whether the file contents actually contained the alleged audio recordings.[9]

"OK. So [Assange] received these phone calls?" Alexandersson asked.

"At least he received some files. I never listened to them so I have no idea what was on there," Thordarson answered.

"You didn't feel like checking it out to hear it? How large was this file?" Alexandersson responded.

"I don't remember. I was doing something at the time so I thought I'd just throw it at Julian, and he'd go over it," Thordarson said.

Thordarson also admitted Assange never "instructed or asked him to access computers in order to find any such recordings."

FBI Deceives Icelandic Authorities

The FBI shared information with Icelandic authorities on June 20, 2011, alleging that a network of computer hackers was planning a cyber attack against government systems in Iceland. According to Iceland's attorney general and the National Commissioner of Police, by July 4, the Ministry of Interior signed off on cooperation with the FBI. A week later, Icelandic police representatives traveled to the US for an FBI meeting.[10]

Icelandic police became aware on August 23 that Thordarson "turned himself in to the US Embassy in Iceland and requested that information be provided to the US authorities." The police received a request from the FBI to enter the country and meet with the informant. US prosecutors from New York and Virginia accompanied the agents.[11]

On August 24, FBI agents and prosecutors arrived in Iceland in a private jet, and Iceland's attorney general and police representatives met with them.[12] The following day, they determined Icelandic police would go with FBI agents to meet with Thordarson. But before the day was over, the State Department "summoned" the attorney general to "discuss the legal request from the US government."[13]

What FBI agents really wanted was not within the scope of the initial request, and Interior Minister Ögmundur Jónasson told the Associated Press in 2013 that he was "upset when he found out that FBI agents had flown to the country to interview an unidentified WikiLeaks associate."

From Jónasson's perspective, FBI agents and prosecutors were in Iceland to "frame" Assange and WikiLeaks, using Thordarson as the bait.

"I, for one, was not aware that they were coming to Iceland," Jónasson recalled. "When I learned about it, I demanded that Icelandic police cease all cooperation and made it clear that people interviewed or interrogated in Iceland should be interrogated by Icelandic police."[14]

Going back to Ryan Gallagher's reporting, Thordarson said the security chief for the US embassy in Reykjavík asked him about the information he allegedly had on the same day he sent his email. Thordarson informed the security chief it was related to the US investigation into WikiLeaks.

Apparently, the security chief denied there was such an investigation yet still asked Thordarson to come to the embassy for a meeting. When Thordarson arrived, he "showed staff a photocopy of Julian Assange's passport" to bolster his allegations.[15]

Thordarson was summoned less than twenty-four hours later. Upon Thordarson's return, the security chief allegedly escorted Thordarson around Reykjavík to ensure they were not followed and then brought the informant to a four-star hotel called the Hotel Reykjavík Centrum. Two men with "American accents" and "FBI credentials" were waiting.[16]

The FBI, according to Thordarson, "asked him a range of questions to 'verify that [he] wasn't full of bullshit.'" Thordarson recalled his chats with Sabu, or Hector Xavier Monsegur, who he did not know was an FBI informant. What Thordarson said about Sabu apparently helped him convince agents that he could be a credible source.[17]

Around this time, Icelandic authorities had given the FBI and Justice Department the cold shoulder. Nevertheless, over "four consecutive days" and at different hotels, FBI agents remained in Iceland. They met with Thordarson to question him about Assange, particularly his life at Ellingham Hall, a ten-bedroom rural estate in Norfolk owned by Frontline journalists' club owner Vaughan Smith, where the WikiLeaks founder lived on bail as he fought extradition to Sweden.

Gallagher said Thordarson told him the FBI agents "wanted information about WikiLeaks' technical and physical security and the locations of WikiLeaks' servers; they asked him, too, for names of individuals linked to WikiLeaks, who might be open to becoming informants if approached by the FBI."

The Ministry of Interior remained firm in its opposition to the FBI's presence. By the end of August, the FBI was pressured to leave Iceland and find another country for a meeting with their new informant.

Meeting With Siggi in Denmark

"[FBI] agents told me that they wanted my data, that they wanted to know more but couldn't operate in Iceland any longer. So they asked me to join them somewhere," Thordarson told the *Reykjavík Grapevine* in 2013.

"They said that I could pick any country in [the] world, any state in the USA. I tell them that I'm not going to the USA—that would be a one-way ticket. I suggest Moscow, Russia, which they didn't find funny, explaining that their relations with the Russian secret service community wasn't so hot. We wound up going to the closest country, Denmark."[18]

According to Thordarson, he had three Denmark meetings with the FBI—two in Copenhagen in October 2011, one in Aarhus in March 2012. He claimed the FBI paid for his flights and hotel rooms. Thordarson also had one FBI meeting in Washington, D.C.

"To the best of my knowledge, the Danish authorities were not involved. I doubt that they would have been happy with the FBI interrogating an Icelandic citizen in Denmark. We stayed there for 24 hours talking, and their technicians cloned some hard drives that I brought with me," Thordarson said to the *Grapevine*.

In his interview with Gallagher, Thordarson claimed that the FBI agents asked him to "wear a recording device and make copies of data stored on laptops used by WikiLeaks staff" during a trip to Ellingham Hall. Thordarson alleged that the agents wanted him to "get Assange to 'say something incriminating about LulzSec.' But he declined to wear a recording device and told his handlers that covertly copying data from computers wouldn't be feasible because 'people literally [slept] with their laptops at Ellingham.'"[19]

Thordarson left WikiLeaks during the same time frame that he was meeting with FBI agents in Denmark. He maintained WikiLeaks owed him money for flights, hotels, and "travel for Assange's bodyguards." In his interview with the *Grapevine*, he asserted Assange approved of him taking money from the WikiLeaks store to cover his costs and buy "computers and supplies for volunteers."

WikiLeaks requested Thordarson repay the money and accused him of embezzling funds. In the organization's version of events, a Canadian volunteer contacted Thordarson and proposed the idea of fundraising by selling T-shirts, coffee mugs, and other merchandise through an online store.

"The Icelander deceived the Canadian volunteer into believing that he was WikiLeaks staff in order to have the funds transferred to his personal account instead of the organization's [account]. When confronted, he admitted the wrongdoing. Because of requests from people close to him and his young age, he was offered the opportunity to repay the stolen funds, which amounted to about $50,000."[20]

The allegations of embezzlement were referred to the Icelandic police and became part of a wider investigation into a string of crimes Thordarson committed, including extortion and fraud.

Thordarson told the *Grapevine* that the FBI "knew that I'd left WikiLeaks at the time but still kept pressuring me to go and visit Julian Assange in the UK. They wanted me to wear a special watch that could record sound. I told them no, just as I had done in August when they brought it up then. They wanted to know if I feared for my safety, if I was afraid Assange would attack me. I told them Assange isn't a violent man."[21]

Gallagher reviewed a message from early February 2012 that showed the FBI encouraged Thordarson to "build relationships with people close to WikiLeaks." It is unclear if they knew WikiLeaks had accused him of embezzling funds.

"A few weeks" after this email, Thordarson flew to Washington, DC, and stayed in a Marriott hotel in Arlington, Virginia. He was near the courthouse for the Eastern District of Virginia, where a grand jury was empaneled in December 2010 to investigate WikiLeaks.

For four days, Thordarson met with FBI agents in a hotel conference room. He told Gallagher the FBI was interested in several individuals allegedly associated with WikiLeaks: Birgitta Jónsdóttir, who was an Icelandic parliamentarian; Jacob Appelbaum, who represented WikiLeaks at the Hackers on Planet Earth (HOPE) conference in 2010; and James Ball, who worked on the Iraq War Logs for WikiLeaks.[22]

"They wanted to know literally everything there was to know about these people," according to Thordarson.

During Thordarson's *Grapevine* interview, he claimed, "Intelligence analysts from all kinds of three-letter-acronym institutions joined. We talked about individuals, about Assange's physical security; who his bodyguards are and such. They were mostly interested in Assange, but also in Icelanders like Birgitta Jónsdóttir, Smári McCarthy, Herbert Snorrason and Kristinn Hrafnsson."[23]

Appelbaum appeared in the 2020 indictment as an unindicted co-conspirator, but there were no allegations in the indictment attributed to Thordarson.

At the time of the FBI's DC meeting, Jónsdóttir was one of the targets of a December 14, 2010, order issued to Twitter that demanded her user data from as early as November 2009.[24] The FBI also subpoenaed Twitter for data from Appelbaum's account.

McCarthy organized the Icelandic Modern Media Initiative

with Assange and Jónsdóttir. The initiative aimed to make Iceland a safe haven for journalists.

Snorrason was a "volunteer chat moderator" for WikiLeaks, which was an informal position within the organization. In August 2011, the FBI issued a subpoena ordering Google to hand over "the content of his Gmail account, calendar data, contact lists, photos, the email addresses that Snorrason corresponded with, and draft and deleted emails."[25]

The last meeting Thordarson had with FBI agents was on March 18, 2012, in Aarhus, Denmark. Gallagher reviewed emails with an "alleged handler, agreeing that he would come equipped with hard drives packed with chat logs, photographs, and other data related to WikiLeaks."

"According to a Justice Department receipt," which Thordarson said "he was provided by the FBI, he turned over eight hard drives." The data totaled 1 terabyte, which Gallagher noted was the "equivalent of about 1,000 copies of the Encyclopedia Britannica."

In July 2014, WikiLeaks filed a criminal complaint in Denmark against Thordarson and the FBI agents who met with him. They also filed a complaint against the Danish Security and Intelligence Service with the Danish Independent Police Complaints Authority.

The organization argued the FBI's actions in Denmark were "illegal," and Danish intelligence was "complicit" in their misconduct.

Hrafnsson said it was "hard to believe" the meetings "took place without permission from the Danish authorities."

Assange stated, "The FBI acquired data that had been stolen from state, friends and associates of WikiLeaks. At least some of the material had been stolen at Ellingham Hall."

Private Intelligence Firm Destroyed So FBI Could Get to WikiLeaks

When DOJ prosecutors broadened the computer conspiracy charge, they added allegations to link Assange to "hackers" affiliated with collectives organized under the banner of Anonymous, AntiSec, LulzSec, and Gnosis, which were primarily active in 2011.[26]

This section of the indictment featured Sabu, the co-founder of LulzSec. The FBI arrested Sabu on June 7, 2011, and he immediately went to work helping agents target individuals involved in hacktivism.

One of the individuals Sabu targeted for the FBI was Jeremy Hammond, an activist who was sentenced to ten years in prison for hacking into computers owned by the Strategic Forecasting intelligence firm (also known as Stratfor). Numerous files from the firm were obtained and later published by WikiLeaks on February 26, 2012. The 2020 indictment painted Assange as a co-conspirator.

"In December 2011," according to the indictment, "Hammond told Sabu that he had been partnering with an individual at WikiLeaks who Hammond believed to be Assange." WikiLeaks allegedly shared links to releases from LulzSec, AntiSec, and Anonymous at the end of December.[27]

The indictment claimed the individual believed to be Assange provided a script that made it easier to search files from Stratfor. Associates of Hammond were allowed to access the script.

Hammond allegedly introduced Sabu to the individual believed to be Assange. On January 16, 2012, Sabu allegedly said, "If you have any targets in mind, by all means let us know," seeking to ensnare Assange in criminal activity. The user, whom Sabu believed was Assange, indicated they could not "give target suggestions for the obvious legal reasons."[28]

Without naming the target, the indictment proceeded to accuse Assange of giving Sabu such a list of targets by mentioning an unnamed "research and investigative firm" that might have files of interest to WikiLeaks.

The indictment alleged Hammond was "indirectly" urged to send a spam email to Stratfor several days before WikiLeaks published the first emails from the firm.

After Stratfor was hacked and its files were published by WikiLeaks, the intelligence consulting company was forced to shut down. Hammond maintained the FBI could have stopped the hack, yet it allowed the firm to be destroyed.

In 2014, the Daily Dot and Motherboard obtained sealed court records that showed the attack on Stratfor was "orchestrated" by Sabu when he was an FBI informant. It affirmed what Hammond had said during his trial: He never heard of Stratfor until Sabu brought it to his attention, and a "skilled hacker" who went by the moniker of Hyrriiya "supplied download links to the full credit card database as well as the initial vulnerability access point to Stratfor's systems."[29]

According to a sealed indictment against individuals involved with LulzSec, the FBI directed Sabu to provide "Hammond and his co-conspirators a computer server in New York, New York, which could be used to store data and to which Hammond and his co-conspirators in fact transferred data."[30]

"Sabu entered into 'conversations with [WikiLeaks] about getting some cash for the leaks,'" Hammond told anthropologist Gabriella Coleman, who documented Anonymous and splinter groups in her 2014 book, *Hacker, Hoaxer, Whistleblower, Spy.*[31]

Coleman described the decision to give the Stratfor files to WikiLeaks. Hammond went to the WikiLeaks internet relay chat (IRC) server without really bothering to inform Sabu. "When talking to WikiLeaks," Hammond recounted, "they first asked to authenticate the leak by pasting them some samples, which I did, [but] they didn't ask who I was or even really how I got access to it. I told them voluntarily that I was working with AntiSec and had hacked Stratfor." Soon after, Hammond "arranged the handoff."

"When Sabu found out, he insisted on dealing with Assange personally. After all, he told Hammond, he was already in contact with Assange's trusted assistant 'Q'"—another FBI informant, Siggi Thordarson.

During the time that Sabu was working with the FBI, he was routinely engaged in criminal activity. Hammond provided many details in his statement to a federal court, which he delivered during his sentencing on November 15, 2013.[32]

Sabu "supplied lists of targets that were vulnerable to 'zero day exploits' used to break into systems, including a powerful remote root vulnerability affecting the popular Plesk software. At his request, these websites were broken into, their emails and databases were uploaded to Sabu's FBI server, and the password information and the location of root backdoors were supplied."[33]

"These intrusions took place in January/February of 2012 and affected over 2000 domains, including numerous foreign government websites in Brazil, Turkey, Syria, Puerto Rico, Colombia, Nigeria, Iran, Slovenia, Greece, Pakistan, and others," Hammond alleged.[34]

He additionally claimed Sabu "infiltrated a group of hackers that had access to hundreds of Syrian systems, including government institutions, banks, and ISPs. He logged several relevant IRC channels persistently asking for live access to mail systems and bank transfer details."[35]

"All of this happened under the control and supervision of the FBI and can be easily confirmed by chat logs the government provided to us pursuant to the government's discovery obligations in the case against me," Hammond declared. He condemned the fact that the majority of documents proving his claims were sealed under a "protective order" and demanded the documents be made public. "I believe the documents [would] show that the government's actions go way beyond catching hackers and stopping computer crimes."

FBI Seizes Assange's Legally Privileged Material

On April 11, 2019, when Assange was arrested and expelled from Ecuador's embassy in London, the FBI enlisted Ecuador's help in obtaining access to legally privileged material that belonged to the WikiLeaks founder.

Gareth Peirce, one of Assange's attorneys, testified during the September 2020 extradition hearing that she immediately contacted the embassy to express dismay over the seizure. Assange wanted the material, in addition to "confidential medical data," to be "identified and released to his lawyers."[36]

"One record of [Assange's] entire archive" was effectively purloined. It contained records related to communications, meetings, and events from 2010 and 2011, which had occurred around a decade earlier. The loss of the archive, according to Peirce, impaired Assange's ability to prepare a defense in his extradition case.[37]

Peirce added, "All legally privileged material was missing save for two volumes of Supreme Court documents and a number of pages of loose correspondence." Photographs of Assange's possessions, including specific files labeled "legally privileged," were leaked by the Ecuadorian authorities to the press.[38]

"Repeated requests by telephone, email, and recorded delivery mail were entirely ignored by the embassy," stated Peirce.

Peirce's law firm, Birnberg, Peirce & Partners, urged the Australian consulate in London to intervene, since Assange is an Australian citizen. The Metropolitan Police in the United

Kingdom declined to help, claiming they had no role in the seizure of any legally privileged material.[39]

During the extradition hearing, Gordon Kromberg, assistant US attorney for the Eastern District of Virginia, where Assange was indicted, maintained that a "taint team" would remove material so the legally privileged material was not used by US prosecutors at trial.

Yet, as Peirce noted, Kromberg made no suggestion during proceedings that the Justice Department had plans to return Assange's archive and other legally privileged material, "even though attention [was] drawn to the existence of recordings of meetings" that could play a part in evidence in the case.

An Immunity Deal for Siggi

Thordarson's fabrications and unfounded claims were not limited to allegations related to hacking Icelandic government institutions. The 2020 indictment also accused Assange and Thordarson of attempting to decrypt a file stolen from an Icelandic bank.

As Bjartmar Alexandersson detailed for *Stundin*, Thordarson admitted he was actually referring to a "well publicized event in which an encrypted file was leaked from an Icelandic bank and assumed to contain information about defaulted loans provided by the Icelandic Landsbanki. The bank went under in the fall of 2008, along with almost all other financial institutions in Iceland, and plunged the country into a severe economic crisis."[40]

"The file was at this time, in summer of 2010, shared by many online who attempted to decrypt it for the public interest purpose of revealing what precipitated the financial crisis. Nothing supports the claim that this file was even 'stolen' per se, as it was assumed to have been distributed by whistleblowers from inside the failed bank," Alexandersson noted.

Furthermore, the indictment accused Assange of obtaining "unauthorized access" through Thordarson to an Icelandic government website "used to track police vehicles."[41]

It turned out, according to the *Stundin* interview, the log-in information belonged to Thordarson. He admitted he was granted "access as a matter of routine due to his work as a first responder while volunteering for a search and rescue team." He also said Assange never requested access to this website.[42]

In May 2019, the FBI granted Thordarson an immunity deal that was signed by US National Security Deputy Assistant Attorney General Kellen Dwyer. *Stundin* obtained a copy of the agreement, which guaranteed the DOJ would not share evidence of crimes with "other prosecutorial or law enforcement agencies," including Icelandic agencies.

The immunity deal apparently emboldened Thordarson to perpetrate more extortion and fraud schemes. He went on to commit a string of new crimes, such as acquiring or forming "legal entities he then used to borrow merchandise, rent luxury cars, [and] even order large quantities of goods from wholesalers without any intention to pay for these goods and services."[43]

Thordarson was jailed in September 2021 after Icelandic police requested that a "rarely invoked" law be used to indefinitely detain him and stop his "crime spree."[44]

The FBI's key witness confessed to *Stundin*, "The idea behind all the companies [that I run in Iceland] is to squeeze out every last penny, knowing it will inevitably lead to bankruptcy at the request of the tax authorities, and the bill would end with them.

"Is it illegal? No, it's just very immoral, that much I would agree with. But I have not heard of anyone being convicted for this sort of thing," Thordarson said.

Alexandersson clarified, "Yet people have been convicted of very similar things in Iceland."

Of course, not everyone is a diagnosed sociopath with an immunity deal from the FBI that makes them believe they have a license to lie, cheat, and steal.

CHAPTER 8

The Abusive Grand Jury

Every breath justifies
Every step that we take to remove what
The powers that be can't prove
And the children will understand why
—CHRYSSIE HYNDE/THE PRETENDERS, "Revolution" (1994)

Chelsea Manning was subpoenaed on January 22, 2019, to testify before a grand jury empaneled in the Eastern District of Virginia to investigate WikiLeaks. Assistant US Attorney Gordon Kromberg ordered Manning—a source—to testify against Julian Assange, the editor-in-chief of the media organization that published documents she submitted.[1]

The grand jury subpoena instructed Manning to appear at the courthouse in Alexandria, Virginia, on February 5. That date was postponed a month. She hired a New York attorney, Moira Meltzer-Cohen, to help her resist the government, and Kromberg vaguely informed her lawyers that he wanted to question her about "past statements."[2]

It was already known that the Justice Department (DOJ) had a sealed indictment against Assange, and an attempt to quash the subpoena prior to Manning's appearance before the grand jury was rejected by a federal judge.

On March 6, she attended grand jury proceedings and informed prosecutors that she would not answer their questions under any circumstances. Judge Claude M. Hilton ordered Manning to return to the courthouse for a contempt of court hearing two days later.

"All of the substantive questions pertained to my disclosures of information to the public in 2010—answers I provided in extensive testimony during my court-martial in 2013," Manning stated. "I responded to each question with the following statement: 'I object to the question and refuse to answer on the grounds that the question is in violation of my First, Fourth, and Sixth Amendment, and other statutory rights.'"[3]

Judge Hilton held Manning in civil contempt. She was taken into custody and jailed at the Alexandria Detention Center. The court informed her she would remain in confinement indefinitely until she "purged" herself of contempt or the grand jury investigation ended.

"I will not comply with this, or any other grand jury," Manning declared after the US government jailed her—again. "Imprisoning me for my refusal to answer questions only subjects me to additional punishment for my repeatedly-stated ethical objections to the grand jury system."[4]

"The grand jury's questions pertained to disclosures from nine years ago and took place six years after an in-depth computer forensics case, in which I testified for almost a full day about these events. I stand by my previous public testimony," she added.

Manning also condemned grand jury investigations in general. "I will not participate in a secret process that I morally object to, particularly one that has been historically used to entrap and persecute activists for protected political speech."

Supporters immediately launched a fundraiser to help Manning sustain her resistance. It was possible she would be confined for a long period.

Manning became the most significant target of a grand jury investigation that had hung over Assange in some form for nearly a decade. Although there was evidence that the investigation into Assange and WikiLeaks already had ramped up under President Donald Trump, the jailing of Manning was the clearest sign yet that the US government was persisting in its campaign against the media organization.

The Inquisition Power of the Grand Jury

The grand jury is composed of a group of citizens who theoretically may help prosecutors determine whether to charge a person with a crime. It developed in England in the twelfth century, and American colonists incorporated the grand jury into their legal structure in 1635. Grand juries were included in the Fifth Amendment of the US Constitution.[5]

The US and Liberia are the only two "common law systems of justice" to still use the process. Several countries and jurisdictions, such as Australia, Belgium, Canada, England, France, Ireland, Japan, New Zealand, Sierra Leone, and Scotland, replaced the grand jury with a "preliminary" hearing system. According to Robert J. Boyle, a New York State attorney and expert on grand juries, who submitted testimony for Assange's extradition trial, "Grand juries operate without adherence to the technical and evidentiary rules of criminal trials." They may "act on unsubstantiated tips and rumors."[6]

The burden is on witnesses, like Manning, to prove a subpoena is improper. Broad investigative power coupled with secrecy makes it difficult for those subpoenaed to prove they are the target of grand jury abuse. Boyle argued, "So long as the government simply asserts that it is investigating whether additional crimes have been committed, the subpoena will be upheld even if the information sought might also help the government's case at trial."

Although a subpoenaed individual may claim the right to avoid self-incrimination, the government can grant "use immunity," which the courts treat as a pledge not to use the testimony against the person in any future criminal proceedings. Still, prosecutors may charge a subpoenaed individual with perjury if they believe false statements were made. "Witnesses cannot base a refusal to testify on their moral or political beliefs or their belief that the grand jury investigation is being used to disrupt legal political dissent," Boyle said.

Grand juries played a role in resistance to the British monarchy, noted Michael Deutsch, an attorney for political activists at the People's Law Office in Chicago. But after the Revolutionary War, President John Adams relied on grand juries to easily secure sedition indictments against his opponents. President Thomas Jefferson also used the grand jury to punish his political enemies, including Aaron Burr.[7]

During and after the American Civil War, Deutsch wrote, "One of the primary roles of the grand jury was to enforce the slavery laws. Frequently, these grand juries indicted outspoken opponents of slavery for sedition or inciting slaves." Southern grand juries suppressed the spread of anti-slavery literature and tried to prevent opponents of slavery from coming to their states. They also charged "people with harboring runaways or with encouraging and assisting fugitives to escape."

"With the urbanization of the United States, the proliferation of crime, and the expansion of federal criminal jurisdiction, the grand jury could no longer exercise even the minimal level of independence that it had been able and willing to exercise in the past," Deutsch added. The "investigative grand jury" was born. It rubber-stamped prosecutors' requests for indictment, and subpoena power became a "valuable tool for wide ranging governmental investigations."[8]

"It is this later inquisitory power that appeared strongly during the Cold War period after World War II. Fueled by the fear of alleged communist subversion that was generated by ambitious politicians, the government used grand jury investigations and indictments as substitutes for a progressive foreign and domestic policy," according to Deutsch. "Loyalty oaths and congressional investigating committees arose to ferret out communists, spies, and sympathizers from all sectors of American society."

During President Richard Nixon's administration, Boyle recalled, more than 1,000 political activists were subpoenaed by more than 100 grand juries investigating "lawful antiwar, women's rights, and Black activist movements. In the 1970s and 1980s, activists from the Puerto Rican Independence Movement were subpoenaed. Upon their refusal to cooperate on moral and political grounds, many were jailed for civil and criminal contempt."[9]

"In the 1980s, numerous subpoenas were served upon activists in the Black liberation movement under the guise of 'investigating' a series of robberies, even though those activists were not suspects. When they refused to testify claiming that the investigation was an improper attempt to gather intelligence on their movement, they, too, were jailed for contempt," Boyle added.

More recently, the DOJ under President Barack Obama exercised this inquisition power. On September 24, 2010, the Federal Bureau of Investigation (FBI) raided the homes of twenty-three antiwar, labor, and international solidarity activists in Chicago, Minneapolis, and other parts of the Midwest. They were issued grand jury subpoenas and informed they were under investigation for "materially supporting" foreign terrorist organizations.

The FBI targeted the activists for their solidarity work with organizers in Colombia and Palestine and for alleged membership in the Freedom Road Socialist Organization. Agents seized notebooks, family photos, membership lists for antiwar groups, and other political documents. The activists later learned an undercover FBI agent had infiltrated their group and attempted to entrap them. No one was ever charged with any crimes, though the threat of prosecution did not end for activists until the statute of limitations passed in 2020.[10]

"Significant" Steps Authorized Against WikiLeaks

On November 29, 2010, WikiLeaks and a handful of media organizations published the first US diplomatic cables. The following day Attorney General Eric Holder told the press he "personally authorized" the DOJ to take "significant" steps in response.[11]

Holder would not specify whether the steps involved search warrants or applications for surveillance under the Foreign Intelligence Surveillance Act, but he made it clear that prosecutors were considering a range of statutes and "tools" in addition to Espionage Act charges.

Two weeks later, DOJ prosecutors were reportedly interested in evidence of collusion between Manning and Assange so they could pursue a conspiracy case against the WikiLeaks founder.

"Justice Department officials have declined to discuss any grand jury activity," the *New York Times* reported. "But in interviews, people familiar with the case said the department appeared to be attracted to the possibility of prosecuting Mr. Assange as a co-conspirator to the leaking because it is under intense pressure to make an example of him as a deterrent to further mass leaking of electronic documents over the Internet."[12]

Around this time, it is generally understood that a grand jury was empaneled and conducted an expansive investigation that involved multiple agencies of the US government. Political pressure also mounted against corporations that provided services to WikiLeaks.

On December 1, Senator Joseph Lieberman persuaded Amazon to remove a copy of the WikiLeaks website from its cloud services.[13] The next day, EveryDNS discontinued the web address for

WikiLeaks, asserting it had no choice but to do so to protect other customers from "intense cyber attacks."[14]

PayPal blocked WikiLeaks from using its service on December 3. The payment processing corporation maintained it did so because the State Department said the media organization's "activities were illegal in the US." However, the State Department denied contacting PayPal.[15]

"What we are seeing here are dangerous moves towards a digital McCarthyism. These actions, and the others like it, are not the result of a legal process, but rather are a result of fear of falling out of favor with Washington," Assange declared.[16]

PostFinance, the financial arm of the Swiss post office, froze Assange's accounts, and three days later, Visa and MasterCard followed PayPal in suspending donations to WikiLeaks.[17]

Donations to WikiLeaks were blocked by Bank of America on December 18, and later the public learned the multinational corporation consulted with Palantir, Berico Technologies, and HBGary Federal on a plan to combat and attack WikiLeaks. Bank of America feared their institution might become a target of WikiLeaks.[18]

Apple removed the WikiLeaks application from its iTunes store. The app provided users with access to the WikiLeaks Twitter feed as well as documents on the WikiLeaks website. A spokesperson for Apple stated, "Apps must comply with all local laws and may not put an individual or targeted group in harm's way."[19]

This censorship was not instigated by the grand jury investigation, but since the DOJ had reportedly compiled a conspiracy case against Assange and WikiLeaks, corporations were convinced to prohibit WikiLeaks' access to their services.

Secret orders for data from Assange, Manning, and several associates of WikiLeaks were signed by US magistrate judges and sent to Twitter, Google, Dynadot, and Sonic.net.

The government ordered Twitter on December 14 to provide data from: Birgitta Jónsdóttir, an Icelandic parliamentarian; Jacob Appelbaum, who represented WikiLeaks at the Hackers on Planet Earth (HOPE) conference in 2010; and Rop Gonggrijp, who worked on the release of the "Collateral Murder" video for WikiLeaks. The order was kept secret until Twitter convinced the government to allow it to notify the targeted users in January 2011.[20]

In March 2012, Google received search warrants for data associated with accounts opened by Joseph Farrell, Sarah Harrison, and Kristinn Hrafnsson, who were journalists and editors at WikiLeaks. Prosecutors were interested in evidence of "espionage," "conspiracy to commit espionage," "theft or conversion of property" belonging to the US government, violations of the Computer Fraud and Abuse Act, and "conspiracy to defraud the United States."[21]

"Google was told to hand over the contents of all their emails, including those sent and received, all draft correspondence and deleted emails," the *Guardian* reported. "The source and destination addresses of each email, its date and time, and size and length were also included in the dragnet.

"The FBI also demanded all records relating to the internet accounts used by the three, including telephone numbers and IP addresses, details of the time and duration of their online activities, and alternative email addresses. Even the credit card or bank account numbers associated with the accounts had to be revealed."

WikiLeaks was not informed of the warrants until December 23, 2014. Michael Ratner, attorney for WikiLeaks, was "astonished and disturbed that Google waited over two and a half years" to notify them. Assange had asked Google CEO Eric Schmidt in April 2011 to stand up for transparency and demand WikiLeaks be informed of any orders for their data, as Twitter had done.[22]

Harrison, who is an unindicted co-conspirator in the Assange case, responded to the search warrant for data from her personal email address. "Knowing that the FBI read the words I wrote to console my mother over a death in the family makes me feel sick."[23]

While the grand jury met regularly, reports surfaced of harassment and intimidation. Appelbaum told the *New York Times* in July 2010 that he had been detained at Newark Liberty International Airport. Agents from Immigration and Customs Enforcement (ICE), along with personnel from the Army's Criminal Investigation Division (CID), asked Appelbaum about Assange. They took his laptop and cellphones but returned the laptop because it did not have a hard drive.[24]

Appelbaum, another unindicted co-conspirator in the Justice Department's indictment, was subjected to suspicionless searches for several years because he associated with WikiLeaks.

"Two American civilians interviewed in recent weeks by the Army's criminal division said that investigators were focusing in part on a group of friends who know [Chelsea] Manning, a leading suspect in the leak. Investigators, the civilians said, apparently believe that the friends, who include students from MIT and Boston University, might have connections to WikiLeaks."[25]

One of those civilians was David House, who co-founded the support network for Manning after she was arrested. Investigators from Army CID, as well as the State Department, came to his home in June 2010. "At the very end of the conversation, they offered me a cash reward in order to, as I said, keep my ear to the ground about WikiLeaks and [Chelsea] Manning," House recalled.[26]

On November 3, 2010, when House was returning from a vacation in Mexico, he was detained by Department of Homeland Security (DHS) agents and missed a connecting flight to Boston. He was forced to hand over his laptop, a USB storage device, a video camera, and a cellphone. The agents did not ask if House consented to a search, and they did not present a search warrant.[27]

The American Civil Liberties Union (ACLU) sent a letter on December 21, 2010, to DHS, ICE, and Customs and Border Protection urging the agencies to return his electronic devices. His devices were returned the day after, and on May 13, 2011, the ACLU filed a lawsuit alleging the government had "targeted House solely on the basis of his lawful association with the Bradley Manning Support Network" and violated his First and Fourth Amendment rights.

Two years later, the government settled with House after a federal judge refused to dismiss the lawsuit. They agreed to "destroy all remaining data copied from House's devices" and "hand over numerous documents, including reports describing Army CID's inspection of House's data as well as the DHS 'Lookout' telling agents to stop House as he entered the country." The government, according to the ACLU, further "agreed to release reports on DHS agents' questioning of House, which included inquiries about whether he knew anything about Manning giving classified information to WikiLeaks."[28]

House remained a high-profile target of the government. The WikiLeaks grand jury subpoenaed him, and he appeared before the grand jury on June 15, 2011, and claimed he had a Fifth Amendment right to remain silent. He also took notes the whole time, which bothered prosecutors. Meanwhile, a WikiLeaks truck driven by a supporter and artist named Clark Stoeckley circled the courthouse and caused the grand jury to laugh each time it passed.[29]

After resisting the grand jury, House read a statement condemning the DOJ for engaging in the "political regulation of journalism" and called the grand jury a "show trial."

"Using Nixonian fear tactics that were honed during the Pentagon Papers investigation, the DoJ is attempting to dismantle a major media organization—WikiLeaks—and indict its editor Julian Assange. The DoJ's ever-widening net has now come to encompass academics, students, and journalists in the Cambridge area. The Administration's goal is to force these individuals to testify against this media organization in an attempt to cast its publications and those of its media partners—the New York Times, the Guardian, Der Spiegel, Le Monde, and El País—as acts of espionage. The government has also violated my Fourth Amendment rights by executing a warrantless seizure on my laptop in an attempt to identify, target and ensnare Cambridge-based supporters of WikiLeaks," House additionally stated.[30]

House changed his mind when Trump's DOJ revived the case against WikiLeaks. He testified for about ninety minutes in 2018 and was reportedly asked about "debates inside WikiLeaks" over redacting the names of individuals in the documents, which he might have heard about during past meetings with Assange.[31]

Reuters reported in January 2019 that American activist and computer scientist Jason Katz, who was living in Iceland, had been contacted by the DOJ. When WikiLeaks needed help accessing a video file provided by Manning, Katz downloaded the file, which supposedly had footage from the 2009 Granai massacre in Afghanistan. He tried to access it with a password-cracking tool, but he was unable to open it.[32]

Immediately, Katz became a person of interest. The grand jury subpoenaed him, and he refused to testify. He told Motherboard, "[W]hen I got raided, they rounded up my entire support network—all of my friends, all of my close family, and just wrecked all of that."

In 2012, he moved to Iceland and "founded the Pirate Party with several former WikiLeaks associates."[33]

The Washington Post reported in November 2013 that Assange was unlikely to face charges because of the "New York Times problem."[34] Nonetheless, the grand jury investigation was never formally shut down by Attorney General Eric Holder.

After Assange's arrest, the German newspaper *Die Zeit* reported that Daniel Domscheit-Berg, a former WikiLeaks spokesperson and yet another unindicted co-conspirator, was sent a letter in March 2018 from Tracy Doherty-McCormick, acting US attorney in the Eastern District of Virginia. It urged Domscheit-Berg to cooperate with a "voluntary interview."[35]

The grand jury charged Assange on March 6, 2018, with conspiracy to commit a computer crime. In November, the US government leaked the fact that Assange had been secretly charged after US prosecutor Kellen Dwyer committed a copy-and-paste error. Dwyer included the details in an unrelated case against someone accused of "enticement and coercion of a minor."[36]

The Grand Juries Empaneled in Response to the Pentagon Papers

The grand jury investigation into WikiLeaks was not the first grand jury investigation to target journalists and undermine press freedom.

After Pentagon Papers whistleblower Daniel Ellsberg, who worked for the RAND Corporation, provided copies of the Pentagon Papers to media organizations, the DOJ convened two grand juries in the Boston area—one in April 1971 that did not return any indictments and another in August 1971.

Prosecutors targeted individuals who possessed copies of the Pentagon Papers and were involved in distributing parts of the study to the press. In August, they subpoenaed Neil Sheehan, the *New York Times* reporter who was the first to write about the Pentagon Papers.

At least thirteen people were subpoenaed, including Noam Chomsky, an MIT linguist and antiwar activist; Richard Falk, an international law professor who was affiliated with the Institute for Policy Studies; and David Halberstam, a journalist.

After entering 4,100 pages of the Pentagon Papers into the congressional record on June 29, Senator Mike Gravel sought to publish a version of the documents edited by Chomsky and Howard Zinn, an activist and historian. Beacon Press, the nonprofit publishing division of the religious Unitarian Universalist Association (UUA), released Gravel's version on October 22. The grand jury turned its attention to Gravel and Beacon Press.

The FBI subpoenaed Gravel and also subpoenaed UUA's financial records from the New England Merchants National Bank. The religious group fought the action until the government withdrew the subpoena on January 17, 1972.[37]

Samuel Popkin, an assistant professor who taught government at Harvard University, endured the most aggressive act of repression. He was jailed after a court found him in contempt.

Ellsberg and Popkin knew each other through their shared interest in the Vietnam War. Popkin had published several articles and informed FBI agents in the summer of 1971, when they questioned him, that he had no knowledge of the leak of the Pentagon Papers.

"I was in Hong Kong when the papers were distributed," Popkin declared. "I discovered the leak, along with Ellsberg's involvement, at the same time as the general public."

Popkin was first subpoenaed in August 1971, and he received multiple subpoenas between then and the fall of 1972.

"Not once was I ever informed about the purpose of the grand jury investigation or why the FBI had focused so inexplicably on me," Popkin stated. "Yet I was repeatedly called to appear before the grand jury and subjected to hours of broad, speculative, and unrestrained questioning.

"Federal prosecutors continued to question me, not about facts, but about my opinions. I was asked to name anyone I had ever interviewed or had a conversation with, who I thought may have had knowledge of the Pentagon Papers study or may have possessed the Pentagon Papers in Massachusetts. I refused to answer this line of questioning."

Popkin added, "I believed answering questions about my suspicions and opinion would have made it much more difficult for me to obtain interviews for future research as sources may be more reluctant to relay sensitive information, or speak at all, if their conversations could be revealed in a government fishing expedition."

As a result of Popkin's resistance, he was held in contempt in March 1972. Popkin fought the contempt charge, but the First Circuit Court of Appeals rejected his argument that a judge should determine whether questions "regarding anything beyond knowledge of a crime" were "relevant" to the proceedings.

Popkin took his case to the Supreme Court. The solicitor general, Erwin Griswold, informed justices on the court that prosecutors would no longer ask for names of "confidential contacts." The assurance led the Supreme Court to decline to hear Popkin's lawsuit; however, prosecutors still requested that he provide "names."

A federal judge ordered Popkin on November 22, 1972, to serve a sentence for contempt at Dedham County Jail in Massachusetts.[38] He was to remain confined until the grand jury concluded, but several days later, the grand jury was "abruptly dismissed." Popkin's release marked the end of a "15-month-long legal tug-of-war."

The government won a victory against press freedom when the Supreme Court ruled that Gravel was immune from providing testimony but that immunity did not extend to those at Beacon Press who had worked on publishing the Pentagon Papers in book form.

The 5–4 decision came exactly one year after Gravel read the papers into the Congressional Record, and Justice William O. Douglas dissented, "To allow the press [to be further] cowed by grand jury inquiries and prosecution is to carry the concept of 'abridging' the press to frightening proportions."[39]

Beacon Press had published a matter in the public record that was fully protected by the speech and debate clause of the US Constitution. Douglas contended, "In light of the command of the First Amendment, we have no choice but to rule that here government, not the press, is lawless."

More than a half century later, a federal appeals court ruled against a lawsuit by *New Yorker* staff writer Jill Lepore to force the release of records from the Pentagon Papers grand juries. Lepore had the support of multiple media organizations and press freedom groups, as well as several individuals, including Popkin, who had received subpoenas.[40]

The DOJ threatened to charge Beacon Press with "receiving, concealing, retaining and conveying stolen government property," and "receiving, retaining, communication and failure to deliver documents relating to the national defense," a violation of the Espionage Act.[41] However, the First Circuit Court of Appeals ruled in favor of grand jury secrecy and blocked records of historical significance from seeing the light of day.

"A Much Worse Prison"

Manning maintained her grand jury resistance and was jailed for one year. On March 12, 2020, Judge Anthony Trenga released her when the grand jury investigating WikiLeaks was dismissed. The order came a day after Manning attempted to commit suicide.

On May 6, 2019, Manning told the court, "The idea I hold the keys to my own cell is an absurd one, as I face the prospect of suffering either way due to this unnecessary and punitive subpoena: I can either go to jail or betray my principles. The latter exists as a much worse prison than the government can construct."[42]

The grand jury's term ended on May 9, 2019, sixty-two days after Manning was jailed. But the DOJ empaneled the grand jury for another term and again subpoenaed Manning to testify. On May 17, she was sent back to jail—six days before the DOJ released an indictment charging Assange with seventeen additional charges under the Espionage Act.

Judge Trenga urged that Manning "reflect on the principles she says she's embracing" as well as "whether those views [were] worth the price she's paying for them." He contended there was "no dishonor" in cooperating with a grand jury because the US Constitution codified the grand jury.

Manning responded with a letter to the court that displayed a firm grasp of grand juries and their history in the United States. In addition to pointing out that slavery, the subordination of women, segregation, and the disenfranchisement of non–property owners were once enshrined in the Constitution, she called attention to the manner in which subpoenas are used by prosecutors to compel witness appearances and the production of documents without having to show probable cause, which undermines the Fourth Amendment.[43]

In addition to jailing Manning, Trenga imposed a fine of $500 per day after thirty days, and then a fine of $1,000 per day after sixty days. Her attorneys told the court Manning's account balances were near zero, and she lacked the financial ability to pay the steep fines. Trenga claimed the fines were "coercive" and not a "punishment" and refused to end the fines when Manning's attorneys challenged them.[44]

"While coercive financial penalties are commonly assessed against corporate witnesses, which cannot be jailed for contempt, it is less usual to see them used against a human witness," Manning's attorneys asserted.

During her time in jail, Manning accumulated $256,000 in fines. Trenga ordered Manning to pay the entire sum. In response, supporters launched a GoFundMe that raised $267,000. They later raised $67,000 more to help Manning rebuild her life.

Another high-profile individual, Jeremy Hammond, was subpoenaed to testify before the grand jury in September. Hammond was in the final months of his sentence at a federal prison in Memphis, Tennessee, which stemmed from his role in hacking the private intelligence firm Stratfor. Hammond resisted the subpoena and was charged with civil contempt. He was jailed at the Alexandria Detention Center.[45]

The Hammond support committee called attention to the fact that Hammond was about two months away from release. He was enrolled in a residential drug abuse program, or RDAP, that involved 500 hours of substance abuse rehabilitation. Participating in this program earned Hammond a one-year reduction of his sentence. But when the DOJ shipped Hammond to Alexandria to testify against Assange and WikiLeaks, he lost his good time credit.

Hammond was sent back to the facility in Memphis when the grand jury was dismissed in March 2020. Since Hammond no longer had his good time credit, he was forced to survive the first wave of the COVID-19 pandemic in prison. Hammond even asked for compassionate release and was denied. He was finally released to a halfway house in the middle of November.[46] DOJ prosecutors were unsuccessful in forcing Manning and Hammond to testify against Assange. Prosecutors wanted Hammond to share details related to chats that he allegedly had with Assange about Stratfor files. But the fact that prosecutors issued a second superseding indictment with new allegations connected to the Stratfor hack showed that they did not need Hammond's testimony. Their goal was to turn a witness supportive of Assange against the WikiLeaks founder.

Similarly, prosecutors wanted to ask Manning about the statement she read during her court-martial in February 2013, when she described her motivations for releasing each set of documents. Prosecutors hoped to question her about the alleged "Most Wanted Leaks" list to bolster their conspiracy theory that Assange "solicited" classified information—something journalists do all the time.

She had previously made it clear. "No one associated with the WLO [WikiLeaks organization] pressured me into giving more information. The decisions that I made to send documents and information to the WLO and the website were my own decisions, and I take full responsibility for my actions."[47]

Manning's grand jury resistance, and the government's failure to break her spirit, left prosecutors with no testimony to use to attack her credibility at Assange's trial.

CHAPTER 9

Retaliation for Exposing Torture, Rendition, and War Crimes

On Battleship Hill, I hear the wind
Say, "Cruel nature has won again"
—PJ HARVEY, "On Battleship Hill" (2011)

The war in Afghanistan turned ten years old on October 8, 2011. A coalition of peace activists in the United Kingdom called Stop the War, founded in September 2001 after President George W. Bush launched the "Global War on Terrorism," gathered in Trafalgar Square. One of the speakers at the rally was Julian Assange, who was living under house arrest at Ellingham Hall.

"Wars are a result of lies," the WikiLeaks founder declared. "The Vietnam War and the push for US involvement was the result of the Gulf of Tonkin incident—a lie. The Iraq War famously is a result of lies. Wars in Somalia are a result of lies. The Second World War and the German invasion of Poland was a result of carefully constructed lies. That is war by media.

"Let us ask ourselves of the complicit media, which is the majority of the mainstream press: what is the average death count attributed to each journalist?"

Assange continued, "When we understand that wars come about as a result of lies peddled to the British public, and the

American public, and the publics all over Europe and other countries, then who are the war criminals? It is not just leaders. It is not just soldiers. It is journalists. Journalists are war criminals."[1]

Those attending the demonstration whooped and hollered in agreement, applauding the WikiLeaks founder for calling out the mass media in Western countries for fueling conflicts throughout the world.

In the span of one year, WikiLeaks did more to expose wars of occupation in Afghanistan and Iraq than most media organizations had accomplished during the previous decade. The media organization also revealed further evidence of human rights abuses against prisoners at the US military prison on Guantánamo Bay, Cuba, and the lengths to which US diplomats would go to protect Central Intelligence Agency (CIA) officers, US soldiers, and government officials implicated in torture and war crimes from accountability.

Very little opposition to WikiLeaks existed before it received documents from Chelsea Manning on the wars in Afghanistan and Iraq. Because WikiLeaks published documents that undermined deliberately crafted war narratives, and Assange went beyond his basic duties as an editor-in-chief to advocate against US wars, they became the target of retaliation by the US government, especially the CIA.

Afghanistan War Logs Reveal US Military Massacres

President Barack Obama, who referred to the Afghanistan War as the "good war," deployed more than 47,000 additional US troops there during his first year in office.[2]

Speaking at the Veterans of Foreign Wars convention on August 17, 2009, Obama insisted the Afghanistan War was not a "war of choice. This is a war of necessity."

Obama maintained, "Those who attacked America on 9/11 are plotting to do so again. If left unchecked, the Taliban insurgency will mean an even larger safe haven from which al Qaeda would plot to kill more Americans."[3]

Americans increasingly believed the war was going badly and was no longer worth fighting.[4] Yet despite widespread doubts about the war at think tanks and among prestige media, Obama still authorized a troop surge.

On July 25, 2010, WikiLeaks published 75,000 military incident reports from the Afghanistan War.

"The disclosures landed at a crucial moment," the *New York Times* contended. "Because of difficulties on the ground and mounting casualties in the war, the debate over the American presence in Afghanistan has begun earlier than expected. Inside the [Obama] administration, more officials are privately questioning the policy."[5]

Obama officials were frustrated with WikiLeaks and did not immediately know how to react. They believed WikiLeaks had unraveled their narrative for a surge in Afghanistan. The White House attempted to deflect responsibility for what was exposed by arguing the files from January 2004 to December 2009 reflected the war under Bush and not Obama.[6]

The "Afghan War Logs" revealed previously unknown civilian deaths, including incidents where troops apparently killed "unarmed drivers or motorcyclists out of a determination to protect themselves from suicide bombers." For example, according to the *Guardian*, one US patrol "machine-gunned a bus" and wounded or killed 15 passengers.[7]

Rachel Reid, a researcher for Human Rights Watch, said "the concealment of civilian casualties," was part of "a consistent trend" by US and North Atlantic Treaty Organization (NATO) forces.

The logs contained examples of "blue on white" events involving the shooting of individual civilians or air strikes on Afghans that resulted in hundreds of casualties. "US and allied commanders frequently deny allegations of mass civilian casualties, claiming they are Taliban propaganda or ploys to get compensation, which are contradicted by facts known to the military," according to the *Guardian*.[8]

One of the more damning revelations involved an assassination squad known as Task Force 373, which was the focus of a cover story in *Der Spiegel*. The kill team was comprised of Navy SEALs and members of the Delta Force. They kept a classified list of "enemies" known as the Joint Prioritized Effects List.[9]

During a mission that was undertaken on June 17, 2007, to kill "prominent al Qaeda functionary Abu Laith al-Libi," Task Force 373 staked out a Quran school, where al-Libi was "believed to be located for several days." They ordered an attack, and the squad killed seven children with five American rockets. Al-Libi was not killed.

Days before this failed assassination attempt, according to a report from the *Guardian*, Task Force 373 "set out with Afghan special forces to capture or kill a Taliban commander named Qarl Ur-Rahman in a valley near Jalalabad. As they approached the target in the darkness, somebody shone a torch on them."[10]

A firefight ensued, and an AC-130 gunship was called in to clear the area. After unleashing their artillery, Task Force 373 found the people they shot in the dark were Afghan police. Seven officers were dead, and four were wounded.

On October 4, 2007, the kill team called in air support to drop 500-pound bombs on what they believed were a group of Taliban fighters in a village called Laswanday. A war log listed the carnage: "two teenage girls and a 10-year-old boy wounded, one girl killed, one woman killed, four civilian men killed, one donkey killed, one dog killed, several chickens killed, no enemy killed, no enemy wounded, no enemy detained."

The Guardian reported that coalition forces falsely claimed "several militants" were killed, and there were no civilian deaths.

They eventually acknowledged "several non-combatants" had died, but senior officials traveled to Laswanday and blamed the villagers for not doing more to "resist the insurgents and their anti-government activities."[11]

Rather than reassess the war in Afghanistan, the Obama administration doubled down on the military occupation. Officials accused WikiLeaks of having "blood on its hands" and demonized the media organization for publishing the documents.

US media organizations showed little interest in digging into the files. The war continued for more than a decade before US troops withdrew, the Taliban took control of Afghanistan, and President Joe Biden's administration imposed sanctions that drove numerous Afghans to sell their children and kidneys for food.[12]

An Order Authorizing US Troops to Ignore Torture

The Iraq War Logs published on October 22, 2010, consisted of more than 390,000 military incident reports and revealed 15,000 civilian deaths that were previously unknown. They also exposed an arrangement US military officers had to ignore allegations of torture.

Collectively, the reports reflected what Patrick Cockburn, the Middle East correspondent for the *Independent*, called the "small change of war."[13]

One log recounted, "The US marine on duty opened fire because he was 'unable to determine the occupants of the vehicle due to the reflection of the sun coming off the windshield.'"

Another report marked the "moment when US soldiers shot dead a man who was 'creeping up behind their sniper position,' only to learn later that he was their own unit's interpreter."

The documents conveyed the reality of war "far better than even the most well-informed journalistic accounts," according to

Cockburn. "Those two shootings were a thousand times repeated, though the reports were rare in admitting that the victims were civilians. More usually, the dead were automatically identified as 'terrorists' caught in the act, regardless of evidence to the contrary."[14]

Iraq Body Count, which collaborated with WikiLeaks on the files, estimated the reports described 23,000 previously unknown incidents in which Iraqi civilians were killed or bodies were found. "The majority of these [newly documented] deaths came from small incidents of one-to-three deaths," which are the type of incidents that attract the least amount of media coverage.

John Sloboda, the co-founder of Iraq Body Count, said the data set remains "the only source of information regarding many thousands of violent civilian deaths in Iraq between 2004 and 2009. . . . [B]y making this information public, Manning and Assange were carrying out a duty on behalf of the victims and the public that the US government was failing to carry out."[15]

The reports contained details related to Frago 242, a military order that appeared more than 1,000 times.[16] As the *Guardian* described, it was issued in June 2004 and instructed "coalition troops not to investigate any breach of the laws of armed conflict, such as the abuse of detainees," unless it directly involved coalition troops. If the alleged abuse was committed by Iraqi forces against Iraqis, an initial report could be filed. "No further investigation" was required unless directed by commanding officers.[17]

Through this policy, US forces relied on the "systematic viciousness" of Iraq's security agencies, which was a feature of Iraq President Saddam Hussein's regime, and benefited from torture by Iraqi forces. Coalition troops established security through a reliance on the "chaotic savagery of the new criminal, political and sectarian groups," which emerged following the invasion. The groups infiltrated Iraq's police and army and used "Iraq's detention cells for their own private vendettas."[18]

Torturers recognized there would be no consequences for their brutality against helpless Iraqis. "Bound, gagged, blindfolded, and isolated," the *Guardian* noted, Iraqis were "whipped by men in uniforms using wire cables, metal rods, rubber hoses, wooden stakes, TV antenna, plastic water pipes, engine fan belts, or chains." Victims were hung by their wrists or ankles. They were "knotted up in stress positions." Detainees faced molestation and rape, or torment with acid, cigarettes, pliers, boiling water, or hot peppers.[19]

Additionally, the documents contained revelations involving the "Wolf Brigade," which was a torture squad that US forces created and supported in an "attempt to re-employ elements of Saddam Hussein's Republican Guard." Brigade members "wore red berets, sunglasses, and balaclavas, and drove out on raids in convoys of Toyota Landcruisers," according to the *Guardian*.[20] They allegedly beat prisoners, traumatized detainees with electric drills, and sometimes executed their captives.

One war log from December 14, 2005, showed that US interrogators threatened to hand over detainees to the Wolf Brigade.

"During the interrogation process, the [redacted] threatened the subject detainee that he would never see his family again and would be sent to the Wolf Battalion, where he would be subject to all the pain and agony that the Wolf Battalion is known to exact upon its detainees," the report recalled.

According to the Bureau of Investigative Journalism, "More than 1,300 individual cases of torture and abuse carried out by Iraqis on Iraqi prisoners at police stations and army bases" were tallied, implicating coalition forces that likely witnessed or reported on the incidents."[21]

One out of fifty Iraqi males were rounded up by US-backed Iraqi forces. "Over 300 classified reports" documented examples of torture and abuse that occurred after the Abu Ghraib torture and abuse scandal in April 2004.[22]

War logs showing torture by Iraqi forces at detention centers sparked a *Guardian*/BBC Arabic investigation that revealed Colonel James Steele, a retired special forces veteran notorious for his participation in dirty wars in Central America, oversaw the detention centers where Shia police commando units carried out torture, which "accelerated [Iraq's] descent into full-scale civil war." Steele was nominated by Defense Secretary Donald Rumsfeld to "help organize paramilitaries in an attempt to quell a Sunni insurgency."[23]

The investigation also uncovered the role of an advisor to General David Petraeus named James H. Coffman in torture. Coffman, a retired colonel, was "sent to Iraq in June 2004 to organize and train the new Iraqi security forces."

"We deplore WikiLeaks for inducing individuals to break the law, leak classified documents, and then cavalierly share that secret information with the world, including our enemies," Pentagon spokesperson Geoff Morrell stated. "We know terrorist organizations have been mining the leaked Afghan documents for information to use against us, and this Iraq leak is more than four times as large.

"By disclosing such sensitive information, WikiLeaks continues to put at risk the lives of our troops, their coalition partners and those Iraqis and Afghans working with us. The only responsible course of action for WikiLeaks at this point is to return the stolen material and expunge it from their websites as soon as possible."[24]

Morrell downplayed the nature of the reports. The leaked documents are "'significant activities' reports," which are "initial, raw observations by tactical units. They are essentially snapshots of events, both tragic and mundane, and do not tell the whole story. That said, the period covered by these reports has been well chronicled in news stories, books and films, and the release of these field reports does not bring new understanding to Iraq's past."[25]

While presenting a false narrative about the newsworthiness of the documents, the US government attacked WikiLeaks for daring to publish materials that "enemies" could mine for "insights" into military operations. Just how field reports offering "snapshots of events" could simultaneously be old news covered in the media but also new and useful information to enemy forces was never made clear.

Meddling in European Justice Systems to Shield the CIA

During the Obama administration's first year, officials ended the CIA's torture program and released memos drafted by the Bush Justice Department to justify torture. But as countries such as Canada, Germany, Spain, and the United Kingdom openly questioned the role their coalition forces played in supporting the torture program, the US thwarted accountability.

A 2010 report from the American Civil Liberties Union (ACLU), compiled before documents were published by WikiLeaks, argued the US was "increasingly isolated in its unwillingness to investigate the roots of the torture program, its refusal to compensate torture survivors, and its failure to hold accountable the senior government officials who authorized interrogators to use torture."[26]

The ACLU described the Obama administration as an "obstacle to accountability for torture." Not only were Obama officials resistant to releasing documents related to the torture program, but they "extinguished lawsuits brought by torture survivors— denying them recognition as victims, compensation for their injuries, and even the opportunity to present their cases."[27]

US diplomatic cables released by WikiLeaks showed officials had meddled in the justice systems of France, Germany, Italy, and

Spain to shield CIA agents, US military officers, and Bush administration officials from prosecution.

In March 2009, under the law of universal jurisdiction, the Association for the Dignity of Spanish Prisoners requested that the Spanish national court indict Alberto Gonzales, former attorney general; David Addington, former chief of staff and legal advisor to Vice President Dick Cheney; William Haynes, former Defense Department general counsel; Douglas Faith, former undersecretary of defense for policy; Jay Bybee, former head of the DOJ's Office of Legal Counsel; and John Yoo, the author of legal memoranda that came to be known as the "torture memos."[28]

A complaint put forward by the organization accused the named officials of conspiring with "criminal intent to construct a legal framework to permit interrogation techniques and detentions in violation of international law." They argued the judiciary had an obligation to prosecute because five Guantánamo prisoners were from Spain.

Arnold A. Chacón, the deputy chief of mission for the US embassy in Madrid, was irked by the organization's attempt to steer the case to Judge Baltasar Garzón, whom Chacón noted had spent the past two decades generating "international headlines with high-profile cases." The "most famous case" was Garzón's "attempt to bring to trial in Spain former Chilean ruler Augusto Pinochet."[29]

By May, US officials succeeded in pressuring Spanish officials, including National Court chief prosecutor Javier Zaragoza. Garzón "bowed" to Spanish prosecutors and abandoned the complaint against Bush administration officials.[30] Zaragoza "challenged Garzón directly and personally," asking if he was "trying to drum up more speaking fees." Garzón informed Zaragoza he was interested "for the record only and would let it die."

Also, Zaragoza shared with US officials his plan to coerce Garzón into backing off prosecutions involving US torture.

Garzón ordered Spanish police in 2004 to visit Guantánamo and collect evidence against "suspected terrorists." When former Guantánamo prisoners reported their mistreatment that same year, Zaragoza claimed Garzón took no action. Zaragoza believed this could be used to embarrass Garzón during a case related to "CIA flights carrying detainees to Guantánamo via Spain."

"The police officers whom Garzón sent to Guantánamo years ago are expected to testify before [Judge] Moreno this month, and Zaragoza hopes their testimony will put on record Garzón's role in the earlier cases," according to Chacón.

Chacón referred to a criminal complaint against Garzón supported by Spanish prosecutors that could be used to remove him from his judicial position. In February 2012, Spain's supreme court banned Garzón from the National Court for eleven years.[31] (Garzón joined Assange's legal team in July 2012, as Assange sought political asylum in the Ecuador embassy.[32])

In Italy, Egyptian imam Abu Omar was kidnapped by the CIA on February 17, 2003. He was tortured, and twenty-six US citizens, primarily CIA agents, were tried for the crime in absentia and convicted by the Italian Supreme Court in 2012 and 2014. Yet, as Italian journalist and WikiLeaks partner Stefania Maurizi reported, Italian politicians neutralized the work of independent Italian prosecutors by refusing to forward extradition requests for the CIA agents to the US government.[33]

One cable on May 24, 2006, from Ronald Spogli, the US ambassador to Italy, described a meeting with Enrico Letta, who was undersecretary to Prime Minister Silvio Berlusconi. "Nothing would damage relations faster or more seriously than a decision by the GOI [Government of Italy] to forward warrants for arrests of the alleged CIA agents named in connection with the Abu Omar case."[34]

A few months later, according to a cable from August 31, 2006, Spogli applauded Italian justice minister Clemente Mastella for

keeping the "lid on recurring judicial demands to extradite presumed CIA officers allegedly involved in a rendition of Muslim
cleric Abu Omar."[35]

On February 12, 2010, a cable sent out regarding Secretary
of Defense Robert Gates's meeting with Italian defense minister
Ignacio La Russa indicated Gates had asked La Russa for "Italian
government advocacy" in recognizing the jurisdiction that NATO
had over Colonel Joseph Romano. "La Russa stated that direct US
intervention during the appeals process would be the best way to
successfully resolve the matter."[36]

According to Maurizi, Romano was head of security at the
NATO base in Aviano, Italy, where Omar was transferred after
his kidnapping before being transferred to Ramstein, a major US
base in Germany. Italian president Giorgio Napolitano pardoned
Romano in 2013.[37]

Cables from Germany provided evidence that the German government caved to pressure from the US government to block the
extradition of members of a CIA rendition team that kidnapped,
detained, and held German citizen Khaled el Masri incommuni-
cado for twenty-three days.

On January 23, 2004, CIA officers handcuffed and blindfolded Masri at Skopje Airport. He was in Macedonia for a family
vacation. The team cut off Masri's clothes, and, according to the
European Court of Human Rights (ECHR), he was "severely
beaten, sodomized, shackled, and hooded, and subjected to total
sensory deprivation—carried out in the presence of state officials
of Macedonia and within its jurisdiction."

Masri recalled that when his blindfold was removed flash pho-
tography "temporarily blinded" him. He then saw seven or eight
men wearing black clothing and black masks. They put him in a
diaper and tracksuit, with a bag over his head and earmuffs. He
was shackled and marched to an aircraft.

"On the plane, I was spread-eagled and my limbs tied to the sides of the aircraft. I was given injections and an anesthetic. I was unconscious for most of the journey," according to a statement Masri submitted for Assange's defense.[38]

Masri eventually realized he was in Afghanistan in a "cold concrete cell" in the winter. He was "humiliated, stripped naked, insulted, and threatened." Interrogators questioned him, and in March, he initiated a hunger strike. On the thirty-fourth day of the hunger strike, Masri said he was dragged from the cell to an interrogation room and "tied to a chair, and a tube [was] painfully forced through [his] nose."

Although the CIA knew his detention was a case of "mistaken identity," it kept Masri confined until May 2004, when interrogators "warned" him "never to mention what happened" or face consequences.

Masri was loaded on an aircraft and subject to a reverse rendition. His captors blindfolded, earmuffed, and chained him to a seat. He landed in Albania, and while his captors informed him he was in a European country, he had no idea where he was and feared he might be shot. Albanian authorities found him and wondered why he was in Albania without permission, as he had a German passport.[39]

In testimony submitted for Assange's defense, John Goetz, who co-authored a report on the cables for *Der Spiegel*, recalled his investigation into what happened. "Only years later, when WikiLeaks published US diplomatic cables," did Goetz find an explanation for "why there were so many difficulties" trying to uncover the truth.[40]

"The US diplomatic cables revealed the extent of pressure brought upon the German authorities (and in parallel, relevant Spanish authorities) not to act upon the clear evidence of criminal acts by the USA," Goetz added.

According to the story from Goetz and Matthias Gebauer, deputy US ambassador John Koenig met with German officials in Chancellor Angel Merkel's office. Koenig urged the officials to "weigh carefully at every step of the way the implications for relations with the US" if investigations into the CIA were pursued. As in the case of Spain, US diplomats invoked the importance of maintaining a "bilateral relationship."[41]

German prosecutors in Munich issued arrest warrants for thirteen CIA operatives suspected of involvement in Masri's kidnapping. As Goetz and Gebauer outlined, on February 1, 2007, American diplomats in Berlin called their contacts in Germany to figure out "how serious German efforts to investigate the CIA abduction were at the time." They shared what they learned with the State Department, DOJ, and National Security Council; the Munich public prosecutor's office, the state government of Bavaria, and the Justice Ministry in Berlin were also troubled.[42]

"Bavaria's top prosecutor, August Stern, told one American diplomat that he had 'felt compelled to act due to media pressure' to issue the arrest warrants," Goetz and Bebauer wrote.

Showing courage, Masri submitted testimony for Assange's defense. "I record here my belief that without dedicated and brave exposure of the state secrets in question what happened to me would never have been acknowledged and understood."

The European Court of Human Rights (ECHR) partly relied on cables published by WikiLeaks in drafting their decision against Macedonia for the country's role in the kidnapping, Masri noted.

As late as 2020, according to Goetz, the US government still refused to accept responsibility and threatened to retaliate against Masri for bringing his case to the International Criminal Court.

"Unreliable Statements" Kept Many Guantánamo Prisoners in Detention

Dozens of prisoners at Guantánamo were released, repatriated, or transferred during President Barack Obama's first two years in office, as part of his plan to close the military prison, which he ultimately failed to complete.

Part of why Obama did not succeed was opposition from Republicans in Congress. His administration also decided forty-eight detainees were "too dangerous to transfer but not feasible for prosecution" and further punished thirty detainees from Yemen by designating them for "conditional detention" because of turmoil in their home country.

When WikiLeaks published the Guantánamo Files, they did not have the same impact as the military reports on the wars in Afghanistan and Iraq or the stream of revelatory diplomatic cables, which made headlines for months. Nevertheless, the detainee assessments were significant because they contained the US military's justification for keeping hundreds of men in confinement without charge or trial.[43]

Journalist Andy Worthington, who partnered with WikiLeaks to cover the files, said the documents showed that "unreliable statements" from eight prisoners who were tortured and abused had formed the basis for many of the justifications for continued detention.

One of these witnesses was Abu Zubaydah, who was waterboarded eighty-three times at a CIA secret prison in Thailand. He spent several years in CIA custody before his transfer to Guantánamo in 2006. In February 2015, the ECHR awarded Zubaydah €100,000 compensation to be paid by Poland for its involvement in his detention.

Abd al Rahim al Nashiri was tortured at the same CIA prison as Zubaydah. Ibn al-Shaykh al-Libi was subjected to a CIA rendition to Egypt and then tortured. As Worthington noted, al-Libi "falsely confessed that al Qaeda operatives had been meeting with Saddam Hussein to discuss obtaining chemical and biological weapons." Both made claims against fellow detainees that were untrue. (Note: In 2014, al Nashiri won his case before the ECHR, which referred to cables published by WikiLeaks.)

The file on Al Jazeera journalist Sami al-Hajj showed he was sent to the prison "to provide information" on the "[Al] Jazeera news network's training program, telecommunications equipment and newsgathering operations in Chechnya, Kosovo, and Afghanistan, including the network's acquisition of a video of [Osama bin Laden] and a subsequent interview" of bin Laden. Al-Hajj was detained for six years.[44]

Twenty-two children were detained at Guantánamo. Pakistani national Naqib Ullah (also known as Naqibullah), for example, was fourteen years old. He was kidnapped from his village in Khan, Afghanistan, while running an errand for his father. Eleven men, known as "Samoud's people," "forcibly raped him at gunpoint," according to Ullah. He was taken to the men's village encampment and "forced to do manual work."[45]

In 2002, three days after his arrival at the camp, US military forces raided it. The men knew ahead of time and ordered Ullah and others to stay behind to fight. Ullah was captured because he had a weapon, though it was never fired. The US military transferred a traumatized child to Guantánamo in January 2003 because they believed he had knowledge of "Taliban resistance efforts and local leaders." He was released around a year later.[46]

General Dick Myers, the chairman of the Joint Chiefs of Staff, defended the detention of children when asked about them in April 2003. "They may be juveniles, but they're not on a little league team anywhere. They're on a major league team, and it's a terrorist team. And they're in Guantanamo for a very good reason—for our safety, for your safety."[47]

With the Guantánamo Files, the world finally saw proof that what Myers said was wild and offensive nonsense.

Cable on Massacre Accelerates Withdrawal of US Forces From Iraq

On March 15, 2006, Philip Alston, the United Nations Special Rapporteur on Extrajudicial, Summary, or Arbitrary Executions, sent a "communications log" to Secretary of State Condoleezza Rice. It was an inquiry about the apparent summary execution of ten Iraqis, including five children, by US-led Multinational Forces (MNF).[48]

When US troops approached the home of Faiz Hratt Khalaf and his wife, Sumay'ya Abdul Razzaq Khuther, the couple was with their three children: five-year-old Hawra'a, three-year-old Aisha, and Husam, five months. Khalaf's mother, sister, two nieces, and a "visiting relative" were also present.

According to the log, which was posted on September 1, 2011, it was believed that shots had been fired from the house, and a confrontation ensued for about twenty-five minutes. The soldiers entered the house, handcuffed all the residents, and executed them. After the forces executed them, an air strike destroyed the house.[49]

Iraqi TV stations broadcast from the scene and showed bodies of the victims (i.e. five children and four women) in the morgue of Tikrit. Autopsies carried out at a hospital morgue indicated that all the corpses were handcuffed and shot in the head.[50]

The US military claimed it "attacked the house to capture members of Mr. Faiz Harrat al Majma'ee's family on the basis that they were allegedly involved in the killing of two MNF soldiers who were killed between 6 to 11 March 2006 in the Al Haweeja area."

After the log was shared widely, Alston said, "[The US] studiously avoided responding to any communications sent to it during this period." He added, "The tragedy is that this elaborate system of communications is in place, but the [UN] Human Rights Council does nothing to follow up when states ignore issues raised with them."[51]

McClatchy Newspapers, a WikiLeaks partner, reported, "At the time, American military officials in Iraq said the accounts of townspeople who witnessed the events were highly unlikely to be true, and they later said the incident didn't warrant further investigation. Military officials also refused to reveal which units might have been involved in the incident."[52]

Remarkably, the incident became known to the world because US-trained Iraqi police at the Joint Coordination Center in Tikrit, "a regional security center set up with American military assistance," were willing to attach their names to a report on the massacre.

In October 2011, the Obama administration announced the US government would stick to a December 31 withdrawal deadline that had been set in 2008. US troops would not be left behind in Iraq, because the Iraqi government refused to agree to a demand by Defense Secretary Leon Panetta and other top military officials to grant immunity for US personnel from prosecution for war crimes.

"The negotiations were strained following WikiLeaks' release of a diplomatic cable that alleged Iraqi civilians, including children, were killed in a 2006 raid by American troops rather than in an airstrike as the U.S. military initially reported," according to CNN.[53]

Writer and scholar Noam Chomsky testified in Assange's defense: "Julian Assange's alleged crime in working to expose government secrets is to violate the fundamental principles of government, to lift the veil of secrecy that protects power from scrutiny, keeps it from evaporating—and again, it is well understood by the powerful that lifting the veil may cause power to evaporate. It may even lead to authentic freedom and democracy if an aroused public comes to understand that force is on the side of the governed, and it can be their force if they choose to control their own fate."[54]

Or, as Assange proclaimed at the end of his speech for the Stop the War rally, "If wars can be started by lies, peace can be started by truth."

If not for Assange (and Manning), the US might have kept a sizable troop presence in Iraq past the withdrawal date. WikiLeaks showed that peace really could be started by the truth.

CHAPTER 10

US Prisons and Truth-Tellers

I am a rebel soldier
And far from my home
—THE FOUR FATHERS, "Rebel Soldier" (2015)

The US government initially lost the battle to extradite Julian Assange when District Judge Vanessa Baraitser denied the request on January 4, 2021. In her decision, she recognized that the mass incarceration system in the United States is inhumane and cruel.

"The detention conditions in which Mr. Assange is likely to be held are relevant to Mr. Assange's risk of suicide," Baraitser determined. "I find that the mental condition of Mr. Assange is such that it would be oppressive to extradite him to the United States of America."[1]

The fact that the Central Intelligence Agency (CIA) backed an espionage operation against Assange while he was in the Ecuador embassy helped convince Baraitser there was a "high level of concern by the US authorities regarding Mr. Assange's ongoing activities." He would likely be confined under restrictive "special administrative measures," or SAMs, which are authorized by the attorney general based on input from law enforcement and intelligence agencies, including the CIA.

She also accepted his attorneys' argument that Assange would be imprisoned in Colorado at the Administrative Maximum Facility (ADX) Florence—a "Supermax" facility that is notorious for its conditions and effects on the mental health of prisoners.

To salvage their extradition case, the US State Department intervened with a "diplomatic note" sent to the United Kingdom's Foreign Office on February 5, 2021.[2] The note contained "assurances" related to how the US government would handle Assange. None of the assurances were offered during the extradition trial, when Assange's defense could test them.

The State Department claimed the government would not designate Assange for SAMs before or after trial. They pledged not to send him to ADX Florence. They indicated they would make sure he was able to receive "clinical and psychological treatment" wherever he was incarcerated. They also said Assange could apply for a prisoner transfer under the Council of Europe Convention on the Transfer of Sentenced Prisons and serve his sentence in Australia.

However, all the assurances contained glaring loopholes. If Assange committed a "future act" that "met the test" for SAMs or imprisonment at ADX Florence, the US would still hold him in these harsh conditions. They did not specify what type of "future act" would be grounds for abandoning their assurances.

The promise to make a psychologist available to him was questionable because US prisons are typically understaffed. Even if Assange saw a qualified doctor, they could deny treatment and prioritize prisoners with more severe mental health problems.

In 2018, data from the US Bureau of Prisons (BOP) itself showed that—despite BOP promises of better care for prisoners with mental health issues—the number of prisoners "designated for higher care levels" had decreased by more than 35 percent over the past four years. The BOP lacked the staff necessary to provide increased care to prisoners with mental health problems. It incentivized staff to "downgrade inmates to lower care levels."[3]

On the question of whether the US government would allow Assange to serve his sentence in Australia, the assurance only said he would be permitted to apply for a transfer. It did not say the US government would grant the application.

David Mendoza was extradited from Spain in 2009 on charges of drug trafficking. A Spanish court made "Mendoza's extradition conditional on prisoner transfer back to Spain to serve any sentence."

The US government offered an assurance similar to the one in the Assange case, but the Justice Department (DOJ) later rejected Mendoza's application for transfer. "When the Spanish court complained of the 'clear breach' of the assurance, the USA retorted that 'the US did not make and therefore could not and did not renege on a promise guaranteeing that Mendoza would comply with the sentence imposed in Spain.'"[4]

The assurances amounted to a cunning tactic to sidestep obstacles to extradition that existed as a result of systematic abuses and inhuman treatment in the US incarceration system. Such abuse and mistreatment was cruelty routinely inflicted on past whistleblowers, whom the US government made an example of through prosecutions under the Espionage Act.

Alleged WikiLeaks Source Detained in "Barbaric" Conditions

One of the glaring reasons to doubt the US government's pledge not to impose "special administrative measures" against Assange is that CIA programmer Joshua Schulte was jailed under SAMs. On July 13, 2022, a jury convicted Schulte of leaking the Vault 7 materials to WikiLeaks. The BOP confined Schulte in the 10 South Unit at the Metropolitan Correctional Center (MCC) in New York after his arrest.

Attorney General Jeff Sessions designated Schulte for SAMs after Schulte contacted reporters at the *Washington Post* and *New*

York Times and shared details from "protected affidavits." The FBI accused him of leaking classified information—revealing the identities of CIA officers, some undercover; filing a handwritten motion for bail that contained classified information related to the CIA; and mailing the motion to his parents and to a Texas attorney whom he asked to assist him on the case.

Schulte was also accused, and later convicted, of making the unauthorized disclosures with contraband cellphones that he arranged to have smuggled into the prison. Sessions deemed him a "significant threat to national security."

Arrested in 2017, Schulte filed multiple complaints in 2019 and 2021 that alleged he was subject to "cruel and unusual punishment" and insisted that prosecutors should end their abuse.

"SAMs inmates are locked in concrete boxes the size of parking spaces with purposefully obstructed views of outside. The cages are filthy and infested with rodents, rodent droppings, cockroaches, and mold," Schulte's defense claimed. "There is no heating or air conditioning in the cages. There is no functioning plumbing. The lights burn brightly 24 hours per day, and the inmates are denied outside recreation, normal commissary, normal visitation, access to books and legal material, medical care, and dental care."[5]

The complaint added, "All attorney-client privilege is also void to SAMs inmates as the prison confiscates, opens, and reads all legal mail. Inmates are forbidden from transferring legal material to and from their attorneys."

During the winter, due to the lack of insulation, Schulte wore "four sets of clothing, five sets of socks, a sweatshirt and sweatpants, two blankets, [and] three sets of socks on his hands." He still froze because the temperature in his cell sometimes plummeted below freezing and water turned to ice in his cell.

Windows were blacked out, and the facility allegedly denied Schulte access to outside recreation.

"Despite Mr. Schulte's congenital heart issues and ongoing cardiologist appointments, he has not seen a doctor since his trial in February 2020. Additionally, Mr. Schulte has not once seen a dentist at MCC," Schulte's defense declared.

The FBI regularly intercepted Schulte's mail to prevent the "alleged dissemination of classified information," which his defense contended was a violation of his Fifth Amendment rights. They urged a federal court to order the FBI to stop reading his incoming mail.

Prisoners in 10 South, where Schulte was jailed, were "shackled from head-to-toe like Hannibal." They were also "often forced to urinate and defecate in plastic bags."

According to the complaint, "During visitation, inmates are moved to a six by six foot cage. Instead of taking the inmate back to his cage after visitation, as would be logical, [Solitary Housing Unit] lieutenants take the visitors back first." This could take anywhere from five to seven hours, which meant prisoners had to go to the bathroom in the plastic bags given to them.

"It is barbaric and inhumane to lock human beings into boxes for years and years," Schulte's defense concluded. "It is a punishment worse than death, and there is no wonder that MCC inmates would rather kill themselves than continue to live in absolute oppression."

Systematic abuse and mistreatment of SAMs prisoners played a decisive role in Baraitser's decision to deny the US government's extradition request against WikiLeaks founder Julian Assange. He would likely be placed under the kind of restrictions Schulte has faced if the US prevailed and brought him to the country for a trial on Espionage Act charges.

The CIA could claim Assange posed an ongoing threat to national security, as District Judge Vanessa Baraitser acknowledged. If the agency did, the attorney general would be under immense pressure to place Assange in confinement conditions that a UK court determined would significantly impact his mental health.

Schulte's first trial ended in a mistrial in March 2020, however, the DOJ pursued a second trial that was held in June 2022. He was convicted on largely circumstantial evidence that stemmed from prosecutors insisting he had used privacy tools to cover his tracks and that was why there was no record of Schulte transferring the CIA hacking materials to WikiLeaks.

Even more troubling, in August 2021, the DOJ shut down MCC New York following reports involving the "rampant spread of COVID-19," "inmates' complaints about squalid conditions," and the death of child sex trafficker Jeffrey Epstein at the facility.

Schulte was eventually transferred to the Metropolitan Detention Center in Brooklyn, but for weeks, the DOJ said prisoners with upcoming trials would be left in the filthy jail. Attorney General Merrick Garland kept Schulte in SAMs.[6]

Assurances Violated in Drone Whistleblower's Case

A federal judge and prosecutors assured drone whistleblower Daniel Hale and his defense attorneys that he would be sent to Federal Medical Center Butner in North Carolina, a low-security facility where he could receive attention for post-traumatic stress disorder (PTSD). Yet after Hale was sentenced, he spent around two months at Northern Neck Regional Jail before authorities transferred him to US Penitentiary Marion, a medium-security prison in southern Illinois.[7]

The BOP placed Hale in a Communications Management Unit (CMU). He was not informed he would be incarcerated in a CMU until he arrived at the facility.

There are two prisons with CMUs—USP Marion and the US Penitentiary in Terre Haute, Indiana. The assurance the State Department offered omitted the possibility that Assange could be sent to either facility and placed in a CMU.

The visitation policy for prisoners designated for a CMU is harsher than the policy for SAMs. Only two four-hour visits per month with "immediate family" are allowed. Contact visits are prohibited. All visits with Assange's wife Stella and his children, Gabriel and Max, would take place through thick plexiglass. He would not be allowed to hug, kiss, or sit next to them.

All phone calls for CMU prisoners are typically restricted to immediate family. Assange would likely face a limit of two scheduled fifteen-minute calls per week. The facility would only permit him to schedule calls when an FBI agent was available to listen to the conversation.

It can take months for prisoners to receive mail. On February 1, 2022, Hale received mail that was postmarked November 5, 2021.

"For any inmate, and many of my clients, the level of monitoring of their lives can—and often does—cause distress leading to significant levels of depression," said Joel Sickler, the head of a criminal defense litigation support firm who testified as an expert on federal prisons during Assange's extradition trial. "In my experience, those inmates who are placed in CMUs experience this exponentially."[8]

The First Step Act, which was signed into law under President Donald Trump, entitles prisoners to accumulate good time credits for early release by enrolling in programs. One may even earn increased minutes for phone calls. Yet someone like Hale, who exposed war crimes, is disqualified from earning benefits. Assange would be ineligible, too.[9]

Maureen Baird was the warden for USP Marion from 2016 to 2017 and oversaw the CMU. She testified at Assange's extradition trial that, due to "limited space for outdoor walking and short of walking in circles, or a short horizontal pattern, it is difficult for an inmate to engage in any meaningful and healthy outdoor exercise." Baird often received "a barrage of complaints" from prisoners related to "the absolute boredom they experienced and lack of meaningful programs in the unit."

The Daniel Hale Support Network relayed on February 14, 2022, "We wish we could share how Daniel is doing, but even the small updates we had been communicating out here have resulted in increased discipline so we are unable to say much more."

Assange would risk similar retaliation if his family or defense committee provided updates on his health or life in incarceration.

The Center for Constitutional Rights filed a federal lawsuit in 2010 against the BOP and officials involved in overseeing CMUs, which violate the due process rights of prisoners.

"Since the BOP secretly opened its first communication management unit in 2006, it has used them as political prisons—to isolate individuals whose ideas the government considers dangerous," declared Rachel Meeropol, a senior staff attorney for the Center for Constitutional Rights who represents prisoners held in CMUs.

Asked about Hale, Meeropol commented, "The BOP has no right to inflict CMU-level isolation and restrictions on anyone without proper procedural protections but especially not an individual struggling with PTSD and depression, and in need of significant medical care."

NSA Whistleblower Kept in Unprecedented Pretrial Confinement

Prior to NSA whistleblower Reality Winner's case, it was almost unthinkable that a person accused by federal prosecutors of violating the Espionage Act would be denied bail.

US Attorney Bobby Christine and his office in the Southern District of Georgia stigmatized the work of Winner, who was a linguist in the Air Force. She was fluent in Farsi, Dari, and Pashto. They claimed she had a "strong and persistent desire to travel to the Middle East, particularly Afghanistan." They said she wanted to meet "leaders of the Taliban."[10]

According to Winner, FBI agents went through her notebooks and journals and found a thesis for a book on the Second Coming of Jesus Christ that was inspired by Salman Rushdie's *Satanic Verses*. Rushdie's novel was important to her father, and she had many conversations about Islam with him after the September 11th attacks.

"I was 24 years old, and I wanted to write something along the lines of a *Satanic Verses* that would be explosive," Winner shared on the podcast *A Song Called Life*. "And so I had a passage in a book that basically the thesis of the book was that the Second Coming of Christ was going to come. The Messiah was going to come back, but he would come back as a fundamental Islamic extremist."[11]

The book, as Winner outlined, would confront Christian nationalists in the US with the question of whether they would accept the Second Coming of Christ if he was not white and if he was in Afghanistan with the mujahideen.

Part of the book had a structure like "Passion of the Christ" that was about Mullah Omar, who founded the Islamic Emirate of Afghanistan, betraying bin Laden.

"I was writing this out to be this really offensive but not illegal sort of novel, and they left out the top portion. And the top portion was, where would Christ be today? Looking for Christ, where would he be, what would his skin color be, like how would he be?" Winner said.

Winner also wrote about how the "Global War on Terrorism" had further entrenched the world in a cycle of extremism.

During the bond hearing, Judge Brian Epps fell for the prosecutors' nefarious description of her writings. In the hopes of diminishing the fear that the government had manufactured, Winner's attorney asked an FBI special agent, who was testifying, to read a top section that prosecutors had ignored. The section made it clear Winner was contemplating where the Messiah would come from in the modern age, not promoting terrorist ideology.[12]

Prosecutors lied about a phone conversation Winner had with her mother while in jail. They insisted Winner confessed she had "leaked documents." They only knew of one leaked document and acted as if she had to remain in jail so they could get to the bottom of this. They later apologized because it was clear they had made it up.[13]

Yet another lie that prosecutors told involved $30,000 in Winner's bank account, which she tried to withdraw to pay her attorneys. She moved the money because she was afraid the government would freeze her account. Prosecutors pointed to the sum because they believed she wanted to deceive the court into believing she was poor so she could obtain a free attorney. Prosecutors eventually apologized for making this false claim as well.

Prosecutors seized upon texts in which Winner said to her sister, "I want to burn the [W]hite [H]ouse down. Find somewhere in Kurdistan to live . . . or Nepal. Ha, ha, maybe," and, "I have to take a polygraph where they're going to ask if I've ever plotted against the government. #gonna fail. . . . Look, I only say I hate America like three times a day. I'm no radical. It's mostly just about Americans' obsession with air conditioning."[14]

When her sister asked her whether she actually "hate[d] America," Winner replied, "I mean, yeah, I do. It's literally the worst thing to happen to the planet. We invented capitalism, the downfall of the environment."

All of the above was construed by prosecutors as evidence that

Winner "hated" America and wanted to burn the White House down. They also highlighted texts, where she seemed to sympathize with Assange and NSA whistleblower Edward Snowden.

The attacks on Winner's character worked. Judge Brian Epps decided she was a flight risk, even though Winner and her parents were willing to subject themselves to a range of restrictions—ankle bracelet, constant monitoring, and so on—whatever it would take to get out of the county jail in Lincolnton, Georgia.

Winner maintained Epps had "no personal knowledge or personal experience in national security or foreign affairs." Prosecutors took advantage and scared him.

An appeals court upheld the decision. "Evidence in the record indicates that Ms. Winner—who is fluent in Farsi, Dari, and Pashto—has long wanted to live and work in the Middle East. She wanted the Air Force to deploy her to Afghanistan; she researched traveling, working, and living in places like Kurdistan, Iraq, Afghanistan, Jordan, and the Palestinian territories; she researched flights to Kurdistan and Erbil; she researched buying a home in Jordan; and she researched how to obtain a work visa in Afghanistan.

"There is, of course, nothing inherently problematic about any of these things, but when they are viewed together and added to the mosaic, they provide an additional reason or motivation for Ms. Winner to not remain in the United States to stand trial. Her demonstrated interest in living and working in the Middle East, and the $30,000 in her bank account makes travel there, under the circumstances, more than a flight of fancy."[15]

To the appeals court, the messages Winner sent to her sister showed she had a "reason to flee" because she lacked "confidence in the government, which has accused her of serious criminal conduct."

The portrait that DOJ prosecutors painted inflicted trauma on Winner. During her time in Lincoln County Jail in Georgia, her bulimia worsened. She engaged in self-harm that left her family afraid that something even more horrible might occur while she was detained. She "began practicing how to commit suicide in jail."[16]

Compounding the abuse was the fact that Winner had to meet with her attorneys in a sensitive compartmented information facility, or SCIF, at the courthouse in Augusta because her case involved classified information. She was kept in shackles for twelve hours each day that she attended a meeting. The shackles were at her waist so she could not use her own two hands to drink from a water bottle. She was subject to humiliating strip searches if she needed to use the bathroom and when she left the SCIF to return to jail.

Winner pled guilty on August 23, 2018, and was transported to Grady County Jail in Chickasha, Oklahoma, where she waited for several weeks until she was moved to Federal Medical Center Carswell. She noticed that the correctional officers had a document with highly sensitive information lying out in the open on a desk in the jail. Or at least her attorneys were told the information was too sensitive to declassify and present it to a jury.

"I saw my name at the bottom and I had this whole little subparagraph under my name," Winner recalled. "Basically, it said broad publicity, and then it went into the leak and what the leak was about and these are things, country names that my lawyers aren't even allowed to say anymore."[17]

"What does this have to do [with] me being transported? It's not like they're going to search my bra and then a whole ream of paper is going to fly out," Winner added.

None of the correctional officers had security clearances, yet here was a document with classified information that Winner was punished for releasing to the media.

Winner received a sixty-three-month prison sentence—the longest sentence ever for an "unauthorized disclosure of national defense information to the media." Attorney Christine boasted, "It appropriately satisfies the need for both punishment and deterrence in light of the nature and seriousness of the offense."[18]

While Winner was imprisoned at Carswell, she survived a major COVID-19 outbreak that infected her entire unit. She was also allegedly sexually assaulted by a guard. Winner filed a claim under the Prison Rape Elimination Act, along with other prisoners, yet Carswell took no meaningful action to protect her.

Bureau of Prisons Marked CIA Whistleblower "Dangerous"

Another example of prosecutors giving an assurance that was later broken occurred in CIA whistleblower John Kiriakou's case.

Kiriakou was sentenced to thirty months in January 2013. The judge, prosecutors, and Kiriakou's attorneys agreed to sending him to a low-security facility in Loretto, Pennsylvania. There he would be incarcerated in the minimum-security camp, which allowed for more freedom of movement. But when he arrived at the prison, a corrections officer notified Kiriakou that the Bureau of Prisons deemed him a "threat to the public safety." He was prohibited from serving his sentence in the camp.

Later, Kiriakou discovered he had been assigned a "public safety factor" designation when he was sentenced for violating the Intelligence Identities Protection Act (IIPA) and marked "dangerous."[19]

According to the BOP, "There are certain demonstrated behaviors, which require increased security measures to ensure the protection of society. There are nine public safety factors (PSFs), which are applied to inmates who are not appropriate for placement at an institution which would permit inmate access to the community [and allow them to be placed in a minimum security camp]."

"The 'greatest severity' public safety factor was placed on inmate Kiriakou by the DSCC [Designation and Sentence Computation Center]," the warden informed him. A program statement for security designations said, "Crimes involving espionage, treason, sabotage, or other related offenses fall within the greatest severity scale."

"My crime should not fall under 'greatest severity' because it is not in any way related to 'espionage, treason, sabotage or other related offenses,'" Kiriakou argued in complaints to officials at Loretto. "Although I was charged with espionage, all of those charges were dropped for the simple reason that I had not committed espionage." (The IIPA is not even in the same section of the US criminal code as the Espionage Act.)

On February 11, 2014, a BOP regional director replied to his complaints to administrators. "Your total offensive behavior is to be considered utilizing the most serious offense or act committed when determining offense security level."[20]

"The security designation has nothing to do with your crime. It has to do with whatever the government accuses you of doing, whether the charges were dropped or not," Kiriakou wrote. "What happened to due process? If I had actually committed the crimes I was charged with, why didn't the government insist on going to trial? Why did they make five different plea offers? Why did they offer to drop four of the five charges? And if I'm so dangerous, why didn't the BOP put me in a maximum security penitentiary?"

Additionally, Loretto officials considered Kiriakou a risk because he had access to the press. He wrote "Letters from Loretto" that were published by Firedoglake. The prison responded by placing Kiriakou under "Central Inmate Monitoring." It meant they could put him under a microscope and disrupt his ability to correspond with journalists and supporters by regularly reading his mail.[21]

On August 30, 2013, Kiriakou said he was "forced to sign" a "memo" from the DOJ that stated he was "legally obligated to clear everything" he wrote "for publication with the CIA's Publication Review Board." The Special Investigative Service, which oversees prisoners with national security designations, demanded Kiriakou give all future "Letters from Loretto" to them to share with the CIA. The service threatened disciplinary action. Kiriakou's attorney suggested he ignore the demand, because it was "illegal, unconstitutional, and unenforceable."[22]

Kiriakou broke his finger two weeks after arriving at Loretto. It took eighteen days after he injured himself to convince the prison to provide him access to medical care. When the prison asked him to report for outside medical consultation, he was escorted to a medical unit and strip-searched. They handed him brown pants, a brown T-shirt, a pair of underwear, socks, and slippers. They took his clothes and watch and locked them in the unit.

Because of his security designation, Kiriakou was handcuffed and shackled around his ankles. "A chain was placed around my waist, which connected to my handcuffs and my leg irons. Then a black steel box about the size of a computer hard drive was locked over the handcuffs so the lock could not be picked."

Two officers instructed Kiriakou to sign a form with "rules," indicating he would be shot if he tried to escape. It also said he must address every person with "sir." Kiriakou resisted their request, so the officers said they would not take him to the doctor. When Kiriakou said fine and called their bluff, "Dumb" and "Dumber" had no idea what to do next. They said, "Forget it," and loaded Kiriakou in a van to receive care for his finger.

CIA Whistleblower Denied Prison Health Care for Heart Condition

In September 2016, staff at Federal Correctional Institution Englewood in Littleton, Colorado, accused CIA whistleblower Jeffrey Sterling of fabricating medical information related to his health, even as he endured chronic heart problems that could have resulted in death.

The symptoms had started on June 21. As Sterling described in a prison letter, he felt a "sudden, very hard heartbeat with a sort of pause." It felt as though his body, breathing, and movement had halted. There were sharp pains in his chest, along with lightheadedness and shortness of breath. Sterling asked prison staff for help, but his health concerns were continually dismissed.

More effort was spent trying to refute him than to provide care. In fact, on June 21, after an EKG was administered, Sterling said medical at Englewood accused him of being "untruthful" in an email to his wife, Holly Sterling, because he claimed a nurse who administered an EKG had found a "blockage." Medical personnel maintained he was "making up the episode" and further asserted there was "no information" in his records to show a "history of atrial fibrillation" or that he was scheduled for an EKG shortly after arriving at the prison.[23]

Holly turned to the press to publicize Sterling's issues with access to medical care and prevent something serious from happening to her husband. On September 19, 2016, Sterling was finally seen by a doctor at Colorado Heart and Vascular.

"For the consult, I was handcuffed, with a waist chain and my ankles were shackled together," Sterling shared. "I was so restrained during the entire visit with the doctor. Salient or [not], it was quite humiliating being paraded on the streets and through the medical facility.

"Not to mention the fact that even though I was completely restrained, I had to sign a statement promising not to go shopping while away from the prison."[24]

Sterling was prescribed a beta blocker and sent back to prison. Whether it constituted care was debatable. Holly believed the doctor "put a band-aid on a gaping wound."

Later, in April 2017, Holly needed the media to pay further attention to Sterling as Englewood staff put her husband in solitary confinement and took away his phone and commissary privileges for thirty days.[25]

According to Sterling, a guard named "Richard" threatened him with physical violence during count. "Do you want to go? Let's go. You're here, so you're not so tough," the guard said. He was taken to a lieutenant's office at the facility and then brought to the Special Housing Unit (SHU), which is solitary confinement.

Sterling was put in solitary confinement because he "spoke during count" and then demanded multiple times to see a lieutenant so that he could report the guard's abuse.[26]

One of the reasons Holly felt powerless to advocate for Jeffrey is the fact that she was isolated. The BOP incarcerated Sterling in a facility nearly 900 miles away from their home in St. Louis.

In the case of Assange, his incarceration would be worse for his wife and children. He would be thousands of miles away, separated by an ocean and several time zones.

Assange may face guards who toy with him because he is on the autism spectrum, and if he disobeys their order, they would probably put him in solitary confinement. If chronic health problems reared their ugly head, it would be as difficult for him as it was for Jeffrey to obtain medical care.

If Assange is imprisoned, the facility where he would be held captive might even be sent the record indicating that Crown prosecutors mercilessly accused him of reading *The BMJ*, the trade journal of the British Medical Association, to learn how to exaggerate his health problems.

"Single-Minded Determination" to Take His Life

To mark the fourth time that her husband spent his birthday (July 3) locked in a cell, Stella Assange penned an op-ed in 2022 that detailed what it was like to visit Julian Assange in Belmarsh prison. Their children, Gabriel and Max, only knew their dad from their prison visits.

"The children walk under razor wire and past layers and layers of security to reach their daddy," Stella recounted. "Guards search inside their mouths, behind their ears, and under their feet. The prison dogs sniff them head to toe, front and back.

"Gabriel slipped some daisies he had picked by the prison walls into his pocket to give to his father. After he passed through the metal detector his daisies were confiscated during the pat-down search by one of the guards, albeit reluctantly.

"During visits, our family is allowed to embrace at the beginning and end. We can hold each other's hands across the table. Julian and I are not allowed to kiss. But Julian would rather kiss his wife and be penalized than have that taken away from him too. So, we kiss."[27]

Belmarsh prison authorities were consistently fearful of any love and affection between Stella and Julian. When they held a marriage ceremony at Belmarsh in March 2022, they were barred from inviting a wedding photographer. Any photographs were deemed a "security risk" because they "could end up on social media or the press."[28]

But the apparent mistreatment at Belmarsh was mild compared to what lies ahead for Julian in a US jail or prison.

"We don't know how long our children have left with their father," Stella declared. "They don't know if they will be able to visit [Julian]. We don't know if we can visit him or even talk to him on the phone. If the extradition goes ahead, US authorities retain the right to put Julian in conditions so cruel that no one in his position is likely to survive."[29]

Dr. Sondra Crosby, an American doctor who focuses on care for asylum seekers and refugees who have experienced torture, met with Julian while he was in the Ecuador embassy. She also visited him in Belmarsh in October 2019 and January 2020. She determined he was at "high risk of completing suicide if he were to be extradited." She also noted severe risks to his physical health that included osteoporosis if he was incarcerated in a US prison.[30]

Julian has concealed the "full extent of his depression and suicide plans" when meeting with prison doctors and mental health specialists, Crosby testified. He worried if he revealed his plans, or the "extent of his suicidal ideations," that he "may be put under more surveillance" or face further isolation.

Dr. Quinton Deeley, who worked for the National Health Service, met with Julian for six hours in July 2020. A test conducted then showed Julian has Asperger's syndrome, a form of autism.[31]

In the cases of Lauri Love and Gary McKinnon, who were both accused of hacking offenses, the US government was blocked from extraditing them. The UK High Court of Justice (in Love's case) and the UK Home Secretary (in McKinnon's case) recognized that their Asperger's syndrome would put them at risk of degrading or inhuman treatment in violation of their human rights. However, this decision was ultimately disregarded by the UK judiciary and UK Home Secretary Priti Patel.

Chelsea Manning was jailed at the Alexandria Detention Center (ADC) while she resisted a subpoena from prosecutors to testify before the WikiLeaks grand jury. In March 2020, she attempted suicide. She had previously attempted suicide while serving a prison sentence at Fort Leavenworth, but that did not apparently make a difference in how staff monitored her. The ADC is where Julian Assange would be held in pretrial confinement.[32]

In District Judge Vanessa Baraitser's decision, she referred to Manning's attempted suicide and Jeffrey Epstein's death. She was convinced that under conditions of "near total isolation and without the protective factors," which prevent him from committing suicide at Her Majesty's Prison Belmarsh, Assange would find a way to commit suicide.[33]

On May 5, 2019, "during a routine search of the cell solely occupied by Mr. Assange, inside a cupboard and concealed under some underwear, a prison officer found 'half of a razor blade,'" Baraitser recalled.

Not one of the assurances put forward by the US government confronted this reality. US assistant attorney Gordon Kromberg, Attorney General Merrick Garland, and President Joe Biden's White House apparently had no qualms about their prosecution resulting in Assange's death.

CHAPTER 11

Standard News-Gathering
Practices

Words of truth give me hope now
Words of truth and blow the rain
—MANU CHAO, "Words Of Truth"

The Crown Prosecution Service, which shepherded the United States government's extradition request through the British courts, took the position that WikiLeaks founder Julian Assange was not comparable to the *New York Times*. They absurdly argued Assange was not charged for publishing, even though more than half of the charges against him apply to the publication of materials.

In making their case, Crown prosecutors referred to the indictment. "WikiLeaks' very purpose and design was to recruit persons to break the law—by circumventing classification restrictions and computer and access restrictions."

"WikiLeaks' purpose was to solicit the provision of classified materials," the indictment claimed. "To an audience of hackers, Assange publicized materials that he would like to be obtained by hacking."

Crown prosecutors continued, "Wikileaks was not merely operating drop boxes [for leaks] but actively in the business of encouraging individuals to hack into computers.

"The allegations against Assange are that he encouraged and assisted Ms. Manning to break the law. A further point of distinction between Assange and the journalists to whom he compares himself, is that Assange encouraged the mass and indiscriminate theft of a vast number of documents."[1]

The fact is, in November 2013 the *Washington Post* reported that the Justice Department (DOJ) had "'all but concluded' it would not bring charges against Assange for publishing classified documents because government lawyers said they could not do so without also prosecuting U.S. news organizations and journalists."[2]

A grand jury in Alexandria, Virginia, that was investigating WikiLeaks remained empaneled. However, unnamed US officials said they faced the "New York Times problem."

"If the Justice Department indicted Assange, it would also have to prosecute the New York Times and other news organizations and writers who published classified material, including The Washington Post and Britain's Guardian newspaper," the *Post* added.

Journalists solicit information all the time. Up until WikiLeaks, it was controversial to suggest that it was a crime for journalists to seek classified information. That is why global press freedom groups from around the world, such as Reporters Without Borders, were so alarmed after Assange was charged with violating the Espionage Act. They consistently demanded that Presidents Donald Trump and Joe Biden drop the charges because they understood news-gathering was under attack.

De-stigmatizing WikiLeaks

Several journalists, along with a prominent journalism professor, testified during Assange's extradition trial in September 2020 and attempted to help his defense demystify and de-stigmatize WikiLeaks.

"WikiLeaks pioneered a secure submission system for journalistic sources prior to 2010. They developed a platform for secure communication between sources and media organizations that was unique at that time and allowed journalists to receive communications from their sources in a way that attempted to ensure that the sources' safety and security were protected," stated Trevor Timm, the director of the Freedom of the Press Foundation.[3]

Italian journalist Stefania Maurizi, who first partnered with WikiLeaks in July 2009, was inspired by the revolutionary idea behind WikiLeaks—making the source material for news reporting available so the public could "assess its value" and determine whether media coverage was "fair and balanced" by viewing the "raw information."[4]

"This publication strategy of making original documents available to the public empowers entire communities: journalists, scholars, the police, human rights activists, [and] victims of human rights abuses," Maurizi added.

Timm noted, "Prior to WikiLeaks, this concept had generally not been attempted before. However, once WikiLeaks began gaining global attention at around the time of the Afghan and Iraq War Logs, mainstream news organizations took notice and started to set up their own secure systems for the same purpose."

The Wall Street Journal and *Al Jazeera* attempted to create submission systems similar to the WikiLeaks system. They soon learned it was rather difficult to manage the systems securely.

According to Maurizi, WikiLeaks was focused on a "number of protections" that became commonplace in journalism. They were concerned about authenticating documents and protecting the integrity of the materials they published so they were not misrepresented or distorted. They were focused on protecting sources who provided the documents, and WikiLeaks was careful to encrypt communications between staff and journalists working on the materials.

A similar secure submission system called SecureDrop was developed by the Freedom of the Press Foundation in 2013. Timm said the organization made it available in ten languages, and as of 2020, "More than seventy media organizations worldwide, including the *New York Times, Wall Street Journal,* Associated Press, *USA Today,* Bloomberg News, CBC, and the *Toronto Globe and Mail*" had systems to "solicit" or encourage sources to provide their organizations with documents.

The International Consortium of Investigative Journalists, which published the "Panama Papers" investigation, included a page on its website that urged potential sources to "leak to us." Numerous news organizations used their social media to advertise their dropboxes.

In the indictment, prosecutors complained, "Assange designed WikiLeaks to focus on information restricted from public disclosure by law, precisely because of the value of that information. WikiLeaks' website explicitly solicited censored, otherwise restricted, and 'classified' materials. As the website stated, 'WikiLeaks accepts *classified, censored,* or otherwise *restricted* material of *political, diplomatic or ethical significance*'" (italics in the original).

Prosecutors seized upon a "Most Wanted Leaks" list to help make their case that Assange committed crimes.

Timm pointed out that "individual journalists often make requests for specific documents. I, myself, have advocated for leaks in cases where the US secrecy system is hiding abuse, corruption, or illegal acts," he confessed. "In 2014, I published an article specifically calling for the leak of the classified version of the Senate Committee report on CIA Torture and tweeted about it. I consider this type of speech advocating for such leaks to be protected by the First Amendment while the prosecution [appears] to view this as a criminal act of 'actively soliciting' classified information," Timm added. (The DOJ never accused Timm of conspiring to violate the Espionage Act.)

Mark Feldstein, a journalism professor at the University of Maryland, contended that "encouraging sources to focus on valued information of political, diplomatic or ethical significance in order to disclose it to the public" was "not only standard journalist practice" but also the "lifeblood" of investigative and national security journalism.[5]

"Like Assange, all reporters prize information with the highest 'value.' Learning to distinguish between what is newsworthy and what is not is a standard part of the journalism school.

"When I was a journalist, I personally solicited sources for confidential or restricted information—on more occasions than I can count," Feldstein recalled. "So has every investigative reporter in the US. I teach journalism students how to cultivate sources to provide information, including about sensitive or secret topics."[6]

If cultivating sources is a criminal act, then US prosecutors are signaling to the world that they believe investigative journalism is a crime.

A History of News Media Publishing Classified Documents

Although the volume of documents published by WikiLeaks greatly surpassed the quantities in prior instances when news media organizations published classified information, Feldstein compiled a list for the British magistrates court that showed the practice in news media is common.[7]

"In 1844, the *New York Evening Post* published President John Tyler's secret proposal to annex Texas, which was then an independent country," Feldstein noted. "In 1871, the *New York Tribune* published a secret treaty between the US and Britain settling claims arising from the American Civil War."

The Washington Post and *New York Times* published a "secret extradition treaty between the US and Britain" in 1890.

"In 1953, the *New York Times* published the entire text—more than 200,000 words—of secret minutes and other records documenting the meeting in Yalta between Winston Churchill, Franklin Roosevelt and Joseph Stalin to divide Europe into spheres of influence after World War II," Feldstein recalled.

Various US media outlets, including the *Times*, reported in 1961 on a US plan to overthrow Cuban President Fidel Castro and claimed it was "imminent." Media included the "locations of training and staging stations, anticipated troop levels, and other military tactics and strategy."

After President Richard Nixon "secretly authorized" the bombing of Cambodia, the *Times* exposed the fact that Nixon was lying about winding down the Vietnam War.

An important leak that was not part of Feldstein's list occurred in 1971, when *Washington Post* reporter Betty Medsger received files from the Citizens' Commission to Investigate the FBI that were stolen by peace activists from an FBI office in Media, Pennsylvania. They were the "first FBI files to ever become public" and exposed COINTELPRO, a program that involved "spying on students, academics, antiwar, and civil rights activists." It revealed that FBI Director J. Edgar Hoover used "disinformation to destroy people" he disliked.[8]

During the "Global War on Terrorism," in 2004, the *New Yorker* magazine published photos of torture by the US military at the Abu Ghraib prison in Iraq, as well as "detailed excerpts of a classified 53-page government report" on the abuse of detainees. *The Washington Post* exposed the CIA's use of secret "black site" prisons as part of the agency's rendition and torture program for alleged terrorism suspects the following year.

All of these examples of published classified information are also examples of information that US government officials typically insist "could harm the national security of the United States" if disclosed without proper authorization. Officials fight to keep such information secret because the records contain evidence of criminal acts or involve policymaking the public might oppose if they knew the finer details.

Jameel Jaffer, the executive director of the Knight First Amendment Institute at Columbia University, provided further testimony on the news-gathering activities criminalized by prosecutors.

The indictment singled out Assange for engaging in "measures to prevent the discovery" of Manning as his source. The "manners and means of the conspiracy" to violate the Espionage Act include the use of an encrypted chat service called Jabber. But Jaffer pointed out that communicating with sources on secure channels is one of several activities that "national security journalists engage in routinely."[9]

Prosecutors took issue with the fact that Assange allegedly cleared logs or used a cryptophone, which allows users to make encrypted calls. They alleged that Assange and Manning had a "code phrase to use if something went wrong," as if that were nefarious.

"This kind of protection of confidential sources is not only standard practice but a crucial professional and moral responsibility for reporters, instilled [by] journalism schools and celebrated in books, movies, and other avenues of popular culture. It is as sacred to journalists as the doctor-patient relationship is to physicians or the attorney-client privilege is to lawyers," Feldstein argued.

"Whistleblowers often take enormous personal risks to supply sensitive information to the public, and reporters have gone to jail rather than betray a source to whom confidentiality has been promised. Indeed, whistleblowers are the linchpin of investigative reporting; without them, the press would be crippled in its ability to serve as an effective check on governmental or corporate wrongdoing.

"Journalists protect confidential sources in a variety of ways: granting anonymity; using code words; encrypting electronic communication; removing digital fingerprints or identifying details from documents; misdirecting suspicion away from sensitive sources to other people; coaching them in how to safely answer suspicious questions; and yes, providing technical advice on how to navigate dropboxes and transmit information without detection," Feldstein added.

Secure Procedures to Protect Documents

US government officials responded to the WikiLeaks publications at issue in this case by claiming the media organization had "blood on its hands," and the indictment accused Assange of knowing that the dissemination and publication of Afghanistan and Iraq War documents would "endanger sources, whom he named as having provided information to US and coalition forces."

The prosecution tried to portray Assange as reckless and indifferent to the sensitive nature of the material that WikiLeaks obtained. However, journalists who partnered with WikiLeaks tell a much different story.

Maurizi met with Assange on September 27, 2010, in Berlin. They discussed how she would report on the Afghan War Logs for *L'Espresso* magazine.

"We immediately started discussing encryption and passwords, and it was interesting to learn from Julian Assange. He also explained to me that it is important to always keep any passwords he shared private, to never ever make them public, because if you make them public you provide insights on their possible weaknesses to actors who want to attack you."[10]

Following the meeting, WikiLeaks provided Maurizi with access to the documents. They were "encrypted and password protected."

WikiLeaks again invited Maurizi to partner with the media organization on the US State Embassy cables.

"I, myself, was given access to 4,189 cables, which could be better assessed and understood with the assistance of a knowledgeable Italian partnership," Maurizi recalled. "I sat down with Mr. Assange and went through the cables as systematically as possible.

"I was given an encrypted USB stick, and once I returned to Italy, I was given the password that would then allow opening the file. Everything was done with the utmost responsibility and attention."

Maurizi shared, "This was the first time I had ever worked in any publishing enterprise involving strict procedures of that kind. Even experienced international colleagues found the procedures burdensome, involving protections considerably beyond those to which any of them were accustomed."

New Zealand journalist Nicky Hager partnered with WikiLeaks on US diplomatic cables from New Zealand and Australia. He traveled to the United Kingdom in November 2010 to cover the release of the first set of cables, and WikiLeaks offered him advanced access.[11]

Hager reported that Assange and WikiLeaks allowed the *New York Times*, the *Guardian, Le Monde*, and other media to make their own decisions about which documents to publicize and which parts they would redact.

"While I was there, WikiLeaks asked the same of me: to read the cables from New Zealand and Australia and to identify any that should not be released for reasons such as personal safety of named people. I found the WikiLeaks staff to be engaged in a careful and responsible process," Hager recalled.[12]

The German weekly news magazine *Der Spiegel* was one of three media organizations WikiLeaks initially planned to partner with on the documents. Journalist John Goetz met with Assange, David Leigh, Nick Davies, and Rob Evans of the *Guardian*, and Eric Schmitt from the *New York Times*, on June 30, 2010.[13] The plan was to develop how the partners would coordinate with each other.

"The task, to understand the amount of data involved, presented an exceptional challenge, and the exercise in which all of the media partners together with WikiLeaks were involved, was to intelligently, imaginatively, and effectively find constructive ways of managing the data leading to its publication in a responsible way.

"There were no written agreements to the best of my recollection at that stage. But the basis of the access to the documents and of the cooperation was that we (WikiLeaks, the Guardian, the NY Times, and Der Spiegel) would all publish at the same time but that we would all do independent stories and our stories would refer to and link to the documents posted on the WikiLeaks web site," according to Goetz.[14]

Goetz said that prior to publishing the Afghan War Logs, he and his colleague Marcel Rosenbach had a detailed discussion with Assange in London about "how the documents might be vetted to prevent risk of harm to anyone." Assange agreed it was important to protect "confidential sources, including certain US and ISAF [International Security Assistance Force] sources.

"We discussed how harm could be minimized, and he explained the approach of WikiLeaks—namely that cases were identified where there might be a reasonable chance of harm occurring to the innocent. Those records, having been identified, were edited accordingly. This approach was understood and agreed to by all of the media partners."[15]

When it came to the release of the Iraq War Logs, Goetz testified that the "redaction process replaced basically all names with blanks or Xs.

"I remember reading stories involving WikiLeaks being criticized publicly for having adopted a process which involved in the view of some others 'over redaction.' Even documents that had been released by the Pentagon as a result of FOIA [Freedom of Information Act] applications provided more information than the redacted WikiLeaks documents."[16]

The Iraq Body Count project offered a "technological solution" for vetting nearly 400,000 documents from the Iraq War. It stirred anxiety among media partners who wanted them to hurry up, even though they had no faster alternative.

"This involved the development of specific software by which a painstaking exercise could be progressed automatically, starting with redaction and working back from that towards unredaction of data. This process took enormous amounts of time," Iraq Body Count co-founder John Sloboda testified.

WikiLeaks was under "multiple pressures to hit the 'publish' button sooner," according to Sloboda, "but stood firm by the principle of adhering to the best solution that could be conceived of to ensure that the released information could not cause danger to any persons."

Assange and WikiLeaks continued to follow a meticulous procedure when handling sets of cables from countries throughout the world.

Never Before Had Prosecutors Charged a Journalist With Violating the Espionage Act

Although the US government previously intimidated, harassed, and threatened to prosecute journalists and media organizations, standard news-gathering activities were historically protected until the Assange case.

At Assange's extradition trial, Carey Shenkman, an attorney and an expert on the Espionage Act, detailed the history of attempts by DOJ prosecutors to put together cases against publishers.

The Chicago Tribune was threatened with prosecution in 1942 after the newspaper "published secrets following the U.S. victory at the Battle of Midway." Ultimately, William Mitchell, the prosecutor handling the case, became "skeptical that the Espionage Act applied to publication by a newspaper."[17]

A small foreign affairs journal based in New York City called *Amerasia* was targeted by President Harry Truman in 1945 after it published an analysis that was critical of postwar policies in Asia. The journal relied on "government sources who were deeply concerned over official policies, particularly in China."[18]

The DOJ under Truman had three journalists and three government sources arrested for conspiracy to violate the Espionage Act, but no indictments were ever issued under the Espionage Act. Outrage among the press played a role.

Shenkman summarized the situation: "Evidence emerged that the Justice Department was heavily influenced by political pressures from multiple factions within the Truman administration. Acting US secretary of state Joseph Grew came under heavy criticism when he indicated that the arrests were 'one result of a comprehensive security program which is to be continued unrelentingly in order to stop completely the illegal and disloyal conveyance of confidential information to unauthorized persons.'"[19]

In 1971, when whistleblower Daniel Ellsberg, who worked for the RAND Corporation, provided copies of the Pentagon Papers to numerous media organizations, not only did the DOJ pursue an Espionage Act prosecution against Ellsberg but prosecutors also were encouraged by Nixon to "destroy" the *New York Times*. The DOJ sought an injunction to prevent the *Times* from publishing the Pentagon Papers and lost in the Supreme Court. There also was a grand jury investigation in the Boston area into individuals whom the prosecutors believed would publish the Pentagon Papers.[20]

Memos from the DOJ reflect the extremism of the Nixon administration. Frederick Lambert, who was in the Office of Legal Counsel (OLC), advised DOJ lawyers, including "future

Supreme Court Chief Justice William Rehnquist," to take the position that the government was "entitled to a heavy presumption that its interests" override the First Amendment.[21]

"It is simply impossible to foresee with clarity the exact manner in which certain sensitive information may damage both defense efforts and foreign relations," Lambert asserted. "The determination of what is prejudicial to the defense of the country simply cannot be left to reporters untrained in assessing the short or long-range impact of disclosing sensitive information."

Thomas Kauper of the OLC advised White House Counsel John Dean that the Espionage Act would allow newspapers, and even "individual reporters," to be prosecuted. Kauper further suggested the *New York Times* could be criminally charged for conspiring and encouraging the theft of the Pentagon Papers. But the US Supreme Court rejected the Nixon administration's view and refused to issue an injunction against the *Times* or the *Washington Post.*[22]

Beacon Press became the target of an investigation in 1971 after it published an edition of the Pentagon Papers, which Senator Mike Gravel read into the congressional record. Jack Anderson, a syndicated columnist who was on Nixon's "enemies" list, was threatened with prosecution after he published the "Anderson Papers," which were classified documents that showed Nixon was "secretly arming Pakistan in a December 1971 war with India despite the White House's claim that the US government would remain neutral."[23]

Nixon and his aides were obsessed with Anderson. Journalism professor Mark Feldstein uncovered evidence that former CIA and FBI agents plotted to assassinate the columnist by "spiking one of his drinks or his aspirin bottle with a special poison that would go undetected in an autopsy, or by putting LSD on his steering wheel so that he would absorb it through his skin while driving and die in a hallucination-crazed auto crash."[24]

President Gerald Ford and his administration were upset when journalist Seymour Hersh and the *New York Times* published an article in 1975 under the headline "Submarines of U.S. Stage Spy Missions Inside Soviet Waters." They considered prosecuting Hersh, but Dick Cheney, an aide to Ford, raised the following concerns: "How do we avoid the 'Pentagon Papers syndrome'? What will the public reaction be? What will the [Capitol] Hill reaction be? Will we get hit with violating the 1st Amendment to the Constitution?"[25]

In 1981, while Ronald Reagan was president, James Bamford published his book on the National Security Agency (NSA), *The Puzzle Palace*. An NSA public relations officer was bothered by the fact that Bamford was not interested in "reassuring" citizens about the "activities of the NSA." He intended to give readers the impression that the NSA and its technical capabilities were "able to monitor at will the communications of individuals—including US citizens—on a worldwide basis." The NSA was upset that the book resulted in "undesirable and unwarranted adverse publicity."[26]

While Bamford obtained "thousands of NSA documents and a top-secret criminal file investigating" the NSA for his book, Shenkman noted US government officials demanded that Bamford return the files and threatened him with prosecution under the Espionage Act.

In fact, according to the *New York Times*, "A 1982 report by a Reagan administration committee recommended that the espionage laws be used to prevent unauthorized disclosure of classified information. It said the laws could be used 'to prosecute a journalist who knowingly receives and publishes classified documents or information.'"[27]

A few years later, in 1986, CIA director William Casey invoked the Espionage Act to scare reporters at the *Washington Post* after the newspaper published details related to "secret US monitoring of Libyan communications." The information was deemed newsworthy by the *Post* because there was evidence the US was planning to invade Libya.

Pentagon Papers Whistleblower Takes the Stand

Ellsberg testified in the extradition proceedings for Assange. Crown prosecutor James Lewis QC tried to distinguish the Pentagon Papers whistleblower from Assange by casting him as a good whistleblower. "When you published the Pentagon Papers, you were very careful in what you provided to the media," Lewis said.[28]

The lead prosecutor highlighted the fact that Ellsberg withheld four volumes of the Pentagon Papers because he did not want to disrupt diplomacy that could end the Vietnam War. But Ellsberg informed Lewis that the thousands of pages he disclosed to the news media contained thousands of names of Americans, Vietnamese, and North Vietnamese. He even named a clandestine CIA officer, who was already well known in South Vietnam.

Nowhere in the Pentagon Papers was an "adequate justification for the killing that we were doing," Ellsberg stated. "I was afraid if I redacted or withheld anything at all it would be inferred I left out" the good reasons why the US was pursuing the Vietnam War.[29]

In the decades since the Pentagon Papers were disclosed, Ellsberg described how he faced a "great deal" of defamation and then "neglect" for someone now regarded as a "clear patriot." He was used as a "foil" against new revelations from WikiLeaks, "which were supposedly very different." Such a distinction is "misleading in terms of motive and effect."

Ellsberg noted Assange withheld 15,000 files from the release of the Afghanistan War Logs. He also requested assistance from the State Department and the Defense Department on redacting names, but US officials refused to help WikiLeaks redact a single document, even though it is a standard journalistic practice to consult officials to minimize harm.

"I have no doubt that Julian would have removed those names," Ellsberg declared, if any officials had helped WikiLeaks.[30]

Rather than take steps to protect individuals, Ellsberg contended US government agencies chose to "preserve the possibility of charging Mr Assange with precisely the charges" that he faces now.

CHAPTER 12

Prestige Media Aid and Abet the Prosecution

CIA feed the propaganda to the television
In the next edition, the pundits preach it in repetition
—R. A. THE RUGGED MAN, "Who Do We Trust?"

Editors for prestige media organizations, including the *New York Times*, *Washington Post*, and even the *Wall Street Journal*, condemned the Espionage Act charges against WikiLeaks founder Julian Assange. They joined a coalition of civil liberties and press freedom organizations in recognizing that the prosecution undermined the First Amendment and criminalized common practices in journalism. Yet for over a decade, these same media organizations had aided and abetted the US government's political case against Assange.

The extradition decision from District Judge Vanessa Baraitser referenced news reports on Assange and WikiLeaks from the *Times*, CNN, and the *Guardian*. Statements from establishment news outlets, which "drew a distinction between their handling of the material and WikiLeaks' treatment of it," were seen by the Crown Prosecution Service in the United Kingdom as evidence that Assange went beyond journalistic acts deserving of protection.

In their rush to avoid opening their organizations up to attacks from the US government, editors and journalists at various media outlets made it easier for powerful factions angry at WikiLeaks to make an example out of a publisher who exposed the United States' wars and global agenda to scrutiny.

The prestige media amplified narratives about Assange that will likely endanger national security journalism for decades.

New York Times Executive Editor Aids Narrative That WikiLeaks Has "Blood on Its Hands"

On July 26, 2010, WikiLeaks published the Afghanistan War Logs. US military officials immediately accused WikiLeaks of having blood on its hands.[1] To avoid being lumped in with WikiLeaks, the editors of the *New York Times* issued a statement differentiating WikiLeaks from the *Times*, the *Guardian*, and *Der Spiegel*.

"The Times and the other news organizations agreed at the outset that we would not disclose—either in our articles or any of our online supplementary material—anything that was likely to put lives at risk or jeopardize military or anti-terrorist operations," the *Times* declared.[2]

"We have, for example, withheld any names of operatives in the field and informants cited in the reports. We have avoided anything that might compromise American or allied intelligence-gathering methods such as communications intercepts. We have not linked to the archives of raw material.

"At the request of the White House, the *Times* also urged WikiLeaks to withhold any harmful material from its website," the newspaper revealed.

A few days later, the *New York Times* went beyond trying to shield itself from any legal action by the US government. It published a blog post by Robert Mackey on July 30 with the headline "Taliban Study WikiLeaks to Hunt Informants."[3] The post was included in FBI special agent Megan Brown's summary of "probable cause" for prosecuting Assange.

"After the release of the Afghanistan War reports, a member of the Taliban contacted the *New York Times* and stated, 'We are studying the report. We knew about the spies and people who collaborate with US forces. We will investigate through our own secret service whether the people mentioned are really spies working for the US. If they are US spies, then we will know how to punish them,'" Brown recalled, referring to Mackey's post.[4] (Note: The Taliban spokesperson had actually contacted the British broadcaster Channel 4, not the *Times*.)

The Taliban spokesperson informed Channel 4 News that they had learned of the "leaked secret documents through media reports."[5] *The New York Times* is far more prominent than WikiLeaks. Taliban militants potentially became aware of the WikiLeaks archive of Afghanistan War documents after reading about it in the *Times*, or militants read other media's coverage of the *Times*' reporting. Either way, if Assange risked the lives of informants, then certainly the *Times* did as well.

Bill Keller, who was the *Times*' executive editor, went a step further in a January 2011 feature for *New York Times Magazine*. "[Assange] was angry that we declined to link our online coverage of the war logs to the WikiLeaks website, a decision we made because we feared—rightly, as it turned out—that its trove would contain the names of low-level informants and make them Taliban targets."[6]

"WikiLeaks's first data dump, the publication of the Afghanistan War Logs, included the names of scores of Afghans that The Times and other news organizations had carefully purged from our own coverage," Keller maintained. "Several news organizations, including ours, reported this dangerous lapse, and months later a Taliban spokesman claimed that Afghan insurgents had been perusing the WikiLeaks site and making a list.

"I anticipate, with dread, the day we learn that someone identified in those documents has been killed," Keller stated melodramatically.

It was not months but days later that a Taliban spokesperson suggested the group would sift through the documents to identify US spies. Media coverage, including reports about US military officials who condemned WikiLeaks for revealing names and putting lives at risk, alerted the Taliban to the possibility that the material contained the names of individuals working with US forces.

Notably, WikiLeaks never called attention to any names in the war logs, but prestige media did so, as they helped the US government stir panic, which distracted from the contents of the historical records.

On August 16, almost three weeks after the war logs were published, Secretary of Defense Robert Gates informed Congress the review had not uncovered any "sensitive intelligence sources and methods compromised" by the disclosure.[7]

Retired brigadier general Robert Carr, who served as chief of the Information Review Task Force that assessed alleged damage from WikiLeaks publications, testified at Chelsea Manning's court-martial. He said, "As a result of the Afghan logs, I only know of one individual that was killed. The individual was an Afghan national. The Afghan national had a relationship with the United States government, and the Taliban came out publicly and said that they killed him as a result of him being associated with the information in these logs."

Major Thomas Hurley, a member of Manning's defense team, objected to this lie. "The individual's name wasn't listed among those names."

The judge, Colonel Denise Lind, asked Carr, "Is [what] you're testifying to tied to the information in any way?"

Carr answered, "The Taliban killed him and tied him to the disclosures. We went back and searched for this individual's name in all of the disclosures. The name was not there."

Lind sustained the objection and sternly instructed military prosecutors to move on. She later told both the prosecution and defense, "I'm going to disregard any testimony about the Taliban killing somebody in accordance with the leak."

The US government never produced a shred of evidence to prove that WikiLeaks was responsible for the death of anyone in Afghanistan.

Furthermore, journalist John Goetz, who worked on the Afghanistan War Logs for *Der Spiegel*, called into question the perception that Assange was callously indifferent to protecting those named in the documents.

"Before publication of the Afghan War Diary, together with my colleague Marcel Rosenbach, I discussed in detail with Assange in London how the documents might be vetted to prevent risk of harm to anyone. He was in agreement as to the importance of protecting confidential sources including certain US and ISAF [International Security Assistance Force] sources," Goetz recalled.[8]

"We discussed how harm could be minimized, and he explained the approach of WikiLeaks—namely that cases were identified where there might be a reasonable chance of harm occurring to the innocent. Those records, having been identified, were edited accordingly. This approach was understood and agreed to by all of the media partners," according to Goetz.

The New York Times did not approach the White House because the newspaper was more responsible and careful with the documents. Goetz said the media partners "agreed it made sense to have just one partner approach the White House. If all of the partners contacted the White House independently, there would be chaos."[9]

Times reporter Eric Schmitt was the person who took on the task of ensuring the *Times* bureau in Washington, DC, arranged a White House meeting. He later emailed Goetz on July 30 to say he had passed along a request from the White House to WikiLeaks to redact names from the documents. WikiLeaks indicated that it had withheld 15,000 documents and would "entertain suggestions from ISAF for names to remove if they'd provide tech assistance."

Rather than negotiate with WikiLeaks, as officials do with all media organizations that obtain government materials, the Pentagon refused to help WikiLeaks protect military informants. The Pentagon joined the *Times* in treating WikiLeaks as if it were not engaged in journalism.

"The only acceptable course is for WikiLeaks to take steps to immediately return all versions of all of those documents to the US government and permanently delete them from its website, computers and records," Pentagon spokesperson Geoff Morrell declared.[10]

In the 2020 indictment against Assange, prosecutors added the following: "On May 24, 2011, a television network [PBS] aired a documentary about WikiLeaks that included an allegation that Assange intentionally risked the lives of the sources named in WikiLeaks publications."

It was a reference to the PBS *Frontline* documentary *WikiSecrets*, which included a story from *Guardian* investigations editor David Leigh, who was part of the team that worked on the documents from WikiLeaks.

"Julian was very reluctant to delete those names, to redact them," said Leigh. "And we said: 'Julian, we've got to do something about these redactions. We really have got to.' And he said: 'These people were collaborators, informants. They deserve to die.' And a silence fell around the table."

Leigh was referring to a private dinner in July 2010 that

occurred a few weeks before the Afghanistan War Logs were published. Goetz, Rosenbach, and Holger Stark, all reporters with *Der Spiegel*, were present. Both Goetz and Stark said Assange never made the remark.

A book by Rosenbach and Stark with a title that translates to *Enemy of the State: WikiLeaks* highlighted the dinner. While it distinguished the media partners from Assange, much like the *Times* did, the book acknowledged that Assange understood lives would be put in danger and "would discredit his organization." He "envisioned a technical solution" and eventually 15,000 documents were withheld.

Nonetheless, Leigh's story was repeated by *Guardian* special correspondent Nick Davies, who also worked on the war logs, and it appeared in director Alex Gibney's documentary *We Steal Secrets*.

"I raised this with Julian, and he said if an Afghan civilian helps coalition forces, he deserves to die. He went on to explain that they have the status of a collaborator or informant." But Davies did not attend the dinner, and it is unclear if this conversation with Assange ever happened.

For what it is worth, neither US prosecutors nor Crown prosecutors quoted this alleged statement from Assange, even though it would have bolstered their case.

Guardian Editor Publishes Password to Cable Archive That Assange Gave Him

The indictment, with seventeen Espionage Act charges against Assange, accused the WikiLeaks founder of publishing more than 250,000 US diplomatic cables, which he knew would endanger sources working with the State Department.

In a letter dated November 27, 2010, from the State Department's legal advisor to Assange and his lawyer, Assange was

informed that, among other things, publication of the State
Department cables would "place at risk the lives of countless
innocent individuals—from journalists to human rights activists
and bloggers to soldiers to individuals providing information to
further peace and security.

"Prior to his dissemination and publication of the unredacted
State Department cables, Assange claimed that he intended 'to
gradually roll [the cables] out in a safe way' by partnering with
mainstream media outlets and 'read[ing] through every single
cable and redact[ing] identities accordingly.'"

Despite collaborating with media organizations as early as
November 2010, the indictment alleged that Assange published
all the cables in August and September 2011 "without redacting
the names of the human sources."

To bolster allegations of recklessness, the Crown Prosecution Service emphasized the condemnation that came from the
Guardian on September 2, 2011, the day WikiLeaks released the
archive without redactions. *The Guardian* stated:

> WikiLeaks has published its full archive of 251,000 secret
> US diplomatic cables without redactions, potentially
> exposing thousands of individuals named in the docu-
> ments to detention, harm or putting their lives in danger.
> The move has been strongly condemned by the five
> previous media partners—the Guardian, the New York
> Times, El Pais, Der Spiegel and Le Monde—who have
> worked with WikiLeaks publishing carefully selected and
> redacted documents.
>
> "We deplore the decision of WikiLeaks to publish the
> unredacted State Department cables which may put sources
> at risk," the organizations said in a joint statement. Our pre-
> vious dealings with WikiLeaks were with a clear basis that

we would only publish cables which had been subjected to a thorough joint edited and clearance process.

We will continue to defend our previous collaborative publishing endeavor. We cannot defend the needless publication of the complete data. Indeed, we are united in condemning it."

Judge Baraitser used the statement condemning WikiLeaks' publication of the cables to illustrate her argument that Assange had not acted as a "responsible journalist."[12]

"Unlike the traditional press, those who choose to use the internet to disclose sensitive information in this way are not bound by a professional code or ethical journalistic duty or practice," Baraitser asserted. "Those who post information on the internet have no obligation to act responsibly or to exercise judgment in their decisions.

"In the modern era, where 'dumps' of vast amounts of data onto the internet can be carried out by almost anyone, it is difficult to see how a concept of 'responsible journalism' can sensibly be applied," Baraitser concluded.

Adding fuel to the US government's narrative for criminalizing WikiLeaks, the *Guardian* released a statement: "When passing the documents to the Guardian, Assange created a temporary web server and placed an encrypted file containing the documents on it. The Guardian was led to believe this was a temporary file and the server would be taken offline after a period of hours."[13]

"However," the *Guardian* continued, "former WikiLeaks staff member Daniel Domscheit-Berg, who parted acrimoniously with WikiLeaks, said instead of following standard security precautions and creating a temporary folder, Assange instead re-used WikiLeaks's 'master password.' This password was then unwittingly placed in the Guardian's book on the embassy cables, which was published in February 2011."

There was nothing "temporary" about the procedure WikiLeaks expected Leigh and the Guardian to follow. Nor is there evidence that WikiLeaks failed to follow "standard security precautions."

Leigh co-authored a *Guardian* book, *WikiLeaks: Inside Julian Assange's War on Secrecy*, which was published on February 1, 2011. One of the chapters covered the work the newspaper did on the cache of more than 250,000 US diplomatic cables. The chapter was subtitled:

"ACollectionOfDiplomaticHistorySince_1966_Tothe_PresentDay#"
Assange's 58-Character Password

The book described the tradecraft WikiLeaks employed while handling the documents. "The Guardian journalist had to set up the PGP encryption system on his laptop at home across the other side of London. Then he could feed in a password."

Assange reportedly wrote the password for the encrypted file on "a scrap of paper." "That's the password," Leigh claims Assange said. "But you have to add one extra word when you type it in. You have to put in the word 'Diplomatic' before the word 'History.' Can you remember that?"

Technically, the "password" was an encryption key. According to WikiLeaks, the extra word was a precaution so if the paper was "seized" it "would not work without Leigh's cooperation." Leigh was illiterate when it came to tools that could keep documents secure and failed to recognize the difference.

In November and December 2010, as acknowledged in Judge Baraitser's extradition decision, WikiLeaks was the target of "online attacks" and encouraged its supporters to "mirror" or copy the website to numerous locations. Christian Grothoff, a computer scientist, informed the court that this meant there were "additional websites" and BitTorrent files that ensured the data would be "broadly available." Some of the mirrors included a copy of the "encrypted archive of the cables given to Leigh."[14]

The encrypted file was available on the internet, but it was "entirely useless without the proper passphrase," according to Grothoff, which was standard.

On August 25, 2011, the German newspaper *Der Freitag* located the encrypted file and opened it with the key that Leigh included in his book. By then, WikiLeaks could no longer release batches of cables in partnership with media organizations throughout the world. WikiLeaks lost control of the archive.

According to Assange's legal team, that same day, Assange contacted the US ambassador to the United Kingdom to warn him of the breach. He also called the State Department and asked to speak with Secretary of State Hillary Clinton to inform her that the unredacted archive was accessible on the internet and vulnerable persons named in the cables were in danger.[15]

While talking to a State Department lawyer, Assange said, "What we want the State Department to do is to step up its warning procedures which it was engaged in earlier in the year" and to notify "any individuals who haven't been warned."

Assange said he also contacted Amnesty International and Human Rights Watch.

But on August 31, Cryptome, a website known for its digital library of government documents, called attention to the passphrase and the encrypted file. A site with a searchable archive of the unredacted cables appeared. WikiLeaks was forced to address the "negligent disclosure" of the encryption key.

"Knowledge of the Guardian disclosure has spread privately over several months but reached critical mass last week," WikiLeaks stated. "The unpublished WikiLeaks' material includes over 100,000 classified unredacted cables that were being analyzed, in parts, by over 50 media and human rights organizations from around the world."[16]

"We entrusted all 251,000 cables to the Guardian so they could read them and do their journalism on them," Assange told the *New Scientist*. "Our security arrangement was perfect, assuming the password was not disclosed."[17]

The Guardian gave government agents and hackers insight into the internal security procedures of WikiLeaks, which would potentially enable malicious actors seeking to disrupt the media organization's future publications.

Leigh also violated their partnership with WikiLeaks by giving the *New York Times* a copy of the "Cablegate" archive, even though the *Times* was not a media partner.[18]

As Assange described, the full archive with no redactions was published so that people who needed to know they were mentioned could potentially learn that their identities were compromised before intelligence agencies did. WikiLeaks also wanted an "authorized version" of the cables online to maintain the organization's credibility. For example, some reports in Pakistan and Tajikistan were based on forged documents. Having all the cables published at WikiLeaks, according to Assange, meant that journalists and the public were able to "check whether a claimed story based on a cable" was true.

Dozens of media partners worked with WikiLeaks on the cables. Only David Leigh and the *Guardian* thought it was a wise choice to include the passphrase in a tell-all book about the squabbles between Assange and the *Guardian*.

Stefania Maurizi partnered on the cables for *L'Espresso*. She was with Assange at Ellingham Hall in Norfolk as he scrambled to deal with the loss of the archive. Maurizi never published the encryption key and the additional word that could be used to open the file because she understood that "keeping passwords private is a very basic security procedure" for journalists to follow, especially when handling sensitive materials.

CNN Launders Information From Security Company That Spied on Assange

Assange's legal team presented the extradition court with stunning allegations of spying by Undercover Global. The surveillance was likely supported by the Central Intelligence Agency (CIA); however, Judge Baraitser dealt with the claims of US surveillance by promoting a "possible alternative explanation"—that Assange "remained a risk" to US "national security."

"In February 2016, WikiLeaks published a series of documents which are said to have shown National Security Agency bugging meetings and intercepting communications with the leaders of governments from around the world," Baraitser recalled.

In March 2017, WikiLeaks published the Vault 7 materials, which contained "a trove of CIA hacking tools" described as "the largest ever publication of confidential documents" on the CIA. (The published documents contained descriptions of the CIA's sophisticated software and techniques, not the "hacking tools" themselves.)

Though it is not entirely clear what Baraitser was referencing, she said reports indicated WikiLeaks was still publishing documents that included "classified Pentagon and State Department materials."

"A CNN report from July 15, 2019, entitled 'Security reports reveal how Assange turned an embassy into a command post for election meddling,' stated, '[d]espite being confined to the embassy while seeking safe passage to Ecuador, Assange met with Russians and world-class hackers at critical moments, frequently for hours at a time. He also acquired powerful new computing and network hardware to facilitate data transfers just weeks before WikiLeaks received hacked materials from Russian operatives.'"

With the help of the CNN report, Baraitser concluded Assange's legal team had not proven that Assange was the "target of a politically motivated prosecution."

"I have no doubt that the intelligence community regard him as a threat to the national defense. They have openly stated this view. However, there is no indication that this has translated into hostility from the Trump administration or that officials from the administration put improper pressure on federal prosecutors to bring these charges," the judge stated.

Baraitser asserted, "I have no reason to find that prosecutors did not make their decisions in good faith."

Yet Baraitser's reliance on the CNN report was troubling because it was a distorted and perplexing assessment of surveillance against Assange, which effectively presented files from UC Global in the light most favorable to the CIA and the DOJ.

The same files were covered by the Spanish newspaper *El País* before CNN, and *El País* handled them much more responsibly.

On July 9, *El País* published a report based on "documents, video, and audio material" that was "used in an extortion attempt against Assange by several individuals." In May, Spanish police arrested journalist José Martín Santos, who had a record of fraud, and a computer programmer for their alleged involvement in an "attempt to make €3 million from the sale of private material."[19]

Reporters for *El País* found the spying on Assange's legal defense meetings to be most significant. They were stunned that a microphone had been planted in the women's bathroom to record attorney-client privileged meetings, which Assange had with his lawyers. Plus, they took note of UC Global's "feverish, obsessive vigilance" toward "the guest," which became more intense after Lenín Moreno was elected president of Ecuador in May 2017.

El País did not make any attempt to connect the files to allegations of meddling in the 2016 presidential election.

In sharp contrast, CNN was hyper-focused on 24/7 news headlines about Trump and Russia. Their reporters pored through the logs, searching for confirmation that Assange collaborated with Russian intelligence assets on the release of emails from John Podesta, who was Hillary Clinton's campaign chairman.

"New documents obtained exclusively by CNN reveal that WikiLeaks founder Julian Assange received in-person deliveries, potentially of hacked materials related to the 2016 US election, during a series of suspicious meetings at the Ecuadorian Embassy in London," CNN claimed. "The documents build on the possibility, raised by special counsel Robert Mueller in his report on Russian meddling, that couriers brought hacked files to Assange at the embassy."[20]

But CNN had no confirmed or verifiable evidence to support its conspiracy theory. The words "potentially" and "possibility" performed heavy lifting, and the story was not an exclusive. Journalists in Spain had the same documents.

CNN's report was the first from prestige media in the United States on UC Global's spying operation. It came well before Yahoo News reporters took an interest and published their report on the CIA "secret war plans" against Assange. Therefore, CNN's report served the CIA by setting a narrative and using UC Global's files to scrutinize the person who was targeted, rather than the company that allegedly aided the CIA.

El País reported, "Security employees at the embassy had a daily job to do: to monitor Assange's every move, record his conversations, and take note of his moods. The company's drive to uncover their target's most intimate secrets led the team to carry out a handwriting examination behind his back, which resulted in a six-page report."[21]

"[UC Global] employees also took a feces sample from a baby's diaper to check whether Assange and one of his most faithful collaborators were the child's parents. This intelligence work had nothing to do with protection duties," *El País* noted.

The fact that UC Global employees took a feces sample was, for CNN, seemingly unimportant and was omitted. Instead, CNN mentioned the Moreno government's wild allegation that Assange "smeared feces on the [embassy] walls out of anger."[22]

"It is not hard to manufacture some kind of supposed evidence of negative behavior when you have somebody under total surveillance for years," WikiLeaks editor-in-chief Kristinn Hrafnsson told *Der Spiegel*. "The security guards and diplomats were instructed to collect selectively negative material. They once found a stain on the light switch of the toilet and alleged it was feces from Julian."[23]

"This report was used by the president of Ecuador as evidence that Julian had been smearing feces all over the walls of the embassy. I mean, how low can you go?" Hrafnsson added.

Not a single photo or video was ever produced to substantiate this slander. The building was under constant surveillance. If Assange had spread poop around the embassy, the world would have seen it.

CNN reported on July 18, 2016, "While the Republican National Convention kicked off in Cleveland, an embassy security guard broke protocol by abandoning his post to receive a package outside the embassy from a man in disguise. The man covered his face with a mask and sunglasses and was wearing a backpack, according to surveillance images obtained by CNN."

The published report contained a grainy frame from a surveillance camera that showed a masked man making a delivery. CNN circumstantially tied the image to WikiLeaks later informing "Russian hackers" that they received files and were prepared to release them, even though CNN had no evidence at all to support this conclusion.

"It's not clear if these incidents are related, and the contents of the package delivered to the embassy are unknown," CNN admitted.

From 2019 to 2022, the cable news network continued to filter its coverage of the Assange extradition case through the lens of the Trump-Russia investigation, despite the fact that charges against Assange had nothing to do with WikiLeaks publications during the 2016 election. They also published columns that professed Assange was not a journalist and claimed the prosecution could ultimately be good for journalism.

"If handled correctly by the courts," CNN contributor Frida Ghitis wrote, "it should result in the development of a functioning definition of what a journalist is, depriving propaganda outlets and government agents of using the label to take cover—and providing the press with the protection it needs to inquire, investigate, and report."[24]

Media gatekeepers such as Ghitis were open to the US government defining who was and was not a journalist through criminal prosecutions because disqualifying Assange could go a long way toward protecting freedom of the press for prestige journalists like those at CNN, who believed they were the ones who actually deserved protection.

Such honesty clarified why so many in the US media establishment were not terribly alarmed every day that the case against Assange dragged on.

CHAPTER 13

Russiagate and WikiLeaks

Early days up with the sun, all the days turn into one
All the sirens beckoning the groove
—BRIAN ENO, "There Were Bells" (2022)

From 2016 to 2019, it was universally accepted among prestige media, security agencies, and the political establishment in the United States that Julian Assange and WikiLeaks had assisted Russian intelligence in their efforts to interfere in the 2016 presidential election. The space for dissenting against these allegations was virtually nonexistent. Yet when the Justice Department (DOJ) unveiled charges against Assange in April and May of 2019, they contained no reference to anything related to Russia and the 2016 election.

That is obviously because all the charges against Assange related to publications in 2010 and 2011.

Prosecutors mentioned that Assange hosted a show, *The World Tomorrow*, that was independently produced by Dartmouth Films and licensed to Russia Today, or RT. The show was billed as a "series of in-depth conversations with key political players, thinkers, and revolutionaries from around the world." Longer versions of the conversations were distributed outside of RT. The rights granted to RT were limited to "first release of 26-minute edits of each episode in English, Spanish, and Arabic," but, according to producers, Assange made "all editorial decisions."[1]

The Crown Prosecution Service never mentioned the "Russiagate" allegations while presenting the DOJ's case to a British district court. Nor did it appear in their closing argument, although Assange's show was mentioned again.

District Judge Vanessa Baraitser referred to the allegations in the extradition decision, but only in her reference to CNN's report from July 15, 2019: "Security reports reveal how Assange turned an embassy into a command post for election meddling." She treated the article based upon materials from Spanish private security company Undercover Global SL as proof that Assange and WikiLeaks were "viewed by the intelligence community as an ongoing threat to national security."

However, breaking news coverage of Assange's arrest and expulsion from the Ecuador embassy consistently asked whether the WikiLeaks founder would face additional charges for publishing emails from the Democratic National Committee (DNC) and Hillary Clinton's presidential campaign.

"An indictment unsealed on Thursday charging Mr. Assange with conspiring to hack into a Pentagon computer in 2010 makes no mention of the central role that WikiLeaks played in the Russian campaign to undermine Mrs. Clinton's presidential chances and help elect President Trump," *New York Times* reporters Mark Mazzetti and Julian E. Barnes wrote. "It remains unclear whether the arrest of Mr. Assange will be a key to unlocking any of the lingering mysteries surrounding the Russians, the Trump campaign and the plot to hack an election."[2]

Leaving aside the fact that Assange was not accused of conspiring to "hack into a Pentagon computer" (see Chapter 1), the assertion was an example of the intrigue that prestige media organizations such as the *Times* tried to inject into a case in order to make it part of the dominant news narrative around Trump and Russia.

The *Times* conceded, "The Justice Department spent years examining whether Mr. Assange was working directly with the Russian government, but legal experts point out that what is known about his activities in 2016—including publishing stolen emails—is not criminal, and therefore it would be difficult to bring charges against him related to the Russian interference campaign."[3]

Time magazine apparently found no way to cover the charges without fixating on the absence of any related to alleged conduct during the 2016 election. The outlet published an explainer, "Why the Charge Against Julian Assange Makes No Mention of Espionage or 2016 Russian Hacking."[4]

The web magazine Business Insider led with the following: "Democrats accuse Assange of being a tool for Russian intelligence, but it remains unclear if he'll face charges over publishing hacked DNC emails." The article included a screen shot of Assange during a 2016 interview for RT.[5]

"Major Democratic figures took to news networks and social media to denounce Wikileaks, which published thousands of stolen emails weeks before the 2016 presidential election in what US intelligence agencies have concluded was a bid to damage the candidacy of Democrat Hillary Clinton," Business Insider added.

"Whatever Julian Assange's intentions were for WikiLeaks, what he's become is a direct participant in Russian efforts to weaken the West and undermine American security," stated Senator Mark Warner, the top Democrat on the Senate Select Committee on Intelligence. "I hope [the] British courts will quickly transfer him to US custody so he can finally get the justice he deserves."[6]

"Now that Julian Assange has been arrested, I hope he will soon be held to account for his meddling in our elections on behalf of Putin and the Russian government," proclaimed top-ranking Democratic senator Chuck Schumer.[7]

Senator Joe Manchin cheered, "We're going to extradite him. It will be really good to get him back on United States soil. So now he's our property, and we can get the facts and truth from him."[8]

This was a bizarre and vengeful remark, especially because Assange is an Australian citizen with no roots in the United States.

Samantha Vinograd, who was part of President Obama's National Security Council and a CNN analyst, tacitly endorsed the prosecution. "I was at the White House when the first release of these documents unfolded as well as the successive stages," she said.[9]

"I can tell you our personnel overseas, including not just military personnel, our diplomats, our sources and methods used in intelligence operations, were put at immediate risk of exposure, retaliation, and more. When we talk about this, let's not just [call] it embarrassing. Let's also call it dangerous," Vinograd urged.

Vinograd argued "Julian Assange and WikiLeaks of 2010 [looked] very different than Julian Assange and WikiLeaks in 2016 and 2019."[10]

"We don't know if there are superseding indictments related to other charges related to election interference in 2016," Vinograd added, as she restated the DOJ's conclusion that WikiLeaks worked with Russian intelligence to release documents from the DNC and Clinton's campaign.

As former US government officials tried to prime Americans for more charges, CNN crime and justice correspondent Shimon Prokupecz said, "We don't see any evidence there's going to be charges related to the Russians."[11]

But CNN senior justice correspondent Evan Perez contradicted his colleague. "Certainly, if [Assange] is extradited, he is going to face additional charges, perhaps including related to the 2016 Russian interference, the hacking charges related to the Russians in 2016."[12]

CNN anchor Jim Sciutto made the side comment, "Julian Assange focuses all his attention on the US government. What has he exposed about Russian government misbehavior? That [goes] to his motivation."[13]

"Could these developments with Assange lead to new information related to the Russia investigation, or maybe even charges for Assange's role in the 2016 election interference?" CNN anchor Brianna Keilar asked. "Because these charges, actually, this has to do with military secrets. This does not have to do with the WikiLeaks involvement in Russian election meddling in 2016."[14]

"Well, I think the one goes together with the other," Democratic representative Gerald Connolly responded. "We know that Assange and WikiLeaks did coordinate with the Russians on the Podesta email leaks. The fact that they had that kind of Russian level of contact makes you wonder, well, what was the comparable, if any, contact with Russians on the military intelligence leaks?"[15]

Connolly continued to weave the indictment against Assange into a totally unfounded conspiracy theory. "One suspects the Russians were certainly interested in the latter. And one suspects they reached out to Assange and WikiLeaks, even if those outreaches were not reciprocated."

"So, as far as we know, Assange wasn't interviewed as part of the Russia investigation. If he's transferred to US custody, do you think that authorities are going to interview him?" Keilar also asked.

"I hope so. I mean, he's been hiding in an Ecuadorian embassy for seven years in London," Connolly replied. "A little hard to interview him as part of the Mueller investigation. Now that he's in British custody and hopefully will be extradited to the United States, I think there is an opportunity for prosecutors to interview him and see what he knows and what he's willing to share."[16]

Early in CNN's coverage, the network's morning news program, *New Day*, spoke with Kristinn Hrafnsson, whom Assange appointed to become WikiLeaks editor-in-chief in October 2018 after Ecuador cut him off from the outside world.

Co-host Alisyn Camerota asked, "How do you know this isn't connected to the 2016 Russian hack of the DNC computers?"[17]

"According to the information from Julian's lawyers who have talked to him, this is pertaining to the publications of WikiLeaks in 2010, which exposed war crimes in Iraq and Afghanistan. That is not a crime. That is journalism," Hrafnsson answered.

"Let me ask you this, the United States says that Russia gave WikiLeaks, gave Julian Assange stolen documents. Is that true?" co-host John Berman asked.[18]

"No," Hrafnsson said.

Hrafnsson tried to focus the interview on the actual indictment against Assange, but Berman persisted. "I'm talk[ing] about in the 2016 election, the United States, Robert Mueller's investigators, the federal government says that WikiLeaks was given stolen documents by Russian intelligence, essentially. If you didn't get those documents from them, where did you get them from?"[19]

To which Hrafnsson replied, "Julian Assange has answered that question. He said the source of the documents that were published in 2016 were not from a state actor and was not from a Russian."

"Did he communicate with Roger Stone or anyone in the Trump campaign about those?" Camerota inquired.[20]

"I mean, it has been published and it has been widely noted that Roger Stone exaggerated the connection he had with Julian Assange," Hrafnsson said.

This was prestige media coverage in a nutshell. Nearly all outlets were reluctant to consider the threat the prosecution posed to press freedom, since there were no Espionage Act charges. They were also disappointed that the indictment did not include charges that would feed their obsession with getting to the bottom of alleged Trump-Russia collusion.

"If You See a Whopper of a Wikileaks"

In July 2016, WikiLeaks published emails from individuals who worked for the Democratic National Committee. In October, the organization followed that publication with the release of emails from Clinton campaign chairman John Podesta's account.

The Podesta emails exposed excerpts of Clinton's paid speeches to Goldman Sachs, efforts to rig parts of the Democratic primary in favor of Hillary Clinton, proposals for turning voters against Democratic presidential candidate Bernie Sanders, and Clinton's duplicity when it came to key progressive issues, including fair trade, clean energy, and raising the minimum wage.

Staff of Clinton's presidential campaign immediately contended the publication was part of a Russian plot, and several campaign individuals said WikiLeaks had published "forged" emails without providing any evidence to back up their claim. Jennifer Palmieri, the campaign's director of communications, warned, "Friends, please remember if you see a whopper of a Wikileaks in [the] next two days—it's probably a fake."[21]

Former CNN contributor Donna Brazile, who forwarded debate questions to Clinton before two CNN events, reacted by saying, "A lot of those emails, I would not give them the time of the day. I've seen so many doctored emails."[22]

"You know, I know, that Russia and other forces would love us to have a debate," Clinton campaign advisor Neera Tanden responded. "This is exactly what they want. They want us to have a debate about the internal structure of Hillary's campaign. What's true, what's not true."

Clinton campaign manager Robby Mook similarly suggested that "the Russians, in an effort to help Donald Trump," wanted people to ask questions. "They're selectively leaking materials at a rate that it is impossible for us to validate them for exactly the purpose of calling things into question, what really happened, who said what, is this true, is this not true. We're not going to verify any of these right now because, again, they're coming thousands a day. It's simply too much for us to do that."

"The Clinton campaign, however, has yet to produce any evidence that any specific emails in the latest leak were fraudulent," PolitiFact noted. However, PolitiFact recognized this was a campaign tactic.[23]

By categorizing the emails as generally inaccurate, it was easier for campaign staff to deny certain realities, such as Clinton's remarks in paid speeches to major banks or how the campaign conspired with the DNC to limit the number of debates and to box out certain candidates, including Sanders.[24]

In January 2017, the CIA, FBI, National Security Agency (NSA), and Office of the Director of National Intelligence (ODNI), which oversees all US intelligence agencies, claimed the Podesta emails were connected to Russian hacking. However, Assange questioned their assertions.

"The US intelligence community is not aware of when WikiLeaks obtained its material or when the sequencing of our material was done or how we obtained our material directly. So there seems to be a great fog in the connection to WikiLeaks," Assange stated.[25]

"The Podesta emails that we released during the election dated up to March [2016]," Assange added. "US intelligence services and consultants for the DNC say Russian intelligence services started hacking DNC in 2015. Now, Trump is clearly not on the horizon in any substantial manner in 2015."

In early 2017, Assange was willing to "provide technical evidence and discussion regarding who did not engage in the DNC releases." He also was willing—before the release of Vault 7 materials from the CIA—to help US agencies address "clear flaws in security systems" that led the US cyber weapons program to be compromised.[26]

Democratic senator Mark Warner learned that DOJ official Bruce Ohr was negotiating some kind of a deal for limited immunity and a limited commitment from Assange. The senator urged FBI director James Comey to intervene.

A potential deal with Assange was stopped, and no testimony was ever collected by investigators, including those working on the Mueller investigation, which might have helped the public better understand what had happened with the DNC and Clinton campaign email publications.

Special Counsel Robert Mueller's investigation considered holding WikiLeaks "liable for ensuring a market for and maximizing the value of the stolen materials." However, investigators were unable to confirm that Assange and Wikileaks had engaged in any criminal activity. They "determined the admissible evidence to be insufficient on both the agreement and knowledge prongs," because many of the communications between purported Russian intelligence (GRU) officers and "WikiLeaks-affiliated actors occurred via encrypted chats."[27]

"Although conspiracy is often inferred from the circumstances," the report noted, "the lack of visibility into the contents of these communications would hinder the office's ability to prove that WikiLeaks was aware of and intended to join the criminal venture" consisting of the purported hacking attempt.

The report added, "While the investigation developed evidence that the GRU's hacking efforts in fact were continuing at least at the time of the July 2016 WikiLeaks dissemination," investigators were unable to "develop sufficient admissible evidence that WikiLeaks knew of—or even was willfully blind to—that fact."[28]

"Absent sufficient evidence of such knowledge, the government could not prove that WikiLeaks (or Assange) joined an ongoing hacking conspiracy to further or facilitate additional computer intrusions," the Mueller investigation concluded.

Democratic Party computers or servers were not backed up so that someone could research alleged hacking and validate specific claims. In fact, Comey said "multiple requests" were made at "different levels" for access to Democratic servers. The FBI did not seize for forensic examination the servers or computers that were allegedly targeted.

The FBI relied on the conclusions of an in-house cyber-response team from CrowdStrike that had worked for the Democrats. But the cybersecurity firm's president, Shaun Henry, admitted that they had no evidence that emails were "actually exfiltrated" by Russia. They only had "circumstantial evidence that that data was exfiltrated off the network."

"Our forensics folks would always prefer to get access to the original device or server that's involved, so it's the best evidence," Comey stated during a Senate Intelligence Committee hearing. Yet the FBI allowed the Democratic Party to rebuff their request for access.

Additionally, the Mueller report maintained they could not "rule out that stolen documents were transferred to WikiLeaks through intermediaries, who visited during the summer of 2016. For example, public reporting identified Andrew Müller-Maguhn as a WikiLeaks associate, who may have assisted with the transfer of these stolen documents to WikiLeaks."

This was wildly misleading. The source for this example was a 2018 profile of Müller-Maguhn by journalist Ellen Nakashima that was published by the *Washington Post*. Müller-Maguhn told Nakashima it "would be insane" to hand-deliver sensitive files, especially when the CIA labeled WikiLeaks a "non-state hostile intelligence service."

"How many of you wouldn't be scared shitless by the head of the CIA declaring you the next target?" Müller-Maguhn quipped.

Müller-Maguhn, who met Assange through the Chaos Computer Club in 2007, sits on the board of the Wau Holland Foundation, which has acted as a fiscal sponsor for WikiLeaks in some capacity since 2010. He characterized the allegation against him as a "lame attempt" by US intelligence agencies to create a pretext in Europe for cutting off the foundation from tax-free donations to WikiLeaks.

Media outlets such as CNN reported that Roger Stone, a political consultant and Trump ally, communicated with WikiLeaks before the Podesta emails were published. However, their coverage misrepresented the exchange that occurred.

In a direct message, Stone wrote on October 13, 2016, "Since I was all over national TV, cable, and print defending WikiLeaks and Assange against the claim that you are Russian agents and debunking the false charges of sexual assault as trumped up BS, you may want to reexamine the strategy of attacking me."[29]

"We appreciate that," the WikiLeaks Twitter account replied. "However, the false claims of association are being used by the Democrats to undermine the impact of our publications. Don't go there if you don't want us to correct you."

The conservative gadfly never met with Assange, and as WikiLeaks put it, Stone kept trolling media to increase his profile. He later admitted in a 2018 MSNBC interview, "It's shtick, please." He reeled off several documents that would prove he never visited Assange in the Ecuador embassy and said he never spoke to Assange "by Skype or phone."[30]

None of the above facts discouraged Democrats from attacking WikiLeaks. Former Clinton campaign rapid response director Zac Petkanas echoed the CIA: "WikiLeaks is not journalism. It's an arm of the Russian intelligence service."

Neera Tanden, one of Clinton's campaign advisors, argued in January 2018, "Every reporter who gleefully trafficked in stolen emails via WikiLeaks abetted a crime. Not illegal activity by itself but unethical and immoral."[31]

"Assange has long professed high ideals and moral superiority," Senator Warner stated. "Unfortunately, whatever his intentions when he started WikiLeaks, what he's really become is a direct participant in Russian efforts to undermine the West and a dedicated accomplice in efforts to undermine American security."[32]

"This Whole Pardon Business"

A widely shared story about Assange and Russia was that Trump offered the WikiLeaks founder a pardon if he "covered up Russian hacking of Democrats."[33] Or, as the *Guardian* reported, "Trump offered Julian Assange a pardon if he would say Russia was not involved in leaking Democratic Party emails."[34]

During a February 2020 extradition hearing, Assange's defense alleged that a "strange interlude" occurred, in which former Republican representative Dana Rohrabacher and right-wing activist Charles Johnson met with Assange at the Ecuadorian embassy. Rohrabacher allegedly discussed a preemptive pardon "in exchange for personal assistance to President Trump."

Headlines made it seem like this was confirmation that Assange was working with Trump all along. They appeared to report that Assange not only aided Russian intelligence in 2016 but also had turned into a full-fledged right-wing propagandist. Except that was not true.

"I spoke to Julian Assange and told him if he would provide evidence about who gave WikiLeaks the emails I would petition the president to give him a pardon," Rohrabacher claimed. "He knew I could get to the president."[35]

According to Rohrabacher, he contacted Trump's chief of staff, John Kelly, after the meeting. Kelly was "courteous," yet did not promise to raise the matter with Trump. In fact, Rohrabacher heard nothing further from Kelly, and he never spoke with Trump about offering Assange a pardon.

"We say that this whole pardon business shows that, just as the prosecution was initiated in December 2017 for political purposes, so too the Trump administration [was] prepared to use the threat of prosecution as a means of extortion to obtain personal political advantage from Mr. Assange," argued Edward Fitzgerald QC, an attorney for Assange.

Jennifer Robinson, another Assange attorney, testified that she was asked to attend the meeting. It was not known ahead of time that Johnson would accompany Rohrabacher.

"[Rohrabacher] said that he regarded the ongoing speculation [around the DNC leaks] as damaging to US-Russian relations, that it was reviving old Cold War politics, and that it would be in the best interests of the US if the matter could be resolved. He and Mr. Johnson also explained that information from Mr. Assange about the source of the DNC leaks would be of interest, value, and assistance to President Trump," Robinson recalled.[36]

Rohrabacher proposed if Assange identified the "source for the 2016 election publications" then he would be rewarded with "some form of pardon, assurance, or agreement, which would both benefit President Trump politically and prevent US indictment and extradition." Both Rohrabacher and Johnson hoped this would end Robert Mueller's investigation.

Assange did not share any information about WikiLeaks sources. To do so would have been against WikiLeaks' policy.

The WikiLeaks founder had an opportunity to secure a deal that might have given him freedom after five long years in the embassy. As it turned out, source protection was more important than finding out whether Rohrabacher could really end his legal limbo.

For the record, Trump actually "entertained the idea" of pardoning Assange before his term ended. However, according to CNN, multiple GOP lawmakers "sent messages through aides that they felt strongly about not granting clemency to Assange." Faced with a Senate impeachment trial after the January 6 riots on Capitol Hill, Trump put himself before freeing Assange (or Edward Snowden).[37]

"Journalists Are Allowed to Request Documents That Have Been Stolen"

The DNC sued Trump's campaign, the Russian Federation, Assange, and WikiLeaks on April 20, 2018, alleging the dissemination of materials "furthered the prospects" of the Trump campaign. They argued that officials "welcomed" the assistance of agents allegedly working for the Russian Federation.

DNC chair Tom Perez accused WikiLeaks of helping to perpetrate a "brazen attack" on democracy. However, Judge John Koeltl of the Southern District of New York saw through the DNC lawsuit and ruled the DNC could not hold WikiLeaks or Assange liable for publishing information that Russian agents were accused of stealing.

Koeltl invoked the Pentagon Papers case, where the Supreme Court held there was a "heavy presumption" against the "constitutional validity" of suppressing the publication of information.[38]

"If WikiLeaks could be held liable for publishing documents concerning the DNC's political, financial, and voter-engagement strategies simply because the DNC labels them 'secret' and trade secrets, then so could any newspaper or other media outlet. But that would impermissibly elevate a purely private privacy interest to override the First Amendment interest in the publication of matters of the highest public concern," Koeltl stated.

"The DNC's published internal communications allowed the American electorate to look behind the curtain of one of the two major political parties in the United States during a presidential election. This type of information is plainly of the type entitled to the strongest protection that the First Amendment offers." That protection extended to "donor lists" and "fundraising strategies."[39]

Koeltl noted the DNC's response. "This case does not threaten freedom of the press because WikiLeaks did not engage in normal journalistic practices by, for example, 'asking foreign intelligence services to steal "new material" from American targets.'"

The DNC alleged that "WikiLeaks sent GRU [Russian military intelligence] operatives using the screen name Guccifer 2.0 a private message, asking the operatives to 'send any new material [stolen from the DNC] here for us to review.'"[40]

Koeltl countered, "This was not a solicitation to steal documents but a request for material that has been stolen. Journalists are allowed to request documents that have been stolen and to publish those documents."

Democrats alleged that WikiLeaks knew the materials were stolen and coordinated with Russian intelligence agents. Therefore, they were "after-the-fact" conspirators in the "theft"—a major allegation which the Mueller investigation never corroborated. But the judge viewed it as "irrelevant" whether WikiLeaks solicited documents from Russian agents or not.[41]

"A person is entitled to publish stolen documents that the publisher requested from a source so long as the publisher did not participate in the theft," Koeltl reiterated. If WikiLeaks were held liable, this would render "any journalist who publishes an article based on stolen information a co-conspirator in the theft."

Koeltl's decision deviated significantly from the position of Trump's Justice Department, which was that Assange was not protected by the First Amendment.

James Goodale, the former general counsel to the *New York Times* who argued the Pentagon Papers case, reacted by stating, "Judge Koetl went out of his way to say that the activities of Assange in releasing that information were fully protected by the First Amendment.

"He decided the First Amendment applies to Julian Assange in this country, and that Julian Assange's activities with respect to the release of information concerning the DNC was protected by the First Amendment."[42]

Prosecutors accused Assange of soliciting information from Chelsea Manning in 2010. According to Koeltl's decision, that was not a crime during the 2016 election. It also was not a crime during the time frame at issue in the prosecution against Assange. What Assange and WikiLeaks did was journalism. (During August 2022, Koeltl was assigned to the lawsuit against the CIA and former CIA director Mike Pompeo for alleged spying on US citizens who visited Assange.)

In the DNC's zeal to hold Assange accountable for the role it believes Assange played in Russiagate, party leaders showed that contempt for press freedom was not limited to the Trump White House. Their overzealousness backfired and gave WikiLeaks a ruling that could help pave the way for its founder's acquittal.

Conclusion

The power to dream, to rule
To wrestle the world from fools
Well it's decreed the people rule
—PATTI SMITH, "People Have the Power" (1988)

Opposition to the US government's case against Julian Assange was widespread around the globe before his extradition.

Dozens of civil liberties, human rights, and press freedom organizations, including Amnesty International, the Committee to Protect Journalists, Human Rights Watch, and Reporters Without Borders, urged President Joe Biden, Attorney General Merrick Garland, and the Justice Department to withdraw the extradition request and drop the charges against Assange.[1]

"The charges against Assange have been condemned by virtually every major American news outlet, even though many of those news outlets have criticized Mr. Assange in the past," the coalition noted.

The International Federation of Journalists, which represents more than 600,000 media workers in 146 countries in journalist trade unions throughout the world, launched a campaign against the prosecution.[2]

"More than 70 members of the German parliament from four political parties" demanded that Biden and the UK government stop the extradition of Assange.[3]

Support for Assange in Latin America was particularly strong.

Evo Morales, former president of Bolivia; Fernando Lugo, former president of Paraguay; Dilma Rousseff, former president of Brazil; Ernesto Samper, former president of Colombia; and Rafael Correa, the former president of Ecuador who granted Assange asylum, each signed on to a letter that urged Biden to protect freedom of expression and abandon the prosecution.[4]

Mexico president Andrés Manuel López Obrador visited the White House on July 12, 2022, and delivered a letter urging Biden to free Assange. López Obrador renewed Mexico's offer to grant Assange asylum. "If they take him to the United States and he is sentenced to the maximum penalty and to die in prison, we must start a campaign to tear down the Statue of Liberty," López Obrador proclaimed.[5]

Lobbying the UK government to block extradition, more than 300 doctors, psychiatrists, and psychologists called attention to the deterioration of Assange's health while in UK custody at Belmarsh prison. They highlighted a "mini-stroke" Assange suffered in October 2021 as evidence of the "chronic stress" caused by "harsh prison conditions" and the fear of confinement in a US prison. They concluded he was at risk of experiencing further episodes that could damage his heart and referred to his extradition as "medically and ethically unacceptable."[6]

The Biden White House shrugged and disregarded all efforts by civil society organizations or influential political leaders to convince the administration to drop the charges. Instead, Biden officials adopted a policy of dodging questions from reporters or responding glibly to any expressed concerns.

For example, on May 12, 2021, in connection with World Press Freedom Day, one reporter said, "The Obama-Biden administration was infamous for taking a heavy hand toward reporters and leaks, including taking the Associated Press's call records and calling a Fox reporter a 'possible conspirator.' But the Obama

Justice Department decided not to prosecute Assange for fear of setting a precedent that could be used to prosecute journalists dealing with classified information. In the name of press freedom, will President Biden be intervening in the Assange case to stop the prosecution? Or will he be allowing the Justice Department and the courts to sort this out?"

White House Press Secretary Jen Psaki flippantly replied, "Well, in the name of independent justice, we will encourage the Justice Department to continue to be an independent Justice Department, which I know is different from what we saw over the last four years so it feels funny to some people."

On June 25, 2021, Secretary of State Antony Blinken participated in a "youth-moderated discussion on democracy and human rights" in Paris. He was asked by a French journalist about the calls throughout France and the rest of Europe to drop the charges against Assange.

"It's not easy for me speak around this issue. There is [an] ongoing legal process, so I will let that legal process continue. I understand the questions, the emotions around this case, but I cannot really speak on this issue," Blinken maintained.[7]

Though it may not have been easy for Blinken to speak about the case, since it undermined the Biden administration's stated commitment to democracy and human rights, it was easy for the US State Department to intervene in the case. Officials sent diplomatic notes to the UK Foreign Office to ensure that the UK High Court of Justice overturned the district judge's decision blocking extradition. Instead of allowing the case to move through the UK courts with the Crown Prosecution Service arguing the case, the State Department meddled in the outcome and saved the US government from a bitter loss.

White House Press Secretary Karine Jean-Pierre was asked on July 8, 2022, if Biden had any response to López Obrador's comment about tearing down the Statue of Liberty if Assange was extradited. Jean-Pierre was petrified. She would not respond to queries about Mexico's asylum offer.

No serious opposition existed in Congress, and few members took any interest in the case. Activism around the case, however, received a boost during the summer and fall when Roger Waters performed his show, "This Is Not a Drill," in numerous major cities in North America. The Pink Floyd bass guitarist used his solo song, "Déjà Vu," to show a clip from the "Collateral Murder" video and bring attention to Assange's case. Waters invited activists, many of them aligned with the Assange Defense Committee, to table at his concerts to raise awareness among his fans.

On October 8, 2022, a human chain that Stella Assange spent months organizing surrounded the UK Parliament. She estimated at least 5,000 people attended the demonstration. The London event inspired solidarity actions in Melbourne, Australia, and several US cities, including Washington, DC, where activists rallied outside the Department of Justice. Organizers saw this global day of action as a model for future demonstrations to free Assange.

Reporters questioned the Biden White House for allowing the Assange case to continue, but because Biden officials were afraid and unwilling to publicly defend the prosecution, it was typically pointless to raise the matter, even though their non-answers illustrated the phoniness of their pronouncements about press freedom.

Biden's Opposition to Assange

The White House's silence made it difficult to know what Biden really thought of the Assange case. Yet, during Biden's 2020 presidential campaign, he was one of several Democratic Party candidates who responded to a *New York Times* questionnaire on executive power, which included a question about the Espionage Act charges against Assange.

"Prosecutors recently expanded a criminal case against Julian Assange to include accusations that he violated the Espionage Act by soliciting, obtaining, and publishing classified documents leaked in 2010 by Chelsea Manning, which could establish a precedent that such common journalistic activities (a separate question from whether Assange counts as a 'journalist') can be treated as a crime in America," the *Times* declared.[8]

"Are these charges constitutional? Would your administration continue the Espionage Act part of the case against Assange?" the *Times* asked.

Without commenting on the specific charges, Biden leaned toward supporting prosecution and answered, "I'm not assuming in any way that Assange is, in fact, a journalist.

"Government officials often have compelling reasons to keep national security information confidential, and professional journalists have long recognized and respected those reasons. Unlike WikiLeaks, responsible journalists historically have declined to publish information when publication would put lives in danger or threaten harm to the national interest."

Biden added, "The First Amendment does not immunize journalists from responsibility for breaking the law. Journalists have no constitutional right to break into a government office, or hack into a government computer, or bribe a government employee, to get information. The perpetrator of a crime should be subject to prosecution."

This answer was nearly identical to the position the Justice Department (DOJ) took when targeting *New York Times* reporter James Risen in the Jeffrey Sterling case. Biden was President Barack Obama's vice president, and prosecutors attempted to force Risen to divulge his confidential sources.[9]

The Fourth Circuit Court of Appeals agreed. "There is no First Amendment testimonial privilege, absolute or qualified, that protects a reporter from being compelled to testify by the prosecution or the defense in criminal proceedings about criminal conduct that the reporter personally witnessed or participated in, absent a showing of bad faith, harassment or other such non-legitimate motive, even though the reporter promised confidentiality to his source."

Although Biden conceded the government should hesitate to "prosecute a journalist who [has] done nothing more than receive and publish confidential information and has not otherwise broken the law," Biden apparently did not view Assange as a journalist. So this statement was irrelevant.

Biden insisted it was inappropriate for him to offer his opinion on an "ongoing criminal prosecution that is now pending in court and about which all the details are not publicly available." But in 2010, when WikiLeaks published the documents at issue in this case and the Justice Department launched a grand jury investigation, Biden did not hesitate to comment. He said Assange probably "conspired to get these classified documents with a member of the US military" and added, "That's fundamentally different than if someone drops [documents] on your lap" and says "you're a press person. Here's classified material."

Biden agreed with Republican Senate majority leader Mitch McConnell that Assange was much more like a "high-tech terrorist" than a journalist.

Moreover, in the 1980s Biden was viewed by CIA director William Casey as an ally in the agency's crackdown on whistleblowers and leaks. Biden introduced the Classified Information Procedures Act (CIPA), which made it harder for individuals facing prosecution to introduce evidence at trial that they were involved in exposing government corruption. It would allow national security cases involving "sensitive intelligence" to hold portions of the trial in secret.[10]

"The press will not like it. Because I'm suggesting they be excluded," Biden said in 1978. "I may end up being the cause of some fairly repressive legislation."[11]

Media Gatekeepers and the Policing of Journalism

The US government's response to WikiLeaks foreshadowed a greater policing of journalism by tech companies, think tanks, and government bureaucrats in the 2020s.

WikiLeaks faced a financial blockade by international banks and payment processors such as Visa, MasterCard, and PayPal, which were pressured by Senator Joe Lieberman. Amazon kicked WikiLeaks off its servers.[12] The Justice Department issued subpoenas to several companies for the private user data of Assange, WikiLeaks staff, and anyone else that federal agents could connect to WikiLeaks.

After the 2016 election, the media organization was routinely referred to as a "tool of Russian intelligence" to discredit WikiLeaks publications.[13] The next year, the CIA mounted a disruption campaign against WikiLeaks and associated individuals because the organization released materials on CIA hacking capabilities. CIA director Mike Pompeo labeled WikiLeaks a "non-state hostile intelligence agency" and insisted Assange had no right to press freedom.

Media gatekeepers helped the US national security state fuel anxiety over the "threat" of WikiLeaks. Editorial boards at newspapers such as the *Washington Post* took the position that WikiLeaks differed "from journalism in methods if not goals" and carelessly "spilled classified government data into the open." They wrongly treated Assange as a "source" who was no different from US Army whistleblower Chelsea Manning, the person who actually disclosed the information.

The New York Times was not a media partner on the US diplomatic cables, yet the *Guardian* went behind the back of WikiLeaks and provided the *Times* access to the cache of files. Scott Shane, who was a national security reporter in the newspaper's Washington, DC, bureau, called the Obama White House in 2010. "We have a quarter million confidential cables, and we plan to publish a lot of them and to write a lot of stories about them," Shane said. The newspaper allowed the State Department to share any objections to the planned reporting.[14]

Journalists at prestige media outlets were more concerned about preserving what Jack Shafer described as the "tradition of horse trading between journalists and government officials behind closed doors."[15]

"No article on a classified program gets published until the responsible officials have been given a fair opportunity to comment. And if they want to argue that publication represents a danger to national security, we put things on hold and give them a respectful hearing. Often, we agree to participate in off-the-record conversations with officials, so they can make their case without fear of spilling more secrets onto our front pages," declared *New York Times* executive editor Bill Keller and *Los Angeles Times* editor Dean Baquet in a joint op-ed published in 2006.[16]

It was the height of the US government's "Global War on Terrorism." Prior to the op-ed, Keller delayed a bombshell Pulitzer Prize–winning report on the National Security Agency's warrantless wiretapping program until after President George W. Bush was reelected in 2004. He effectively sat on a story about the Bush administration committing impeachable offenses.

In 2013, Baquet was now the *New York Times* managing editor. The newspaper helped the US government hide the existence of a base in Saudi Arabia used by the CIA to launch drone strikes. Baquet shared the US government's concern that the "Saudis might shut it down because the citizenry would be very upset." He insisted, "We have to balance that concern with reporting the news." However, *Times* public editor Margaret Sullivan disagreed. "The need to tell this particular story accurately trumped the government's concerns."[17]

When Dana Priest exposed the CIA's network of "black site" prisons for terrorism detainees, the *Washington Post* undermined her reporting and withheld the names of countries to protect the CIA's program of rendition, detention, and torture from being disrupted. "The Washington Post is not publishing the names of the Eastern European countries involved in the covert program, at the request of senior US officials," the newspaper stated.[18]

Raymond Davis, a former US soldier and CIA contractor working for Blackwater, killed two men in Pakistan in 2011. *The New York Times*, the *Post*, and the Associated Press each concealed information about Davis's identity "at the US government's request," despite the crisis it sparked. They allowed President Barack Obama to lie and refer to him as a diplomat until the *Guardian* defied the US government and published a story revealing the truth about Davis.[19]

Many of the US news media helped the US government make the case for wars in Afghanistan and Iraq, which WikiLeaks exposed to unparalleled scrutiny. In particular, the *Times* published disinformation on aluminum tubes and relied on unreliable sources opposed to Iraq President Saddam Hussein, such as Iraqi exile Ahmad Chalabi, who was "a favorite of hard-liners within the Bush administration."[20]

Prestige media constantly harped on WikiLeaks for what they viewed as an unfair focus on the US government. "Much of the material that you have published, as you said, a lot if it is English language. And a lot if it does target the West," *Times* reporter Jo Becker declared during a live interview with Assange that was broadcast on the newspaper's Facebook page in August 2016.[21]

"No, it doesn't target the West, please," Assange replied. "We are an investigative publisher. We also represent whistleblowers who want to speak to the public, like a lawyer presenting to the greatest court of all—the court of public opinion. We don't target anyone."

Becker continued her line of questions. "To the extent that the leaks that have been published so far are embarrassing to the West and can be seen in a number of cases as potentially being helpful to say Russia, [what do you say]?"[22]

"What do you mean by the West? WikiLeaks has published more than 10 million documents. It has a perfect record in the accuracy of the documents it's published. The documents that we have published have gone on to be used to put the guilty in prison, to free the falsely accused from prison, [and] to engage in international civil litigation," Assange claimed, the last phrase referring to the lawsuit CIA torture survivor Khaled el Masri pursued in the European Court of Human Rights.

Assange added, "I would hope that the New York Times would aspire to something like that in its desire to publish, to educate," and suggested, "The public does not feel targeted. The public loves it when they get a glimpse into the corrupt machinery that is attempting to rule them."[23]

As a media gatekeeper, Becker could not bring herself to move on to another question. "To the extent that certain leaks benefit other countries, and I'm thinking particularly—I'll give you an example. A lot of the trade leaks were about trade pacts that were opposed by certain countries, including Russia. Is that a coincidence?"

"This is absurd. This is like saying the New York Times publishes something. Oh my god, is [Russia president Vladimir] Putin going to use it as a talking point? Ridiculous. What kind of consideration is that to take into account if you have a mission to publish suppressed documents from whistleblowers and others to educate the public? You obviously can't be second-guessing yourself at the editorial level like that."[24]

Nothing Assange said mattered because Becker and the *Times* already had their narrative, which aligned with the ideology of high-ranking CIA officials, and they stuck to it. Hours after talking to Assange, the newspaper published a report, "How Russia Often Benefits When Julian Assange Reveals the West's Secrets." The subhead told readers, "American officials say Mr. Assange and WikiLeaks probably have no direct ties to Russian intelligence services. But the agendas of WikiLeaks and the Kremlin have often dovetailed."[25]

The 2016 US presidential election and the 2022 Russian invasion of Ukraine only intensified this shared perspective among many US journalists. They sounded the alarm over the perceived problem of disinformation, which developed into a moral panic much like the Red Scare of the late 1940s and 1950s.

Major tech companies streamlined processes for removing independent content creators from their platforms. Google adopted a YouTube policy in August 2020 against the publication of videos containing "hacked information about a political candidate shared with the intent to interfere in an election." The new policy came a couple months before Election Day. It was clearly aimed at independent media, which might have published emails from campaigns or political organizations when the material would have the most impact (as WikiLeaks did). Google seemingly ignored the fact that a federal judge in the Southern District of New York had defended the right to publish materials allegedly hacked or stolen as covered by the First Amendment.[26]

A proliferation of disinformation tracking tools was supposed to empower news consumers with the ability to protect themselves from "fake news." NewsGuard, which had an advisory board that included Tom Ridge, the first Homeland Security secretary, and Michael Hayden, a former CIA and NSA director, labeled WikiLeaks with a red caution sign.[27]

"This website fails to meet several basic standards of credibility and transparency," NewsGuard deceitfully stated. A "nutrition label" described WikiLeaks as a "publisher of confidential documents, often acquired from leakers and hackers. WikiLeaks published hacked emails, traced to the Kremlin, that hurt Democrats ahead of the 2016 presidential election."

NewsGuard acknowledged that WikiLeaks did not "repeatedly publish false content" and, in fact, revealed who is in charge, including "any possible conflicts of interest." It did not publish "deceptive headlines." Yet the tracking tool maintained the site failed to gather and present information responsibly and did not handle the "difference between news and opinion responsibly," which are common responses from the US national security state to undermine the credibility of independent media organizations that challenge dominant narratives.

In early May 2022, PayPal banned Consortium News and MintPressNews from using its services. Editors for both outlets learned they were blocked but received no explanation. Both were known for publishing content critical of US wars and foreign policy, including US actions in the war in Ukraine.

Consortium News had dedicated a team to covering the Assange case. This financial censorship was nearly identical to what WikiLeaks experienced in 2010.[28]

"If You Open the Door to Anyone Who Blogs"

By charging Assange, the US government assumed and expanded its authority to decide who is and is not a journalist and when a person ceases to be a journalist.

Congress did not object to the unprecedented nature of this prosecution. In fact, Senate Majority Leader Chuck Schumer and Dianne Feinstein, ranking member of the Senate Select

Committee on Intelligence, were part of a group of influential Democrats who urged Secretary of State Mike Pompeo in December 2018 to escalate pressure on Ecuador to end Assange's "presence" in their London embassy.[29]

Schumer and Feinstein were outraged to learn that Fox News reporter James Rosen was labeled an "aider, abettor, and conspirator" during the leak investigation against State Department employee Stephen Kim. They supported a shield law to protect journalists from "unwarranted intrusion" in their work. But they made certain that "covered journalists" would exclude individuals at WikiLeaks-type organizations or "a seventeen year-old who drops out of high school, buys a website for five dollars and starts a blog."[30]

"If you open the door to anyone who blogs, you have opened the door in terms of national security and safety far wider than I think it should be," declared Democratic senator Dick Durbin. Feinstein said, "If a Snowden were to sit down and write this stuff, he'd have a privilege, and I'm not gonna go there." (Which is false, given that Snowden was a government contractor who signed a nondisclosure agreement with the National Security Agency.)

The proposed shield law excluded any organization or person "whose principal function, as demonstrated by the totality of such person or entity's work, is to publish primary source documents that have been disclosed to such person or entity without authorization."[31]

Although the shield law never passed, it was a preview of where we find ourselves. Senators were willing to include filmmakers and nonfiction book authors. They were open to including individuals who use mobile applications for journalism. However, they refused to include "citizen bloggers" and effectively attempted to create special carve-outs to exclude certain persons from press freedom protections—exclusions US prosecutors have endorsed in Assange's case.

It is wrong to take the position that Julian Assange is not a journalist simply because we believe that makes it easier to build opposition to the political case. That dilutes solidarity and cedes ground to the US and UK governments, which have denied him the journalist label to justify their punishment by process.

Few dispute that Assange engaged in journalism when he published the leaks that are at issue. Instead, prosecutors argue that Assange committed offenses because he "irresponsibly" handled material shared with WikiLeaks. But even though the *New York Times* and *Washington Post* would never publish an entire archive of documents from a classified database, it is not a crime in the US to make such information accessible to the world.

The First Amendment of the US Constitution explicitly protects freedom of the press because those who colonized the United States viewed the Fourth Estate as essential to the ability of the governed to hold those in power accountable. US citizens are supposed to have the right to share information and be free from censorship. If a non-US citizen such as Assange is subject to US laws, which on its own is an extraordinary and troubling development, then at the very least he should be afforded the same constitutional rights every US citizen supposedly enjoys.

Prosecuting Assange significantly undermines freedom of expression for journalists around the world. It gives governments with influence or regional power—such as Brazil, China, India, Israel, Russia, Saudi Arabia, and Turkey—the green light to assert similar control over their state secrets, and to target journalists, especially if the further release of information would delegitimize their rule.

Journalists at well-known prestige media organizations are not safe either. The same class of media professionals, who have done the bare minimum to support Assange, could see one of their colleagues prosecuted if the climate in Washington became even more chilly than it was under Trump.

New York Times and *Washington Post* reporters received a Pulitzer Prize for their work on alleged Russian government interference in the 2016 presidential election and possible "Russian connections" to Trump's campaign. Trump believed those reporters were out to destroy his presidency. A future president who follows in the footsteps of Trump could go beyond labeling *Times* and *Post* reporters "enemies" and enlist the attorney general to make an example out of a reporter for "intending" to "injure the United States."[32]

At stake is whether the US government is allowed to criminalize journalism when it challenges the most powerful country in the world.

Let's expand our imagination. Most people use social media applications, which allow them to share anything newsworthy that they obtain firsthand. Just about anyone can commit an act of journalism by publishing content. The universe of what US officials deem dangerous does not have to remain limited to information covered by the Espionage Act.

Even if Julian Assange is not convicted at trial, this political case has already set an alarming precedent. We could all be guilty of journalism.

Thirty WikiLeaks Files the US Government Doesn't Want You to Read

Since WikiLeaks launched its website in 2006, the media organization has published several million documents that have generated news headlines. This list highlights thirty files (cables, emails, and intercepts) that go beyond the revelations of torture, rendition, and war crimes explored in this book. From US meddling in other nation's domestic politics to the influence of multinational corporations, these files reflect the positive impact that WikiLeaks has had by boosting our shared knowledge of a government that rules the most powerful country in the world.

Climate Change and the Environment

—NSA spied on Japanese and German diplomats to help the US government overcome each country's demands for a stronger deal at the Copenhagen climate summit (2016) [Source: https://wikileaks.org/nsa-un/intercepts/ - intercept2]

—Trans-Pacific Partnership international trade agreement negotiated in secret included an environment section that did not mention climate change (2015) [Source: https://wikileaks.org/tpp-sacrificing-the-environment.html]

—US government negotiated a deal at the Copenhagen climate summit that allowed rich countries to emit almost twice as much carbon as developing countries (2009) [Source: https://wikileaks.org/wiki/Draft_Copenhagen_climate_change_agreement,_8_Dec_2009]

—As the Earth warmed, US diplomatic cables revealed race between nations to take advantage of melting Arctic and secure control of oil reserves (2009) [Source: https://wikileaks.org/plusd/cables/09MOSCOW1346_a.html]

—Iraq's main port city Basra faced a "ticking time bomb" as a result of environmental damage (including depleted uranium, oil, sewage) from three wars (2006) [Source: https://wikileaks.org/plusd/cables/06BASRAH107_a.html]

Corporate Power

—US government backed US corporations in effort to stop Haiti from raising the minimum wage to $5 per day (2009) [Source: https://wikileaks.org/plusd/cables/09PORTAUPRINCE553_a.html]

—Pfizer hired "investigators" in Nigeria to blackmail the Nigerian attorney general so he would drop lawsuits against the corporation's drug testing on children (2009) [Source: https://wikileaks.org/plusd/cables/09ABUJA671_a.html]

—US government in France planned trade war against Europe for refusing to adopt agricultural biotechnology from Monsanto (2007) [Source: https://wikileaks.org/plusd/cables/07PARIS4723_a.html]

—Saudi Arabian king requested US government make his plane like Air Force One if they wanted him to purchase a fleet of Boeing aircraft; US authorized an upgrade (2006) [Source: https://wikileaks.org/plusd/cables/06RIYADH8234_a.html]

—US government pressured the India government to drop claims against Dow Chemical related to the 1984 Bhopal disaster (2007) [Source: https://wikileaks.org/plusd/cables/07NEWDEL-HI4272_a.html]

Human Rights Abuses

—US government aware of Israeli military force's cruel methods for repressing Palestinian protests, including spraying chemically-treated "skunk" water (2010) [Source: https://wikileaks.org/plusd/cables/10TELAVIV344_a.html]

—Yemen President Ali Abdullah Saleh pledged to continue helping the US government conceal drone strikes (2010) [Source: https://wikileaks.org/plusd/cables/10SANAA4_a.html]

—US government withdrew military forces and supported Sunni mercenaries in fight against al Qaeda, but when the Shia-led Iraqi government would no longer pay them, further sectarian violence fueled the country's disintegration (2009) [Source: https://wikileaks.org/plusd/cables/09BAGHDAD899_a.html]

—After Afghanistan signed treaty banning cluster bombs, US government sought loophole to continue using cluster bombs in Afghanistan War (2008) [Source: https://wikileaks.org/plusd/cables/08STATE134777_a.html]

—Israeli officials pledged to keep Gaza economy on "brink of collapse" (2008) [Source: https://wikileaks.org/plusd/cables/08TELA-VIV2447_a.html]

—Israel sought to coordinate Operation Cast Lead in Gaza with Egypt and Palestinian Authority (2008) [Source: https://wikileaks.org/plusd/cables/08TELAVIV2447_a.html]

—FBI trained members of Egyptian police service responsible for torture (2007) [Source: 07CAIRO3348_a]

—US government aided Turkey's massacres of Kurdish people; tens of thousands of civilians were killed (2006) [Source: https:// wikileaks.org/plusd/cables/06ANKARA3352_a.html]

—Flouting ban in Philippines' constitution, US government pushed for direct military involvement in country's counterterrorism operations in Mindanao (2006) [Source: https://wikileaks. org/plusd/cables/06MANILA3401_a.html]

—Turkey authorized use of Incirlik Air Base for CIA rendition flights to Guantánamo (2002) [Source: https://wikileaks.org/ plusd/cables/02ANKARA8305_a.html]

Regime Change

—US recognized that the coup against Honduran President Manuel "Mel" Zelaya was illegal (2009) [Source: https://wikileaks. org/plusd/cables/09TEGUCIGALPA645_a.html]

—US trained and funded violent student protesters who led demonstrations against Venezuela President Hugo Chávez's administration (2006) [Source: https://wikileaks.org/plusd/ cables/06CARACAS2104_a.html]

—US government supported violent opposition against Bolivia President Evo Morales, which had plans to blow up gas pipelines (2008) [Source: https://wikileaks.org/plusd/ cables/08LAPAZ2004_a.html]

—US government organized and funded opposition to President Daniel Ortega in Nicaragua through NGOs (2007) [Source: https:// search.wikileaks.org/plusd/cables/07MANAGUA493_a.html]

—US government singled out Ecuador President Rafael Correa as a top "threat" to US government interests prior to Correa's election (2006) [Source: https://wikileaks.org/plusd/cables/06QUITO2150_a.html]

—US government backed opposition groups in Syria to further regime change operations (2006) [Source: https://wikileaks.org/plusd/cables/06DAMASCUS701_a.html]

Foreign Policy

—US government knew Iran had "no ballistic missiles capable of carrying nuclear weapons," despite hyping the so-called threat of Iran nuclear missiles to the Middle East and Europe (2010) [Source: https://wikileaks.org/plusd/cables/10STATE17263_a.html]

—US officials were well aware of Tunisia President Ben Ali and his family's corruption and "potent outrage" among Tunisians outraged by their "displays of wealth" (2008) [Source: https://wikileaks.org/plusd/cables/08TUNIS679_a.html]

—US ambassador William Burns, who was CIA director under President Joe Biden, outlined why Russia viewed NATO encirclement as a military threat (2008) [Source: https://wikileaks.org/plusd/cables/08MOSCOW265_a.html]

US Politics

—Hillary Clinton's Democratic presidential campaign adopted a "Pied Piper" strategy that boosted extreme Republican candidates like President Donald Trump (2015) [Source: https://wikileaks.org/podesta-emails/emailid/1120]

ACKNOWLEDGMENTS

The book was initially passed on by a publisher that had already released several books on WikiLeaks; throughout 2021, the project languished until I mentioned it to Mickey Huff, the director of Project Censored. Mickey was interested, and from that point onward, the opportunity to write my first book became a reality.

Mickey, along with associate director Andy Lee Roth, believed in this project every step of the way. Andy deserves credit for reading the first draft of every chapter of the book and providing his immediate reactions so I could be confident in the way I presented key ideas. Mickey and Andy spent lots of time going over the finer details to help me convert my ongoing research and reporting into a book.

I am immensely grateful for Elizabeth Bell, who edited the manuscript. Thanks also to the fine people at The Censored Press and Seven Stories Press—including Dan Simon, Ruth Weiner, and Jon Gilbert at Seven Stories and Lorna Garano at The Censored Press—who were enthusiastic about this project and have ensured that the book is well designed, distributed, and publicized. Thanks also to Shealeigh Voitl, Reagan Haynie, Gavin Kelley, and Vikki Vasquez for their help proofreading the manuscript.

Abby Martin is a fierce reporter and humanitarian. She made time while producing a film project to write the book's foreword, for which I am grateful.

I met Mr. Fish, a satirical cartoonist, at a dinner in Washington, DC. When we met, I did not know he was the artist who had created the image of Assange featured on this book's cover. As I showed guests the online listing for *Guilty of Journalism*, Fish said, "That's my art." We marveled at the serendipitous nature of our meeting, and he kindly agreed to work on more illustrations for the book.

I am much too young to call this a memoir; however, writing the book offered moments to reflect on the past work I have accomplished. Several mentors who taught me how to be a professional journalist deserve my gratitude.

Rob Kall at *OpEdNews* gave me a platform while I was in college to write about antiwar activism, national security, and civil liberties. In 2011, *The Nation* offered me an internship after reading my articles at OEN. That internship gave me valuable newsroom experience. I had the privilege of working with Greg Mitchell, who encouraged me to take initiative and produce posts that were highlighted in his daily blog on WikiLeaks.

After my Nation internship concluded, I was granted a Democracy For America fellowship to attend the Netroots Nation conference in Minneapolis, Minnesota. I recall meeting some young Democrat during a mixer who asked about what I did, and I made the mistake of talking about WikiLeaks' "Collateral Murder" video. They stopped talking with me. I quickly realized this was not my scene, but everything changed when Firedoglake founder Jane Hamsher invited me to lunch the next day. I was offered a salaried position covering civil liberties for the progressive website.

I am deeply indebted to Jane. She and her poodles welcomed me into their home near Washington, DC, where I lived for an entire summer in 2013 while the trial against Chelsea Manning unfolded. She gave me full editorial control to choose what stories I wanted to cover for my column, The Dissenter. She promoted fundraisers, which brought in donations from prominent individuals, such as Graham Nash and Roger Waters. Jane took care of my basic needs, and that allowed me to keep up with an intense schedule without having to worry about food, lodging, or transportation.

Through my work for Jane, I met whistleblowers and whistleblower advocates including Daniel Ellsberg, Michael Ratner, Thomas Drake, John Kiriakou, Jesselyn Radack, Jeffrey Sterling, and Glenn Green-wald, who later helped Edward Snowden reveal NSA documents that exposed the United States' global system of mass surveillance. The ability to connect with these people expanded my understanding of many of the issues that are central to this book.

Daniel was very kind, generous with praise, and consistently willing to support my reporting on Manning, Julian Assange, WikiLeaks, and various whistleblower cases. The same applies to Michael, who was president of the Center for Constitutional Rights and an attorney on the WikiLeaks legal team. Michael always made himself available to give me a quote for my coverage of WikiLeaks.

Rania Khalek, a good friend, BreakThrough News anchor, and co-host with me of the "Unauthorized Disclosure" podcast, amplified my reporting on Assange and gave me access to various platforms to share my work with a wider audience.

Sometimes it really helped to have a conversation about the status of the book and the many creative dilemmas that popped up while developing each chapter. Brian Sonenstein, another good friend who co-founded Shadowproof with me, listened and helped me stay on track. He always responded with excitement when I shared updates on the book, which reinforced my confi-dence in the project.

Thank you to all the people who contributed endorsements: Daniel, Rania, Medea Benjamin, Noam Chomsky, John Pilger, Ryan Grim, Chris Hedges, Stefania Maurizi, Tom Mueller, Carey Shenkman, Trevor Timm, and Ann Wright. Nathan Fuller deserves a special mention as well for his assistance.

Shadowproof donors and paid subscribers of The Dissenter Newsletter, especially Feroz, Patrick Wang, Pat Kenzler, Pascale

Vielle, Tom Bradburn, Laine Duffy, Terry Lustig, Rosemary Kean, Theresa Barzee, Raymond McGovern, Cloudy, Joanne Lukacher, Robert Kolkebeck, Priscilla Felia, and Jeanie Schmidt and Todd Seller deserve thanks for funding my journalism.

I nearly suspended The Dissenter Newsletter entirely while I wrote the book, but Mohamed Elmaazi and Kit Klarenberg, who are both based in the United Kingdom, contributed stories that made it possible for me to keep the newsletter going during that time.

Without my wife Julie, this book might not exist. I would still be slogging through the first few chapters and grumbling about how it would never get done because of too many distractions.

Finally, on October 2, 2020, after the main extradition hearing against Assange wrapped, I asked on Twitter if people would read a book about the Assange case. Matt Kennard, journalist and co-founder of Declassified UK, responded, "I think it would be a vital piece of work without which the historical record would remain incomplete. And I don't think anyone is better placed to write it. No pressure."

Matt gave me the determination to make this project real. And I hope this book demonstrates why I was best placed to produce a chronicle of the Assange case.

NOTES

INTRODUCTION

1. Ben Jacobs and Spencer Ackerman, "Trump Decries 'Criminal' Leaks Exposing Michael Flynn's Russia Cover-up," *The Guardian*, February 15, 2017.
2. Rebecca Savransky, "Trump: Spotlight Is on 'Low-life Leakers,'" *The Hill*, February 16, 2017.
3. Jonathan Alter, *The Promise: President Obama, Year One* (New York: Simon & Schuster, 2010), 154–155.
4. John Glaser, "Cables Reveal 2006 Summary Execution," Antiwar.com, August 29, 2011.
5. Matthew Schofield, "WikiLeaks: Iraqi Children in US Raid Shot in Head, UN Says," *McClatchy Newspapers*, August 31, 2011.
6. Amy Goodman, interview with Matthew Schofield, "Another Civilian Massacre? U.S. Launches Investigation After Iraqi Police Accuse U.S. Troops of Murdering 11 Men, Women and Children Last Week," *Democracy Now!*, March 23, 2006.
7. "Obama: Iraq War Will Be Over by Year's End; Troops Coming Home," CNN, October 21, 2011.
8. Arun Rath, "The 'Indie' Journalists At the Center of the Bradley Manning Trial," PBS *Frontline*, March 15, 2013.
9. Margaret Sullivan, "The Times Should Have a Reporter at the Bradley Manning Hearing," *New York Times*, December 5, 2012.
10. Margaret Sullivan, "An Empty Seat In the Courtroom," *New York Times*, December 8, 2012.
11. Amy Goodman and Nermeen Shaikh, interview with Kevin Gosztola, "Behind The Scenes of the Bradley Manning Trial," *Democracy Now!*, July 10, 2013.
12. Jules Boykoff, *Beyond Bullets: The Suppression of Dissent in the United States* (Oakland: AK Press, 2007), 27.
13. Kevin Gosztola, "'Another Dark Day': UK Government Approves Assange's Extradition to United States," The Dissenter, June 17, 2022.
14. *US v. Assange: Judgment*, District Judge Vanessa Baraitser, January 4, 2021.
15. *US v. Assange, Judgment*, Chief Justice Ian Burnett, December 10, 2021.
16. Amnesty International, "US/UK: US 'Assurances' Leave Julian Assange at Risk of Ill-treatment if Extradited from UK," July 13, 2021.
17. *US v. Assange, Judgment*, Burnett.
18. Matt Kennard and Mark Curtis, "Assange Judge Is 40-Year 'Good Friend' of Minister Who Orchestrated His Arrest," Declassified UK, December 2, 2021.

19. Ibid.
20. Kevin Gosztola, "Assange Appeals Extradition To The United States With Two Appeals," The Dissenter, July 15, 2022.
21. Megan Specia, "Less Than 1 Percent of Britain's People Voted on the New Prime Minister. Here's Why," *New York Times*, September 5, 2022.

CHAPTER 1: CHARGES AND ALLEGATIONS

1. Committee to Protect Journalists, "Methodology," undated [accessed on June 7, 2022].
2. Kevin Gosztola, "For Third Year, Committee to Protect Journalists Excludes Assange from Jailed Journalist Index," The Dissenter, December 20, 2021.
3. Article 19 and Liberty, "Secrets, Spies and Whistleblowers: Freedom of Expression in the UK," November 2000.
4. *US v. Assange, Indictment*, Tracy Doherty-McCormick, Kellen S. Dwyer, Thomas W. Traxler, March 6, 2018.
5. US Department of Justice, "WikiLeaks Founder Charged in Computer Hacking Conspiracy," Press Release, April 11, 2019.
6. Charlie Savage, "Press Freedoms and the Case Against Julian Assange, Explained," *New York Times*, April 11, 2019.
7. "Why Julian Assange Should Be Extradited," *The Economist,* April 17, 2019.
8. Jack Shafer, "Julian Assange Might Have Already Won," *Politico*, April 11, 2019.
9. Michael Weiss, "Julian Assange Got What He Deserved," *The Atlantic*, April 12, 2019.
10. Kevin Gosztola, "FBI Affidavit in Assange Case Shows Government Is Criminalizing the Publication of Afghanistan War Logs," Shadowproof, April 16, 2019.
11. Robert Mackey, "Taliban Study WikiLeaks to Hunt Informants," *New York Times*, July 30, 2010.
12. See, for example, C.J. Chivers, "Foot on Bomb, Marine Defies a Taliban Trap," *New York Times*, January 23, 2010; and Dexter Filkins, "Bomb Material Cache Uncovered in Afghanistan," *New York Times*, November 10, 2009.
13. US Embassy Reykjavík, Iceland, "Looking for Alternatives to an Icesave Referendum," January 13, 2010.
14. *US v. Assange, Indictment*, Tracy Doherty-McCormick, Kellen S. Dwyer, Thomas W. Traxler, Gordon Kromberg, May 23, 2019.
15. Ibid.
16. Charlie Savage, "Assange Indicted Under Espionage Act, Raising First Amendment Issues," *New York Times*, May 23, 2019.
17. Natasha Bertrand, "DOJ Accuses Assange of Violating Espionage Act," *Politico*, May 23, 2019.
18. Society of Professional Journalists, "SPJ: Assange Indictment Raises Serious Concerns for Press Freedom," Press Release, May 24, 2019.
19. Savage, "Press Freedoms and the Case Against Julian Assange, Explained."

20. Michael M. Grynbaum and Marc Tracy, "'Frightening': Charges Against Julian Assange Alarm Press Advocates," *New York Times*, May 23, 2019.
21. Camille Fassett, "Press Freedom Advocates and News Outlets Strongly Condemn New Charges Against Julian Assange," Freedom of the Press Foundation, May 24, 2019.
22. Barton Gellman, Twitter Post, May 23, 2019, 4:11 p.m.
23. Reporters Committee for Freedom of the Press, "Reporters Committee Statement on Latest Assange Indictment," Press Release, May 23, 2019.
24. Tom McCarthy, "Assange's Indictment Escalates Trump's Attacks on Free Speech, Experts Say," *The Guardian*, May 24, 2019.
25. Fassett, "Press Freedom Advocates and News Outlets Strongly Condemn New Charges Against Julian Assange."
26. Jon Swaine, "New US Charges Against Julian Assange Could Spell Decades Behind Bars," *The Guardian*, May 23, 2019.
27. US Department of Justice, "WikiLeaks Founder Charged in Superseding Indictment," Press Release, June 24, 2020.
28. Ibid.
29. *US v. Assange, Second Superseding Indictment*, G. Zachary Terwilliger, Tracy Doherty-McCormick, Kellen S. Dwyer, et al., June 24, 2020.
30. Dell Cameron, "How an FBI Informant Orchestrated the Stratfor Hack," Daily Dot, May 31, 2021.
31. US Department of Justice, "New Allegations Assert Assange Conspired with 'Anonymous' Affiliated Hackers, Among Others," Press Release, June 24, 2020.
32. Kevin Gosztola, "Judge Railroads Assange as Legal Team Objects to Fresh Extradition Request," The Dissenter, September 7, 2020.

CHAPTER 2: CHELSEA MANNING'S COURT MARTIAL

1. Kevin Gosztola, "Military Judge Announces Rationale Behind Verdict in Bradley Manning's Trial," Shadowproof, August 16, 2013.
2. US Congress Select Committee on Intelligence United States Senate, *Russian Active Measures Campaigns and Interference in the 2016 U.S. Election: Volume 5: Counterintelligence Threats and Vulnerabilities*, 116th Cong., 1st session, August 18, 2020.
3. US Department of Justice, "WikiLeaks Founder Charged in Computer Hacking Conspiracy," Press Release, April 11, 2019.
4. Alexa O'Brien, "Bradley Manning's Personal Statement to Court-Martial: Full Text," *The Guardian*, March 1, 2013.
5. Ibid.
6. Ibid.
7. Ibid.
8. Ibid.
9. Ibid.

10. US Embassy Reykjavík, Iceland, "Looking for Alternatives to an Icesave Referendum," January 13, 2010.
11. Ibid.
12. O'Brien, "Bradley Manning's Personal Statement to Court-martial."
13. "Draft: The Most Wanted Leaks of 2009," WikiLeaks, undated [accessed on May 30, 2022].
14. *US v. Manning*, Morning Session, Vol. 22, July 26, 2013, unofficial transcript, Freedom of the Press Foundation.
15. Ibid.
16. *US v. Assange, Second Superseding Indictment*, Tracy Doherty-McCormick, Kellen S. Dwyer, Thomas W. Traxler, Gordon Kromberg, Alexander P. Berrang, June 24, 2020.
17. Ibid.
18. Ibid.
19. Ibid.
20. O'Brien, "Bradley Manning's Personal Statement to Court-Martial."
21. Jan Wolfe and Nathan Layne, "Assange Hacking Charge Limits Free Speech Defense: Legal Experts," Reuters, April 11, 2019.
22. Kevin Gosztola, "Prosecutors' Password-Cracking Conspiracy Theory Against Assange Unravels at Extradition Trial," The Dissenter, September 26, 2020.
23. *US v. Manning*, Afternoon Session, Vol. 6, June 12, 2013, unofficial transcript, Freedom of the Press Foundation.
24. *Extradition Hearing, Westminster Magistrate's Court*, Patrick Eller, President and CEO, Metadata Forensics, LLC, 2020.
25. *US v. Manning*, Afternoon Session, Vol. 21, July 25, 2013, unofficial transcript, Freedom of the Press Foundation.
26. Ibid.
27. *US v. Manning*, Afternoon Session, Vol. 37, August 19, 2013, unofficial transcript, Freedom of the Press Foundation.
28. Chelsea Manning, "Chelsea Manning: 'I'm Still Bound to Secrecy,'" *New York Times*, October 8, 2022.

CHAPTER 3: HOW THE US GOVERNMENT VIEWED WIKILEAKS

1. *National Defense Authorization Act for Fiscal Year 2020*, S. 1790, 116th Session.
2. Kevin Gosztola, "US Government Accuses Bradley Manning of Aiding Al Qaeda," Shadowproof, December 22, 2011.
3. Ibid.
4. Kevin Gosztola, "How the Government Hopes to Argue Bradley Manning's Alleged Leaks Aided Terrorism," Shadowproof, January 9, 2013.
5. Ibid.
6. *US v. Manning*, Afternoon Session, Vol. 18, July 15, 2013, unofficial transcript, Freedom of the Press Foundation.
7. Floyd Abrams and Yochai Benkler, "Death to Whistle-Blowers?" *New York Times*, March 13, 2013.

8. *US v. Manning*, Afternoon Session, Vol. 17, July 10, 2013, unofficial transcript, Freedom of the Press Foundation.
9. Ibid.
10. Ibid.
11. Ibid.
12. New York Times Editorial Board, "Stifling Online Speech," *New York Times*, February 21, 2008.
13. Joseph Lieberman, "Lieberman Urges Better Public Access to CRS Reports," Press Release, March 4, 2009
14. Rebecca Neal, "Congressional Research Sees Light of Day," *Federal Times*, February 23, 2009.
15. Frontline Club, "WikiLeaks Release of Classified War Documents," C-SPAN, 1:04:00, July 26, 2010.
16. Eric Schmitt, "U.S. Tells WikiLeaks to Return Afghan War Logs," *New York Times*, August 5, 2010.
17. *US v. Manning*, unofficial transcript, Afternoon Session, July 15, 2013.
18. Ibid.
19. Ibid.
20. Ibid.
21. *US v. Manning*, Morning Session, Vol. 17, July 10, 2013, unofficial transcript, Freedom of the Press Foundation.
22. Michael D. Horvath, "Wikileaks.org—An Online Reference to Foreign Intelligence Services, Insurgents, or Terrorist Groups?" United States Army Counterintelligence Center, March 18, 2008.
23. Ibid.
24. *US v. Manning*, Afternoon Session, Vol. 5, June 11, 2013, unofficial transcript, Freedom of the Press Foundation.
25. *US v. Manning*, Afternoon Session, Vol. 4, July 10, 2013, unofficial transcript, Freedom of the Press Foundation.
26. Horvath, "Wikileaks.org—An Online Reference to Foreign Intelligence Services, Insurgents, or Terrorist Groups?"

CHAPTER 4: THE ESPIONAGE ACT

1. David G. Savage, "Clinton Vetoes Bill on Leaking of U.S. Secrets," *Los Angeles Times*, November 5, 2000.
2. Sharon LaFraniere, "Math Behind Leak Crackdown: 153 Cases, 4 Years, 0 Indictments," *New York Times*, July 20, 2013.
3. Ibid.
4. Ibid.
5. *Extradition Hearing, Westminster Magistrate's Court*, statement of Carey Shenkman, Law Office of Carey Shenkman, 2020.
6. Chip Gibbons, "Repressing Radicalism," *Jacobin*, June 15, 2017.
7. Joshua Waimberg, "Schenck v. United States: Defining the Limits of Free Speech," National Constitution Center, November 2, 2015.

8. Anthony Lewis, "Abroad at Home; Spies and Non-Spies," *New York Times*, November 28, 1985.

9. Stephen P. Mulligan and Jennifer K. Elsea, "Criminal Prohibitions on Leaks and Other Disclosures of Classified Defense Information," March 7, 2017, Congressional Research Service.

10. *US v. Steven J. Rosen*, Keith Weissman, 445 F. Supp. 2d 602 (E.D. Va.), 2006.

11. Ibid.

12. US Department of Justice, *Motion to Dismiss Superseding Indictment, US v. Steven Rosen*, Keith Weissman, by Dana Boente, James Trump, W. Neil Hammerstrom Jr., Thomas Reilly, May 1, 2009.

13. LaFraniere, "Math Behind Leak Crackdown."

14. Peter Maass, "Destroyed by the Espionage Act," The Intercept, February 18, 2015.

15. Steven Aftergood, "Court Eases Prosecutors' Burden of Proof in Leak Cases," Secrecy News, July 29, 2013.

16. Kevin Gosztola, "When the Justice Department Pursues Reporters as Spies," Shadowproof, May 21, 2013.

17. Ibid.

18. *US v. Shamai Leibowitz, Indictment*, Rod Rosenstein, December 4, 2009.

19. US Department of Justice, "Former FBI Contract Linguist Pleads Guilty to Leaking Classified Information to Blogger," Press Release, December 17, 2009.

20. Shamai Leibowitz, "Blowback from the White House's Vindictive War on Whistleblowers," *The Guardian*, July 5, 2013.

21. Ibid.

22. Scott Shane, "Leak Offers Look at Efforts by U.S. to Spy On Israel," *New York Times*, September 5, 2011.

23. Kevin Gosztola, "NSA Whistleblower Compares Case to CIA Officer Convicted of Leaking Name of Undercover Officer," Shadowproof, January 8, 2013.

24. Steven Aftergood, "Handling of Drake Leak Case Was 'Unconscionable,' Court Said," Secrecy News, July 29, 2011.

25. Ibid.

26. *US v. Jeffrey Sterling, Indictment*. Neil MacBride, William Welch, Timothy Kelly, James Trump, December 22, 2010.

27. Jeffrey Sterling, "The Assange Prosecution: A Haunting Reminder of What Happened in My Espionage Act Case," The Dissenter, December 14, 2020.

28. *US Court of Appeals for the Fourth Circuit, Opinion*, J. Harvie Wilkinson. August 3, 2005.

29. Ibid.

30. US Department of Justice, "Former CIA Officer John Kiriakou Indicted for Allegedly Disclosing Classified Information, Including Covert Officer's Identity, to Journalists and Lying to CIA's Publications Board," Press Release, April 5, 2012.

31. Kevin Gosztola, "CIA Whistleblower John Kiriakou, Sentenced to 30 Months in Jail, Wears Conviction as 'Badge of Honor,'" Shadowproof, January 25, 2013.
32. Ibid.
33. Chip Gibbons, "Jailing the Messenger: The CIA's Torture Whistleblower Featuring John Kiriakou," *Primary Sources* (podcast), September 8, 2021.
34. Ibid.
35. Nick Miller, "'You Don't Stand a Chance': How the Press Freedom Argument Will Go For Assange," *Sydney Morning Herald*, June 9, 2019.
36. Connor Simpson, "Joe Biden Is on Edward Snowden's Case," *The Atlantic*, June 29, 2013.
37. "Ecuador's Correa Says Biden Asked Him to Deny Edward Snowden Asylum," *The Guardian*, June 29, 2013.
38. Matthew v. Lee, "AP Source: NSA Leaker Snowden's Passport Revoked," Associated Press, June 24, 2013.
39. Jamie Grierson, "Edward Snowden Would Be Willing to Return to US for Fair Trial," *The Guardian*, February 21, 2016.
40. Kevin Gosztola, "US Government's Censorship System Claims Victory Against NSA Whistleblower Edward Snowden," Shadowproof, December 18, 2019.
41. Ed Pilkington, "Chelsea Manning: Government Anti-Leak Program a 'Blank Check for Surveillance,'" *The Guardian*, March 18, 2016.
42. Ibid.
43. Chelsea Manning, "When Will the US Government Stop Persecuting Whistleblowers?" *The Guardian*, March 18, 2016.
44. Project on Government Oversight, "22 Organizations Ask the IC IG to Investigate Insider Threat Program," Press Release, January 6, 2016.
45. LaFraniere, "Math Behind Leak Crackdown."
46. Kevin Gosztola, "President Donald Trump's Vengeful Pledge To Pursue 'Low-Life Leakers,'" Shadowproof, February 17, 2017.
47. Kevin Gosztola, "Facing Crisis of Legitimacy, Trump Administration Pledges to Intensify War on Leaks," Shadowproof, August 4, 2017.
48. Ben Smith, "The Intercept Promised to Reveal Everything. Then Its Own Scandal Hit," *The New York Times*, September 13, 2020 (updated June 14, 2021).
49. US Department of Justice, Federal Bureau of Investigation, *United States v. Reality Winner, Verbatim Transcription*, June 3, 2017.
50. Kevin Gosztola, "NSA Whistleblower Receives Longest Sentence Ever for Unauthorized Disclosure," Shadowproof, August 23, 2018.
51. Kevin Gosztola, "After Reality Winner's Sentencing, One of Her Attorneys Speaks About the Case," Shadowproof, August 24, 2018.
52. *US v. Reality Winner. Government's Response to Defendant's Brief Regarding the Elements of the Offense*, R. Brian Tanner and Julie A. Edelstein, October 13, 2017. Accessible online at The Intercept.

53. US Press Freedom Tracker, "Former FBI Agent Terry Albury Accused of Leaking Documents to The Intercept," Freedom of the Press Foundation, October 18, 2018.

54. Janet Reitman, "'I Helped Destroy People,'" *New York Times Magazine*, September 1, 2021.

55. *US v. Daniel Hale, Motion for Leave to File Amicus Curiae Brief on Behalf of CAIR Foundation*, Lena F. Masri, Gaderir I. Abbas, and Justin Sadowsky, July 12, 2021.

56. *US v. Daniel Hale. Government's Motion in Limine to Exclude Certain Evidence, Argument, or Comment at Trial*, G. Zachary Terwilliger, Alexander P. Berrang, Gordon D. Kromberg, and Heather M. Schmidt, September 16, 2019.

CHAPTER 5: THE CIA'S WAR ON WIKILEAKS

1. WikiLeaks, Twitter Post, June 7, 2014, 12:12 a.m.

2. WikiLeaks, "Vault 7: CIA Hacking Tools Revealed," Press Release, March 7, 2017.

3. Zach Dorfman, Sean D. Naylor, and Michael Isikoff, "Kidnapping, Assassination and a London Shoot-out: Inside the CIA's Secret War Plans Against WikiLeaks," Yahoo News, September 26, 2021.

4. US Congress, Senate, Select Committee, Hearings before the Committee on Nomination of Hon. Mike Pompeo To Be Director of the Central Intelligence Agency, 115th Cong., 1st session, 2017.

5. Victor Marchetti and John D. Marks, *The CIA and the Cult of Intelligence* (New York: Alfred A. Knopf, 1974).

6. WikiLeaks, "CIA Espionage Orders for the Last French Presidential Election," Press Release, February 16, 2017.

7. WikiLeaks, "Vault 7: CIA Hacking Tools Revealed."

8. Arjun Kharpal, "WikiLeaks Dump: Apple, Samsung, Microsoft React to Claims CIA Hacked iPhones, TVs," CNBC, March 8, 2017.

9. Ibid.

10. "Hive," WikiLeaks, undated [accessed on June 1, 2022].

11. "Marble Framework," WikiLeaks, undated [accessed on June 1, 2022].

12. "CIA Says WikiLeaks 'Equips Our Adversaries'; Assange Sees 'Incompetence,'" Radio Free Europe/Radio Liberty, March 9, 2017.

13. WikiLeaks, "Vault 7: CIA Hacking Tools Revealed."

14. Mike Pompeo, "A Discussion on National Security," transcript of speech delivered at Center For Strategic & International Studies (CSIS) Headquarters, Washington, DC, April 13, 2017.

15. Dorfman, Naylor, and Isikoff, "Kidnapping, Assassination and a London Shoot-out."

16. Ibid.

17. Ibid.

18. Mike Pompeo, "Mike Pompeo Speech at Hillsdale College," YouTube video, 1:00:00, posted by Hillsdale College, September 27, 2021.
19. Glenn Beck, Twitter Post, September 7, 2021, 11:29 a.m.
20. "Mike Pompeo on Whether US Plotted to Kill Julian Assange," YouTube video, 38:45, posted by Megyn Kelly, September 29, 2021.
21. Mike Pompeo, "Secretary Pompeo Participates in Q&A Discussion at Texas A&M University," YouTube video, 28:50, posted by U.S. Department of State, April 15, 2019.
22. Amy Goodman, interview with Alex Gibney, "'We Steal Secrets': Alex Gibney's New Documentary Explores the Story of WikiLeaks," *Democracy Now!*, January 23, 2013.
23. Julian Assange, "Julian Assange: The CIA Director Is Waging War on Truth-Tellers Like WikiLeaks," *Washington Post*, April 25, 2017.
24. Deb Riechmann, "CIA Director Cancels Harvard Speech Over 'Traitor' Manning," Associated Press, September 14, 2017.
25. David Smith, "Arresting Julian Assange Is a Priority Says US Attorney General Jeff Sessions," *The Guardian*, April 20, 2017.
26. Evan Perez, Pamela Brown, Shimon Prokupecz, and Eric Bradner, "Sources: US Prepares Charges to Seek Arrest of WikiLeaks' Julian Assange," CNN, April 20, 2017.
27. Dorfman, Naylor, and Isikoff, "Kidnapping, Assassination and a London Shoot-out."

CHAPTER 6: THE SPYING OPERATION AGAINST ASSANGE

1. "WikiLeaks—USA against Julian Assange," YouTube video, 30:00, posted by ARD, September 15, 2020.
2. Ibid.
3. Ibid.
4. *Extradition Hearing, Before Westminster Magistrates' Court*, Aitor Martinez, Lawyer, ILOCAD SL, Baltasar Garzón Abogados, 2020.
5. Ibid.
6. Ibid.
7. Ibid.
8. Chip Gibbons, "Secret Documents Have Exposed the CIA's Julian Assange Obsession," *Jacobin*, September 17, 2022.
9. *Extradition Hearing, Before Westminster Magistrates' Court*, Witness 1, UC Global Employee, 2020.
10. Robert D. McFadden, "Sheldon Adelson, Billionaire Donor to G.O.P. and Israel, Is Dead at 87," *New York Times*, January 12, 2021.
11. Extradition Hearing, Westminster Magistrates' Court, Witness 1, 2020.
12. Ibid.
13. Ibid.
14. *Extradition Hearing, Before Westminster Magistrates' Court*, Witness 2, UC Global Employee, 2020.

15. Ibid.
16. Ibid.
17. Ibid.
18. Ibid.
19. Ibid.
20. Ibid.
21. Extradition Hearing, Westminster Magistrates' Court, 2020, Witness 1.
22. Extradition Hearing, Westminster Magistrates' Court, 2020, Witness 2.
23. Ibid.
24. Ibid.
25. Ibid.
26. José María Irujo, "Spanish Firm that Spied on Julian Assange Tried to Find Out If He Fathered a Child at Ecuadorian Embassy," *El País*, April 15, 2020.
27. Extradition Hearing, Westminster Magistrates' Court, Witness 2, 2020.
28. Zach Dorfman, Sean D. Naylor, and Michael Isikoff, "Kidnapping, Assassination and a London Shoot-out: Inside the CIA's Secret War Plans Against WikiLeaks," Yahoo News, September 26, 2021.
29. Extradition Hearing, Westminster Magistrates' Court, Witness 1, 2020.
30. José María Irujo, "Russian and US Visitors, Targets for the Spanish Firm that Spied on Julian Assange," *El País*, October 8, 2019.
31. Ibid.
32. Ibid.
33. Ibid.
34. Ibid.
35. Kevin Gosztola, "Journalists Who Visited Julian Assange Targeted by Company Spying on CIA's Behalf," Shadowproof, October 9, 2019.
36. Gonzalo Solano, "Ecuador Cuts WikiLeaks Founder Julian Assange's Internet at Embassy," Associated Press, March 28, 2018.
37. John McEvoy and Pablo Navarrete, "'A Lot of Mistakes': The Guardian and Julian Assange," MintPress News, November 27, 2021.
38. Ibid.
39. Ibid.
40. Ibid.
41. Sondra Crosby, Affidavit, March 1, 2019.
42. Nils Melzer, Twitter Post, June 12, 2019, 1:22 p.m.
43. "Why Ecuador Ended Asylum for 'Spoiled Brat' Julian Assange," Associated Press, April 12, 2019.
44. *US v. Assange, Prosecution Closing Submission*, November 20, 2020.
45. *US v. Assange, Judgment*, District Judge Vanessa Baraitser, January 4, 2021.
46. Kurt Andersen, host, Episode Six: "Off the Rails," *Nixon at War* (podcast), July 19, 2021.
47. Ari Melber, Noel Hartman and Liz Johnstone, "NBC News Exclusive: Memo Shows Watergate Prosecutors Had Evidence Nixon White House Plotted Violence," NBC News, June 18, 2017.
48. "Text of Ruling by Judge in Ellsberg Case," *New York Times*, May 12, 1973.

49. *Robinson v. United Kingdom, Decision*, European Court of Human Rights, Fourth Section, May 19, 2022.
50. Steve Sweeney, "Mike Pompeo Summoned by Spanish Court to Explain Assange Assassination Plot," *Morning Star*, June 5, 2022.

CHAPTER 7: THE FBI'S ROLE IN THE CASE

1. "Siggi 'The Hacker' Charged with Multiple Sexual Offences Against Minors," *Iceland Monitor*, July 11, 2015.
2. "Former WikiLeaks Volunteer 'Siggi the Hacker' Sentenced to Prison for Sexually Violating Teenage Boys," *Iceland Magazine*, September 25, 2015.
3. Andie Sophia Fontaine, "'Siggi Hacker' Charged with Multiple Fraud and Theft Counts," *Reykjavík Grapevine*, June 11, 2014.
4. Ryan Gallagher, "WikiLeaks' Teenage Benedict Arnold," Slate, August 9, 2013.
5. Ibid.
6. Ibid.
7. Ibid.
8. Bjartmar Oddur Þeyr Alexandersson and Gunnar Hrafn Jónsson, "In His Own Words: Assange Witness Explains fabrications," *Stundin*, September 7, 2021.
9. Ibid.
10. Iceland Attorney General's Office, "Summary of the State Prosecutor and the National Commissioner of Police Regarding the Arrival of FBI Employees and Two Prosecutors in Iceland in August 2011," Press Release, February 4, 2013.
11. Ibid.
12. Bo Elkjær, "The FBI Spied on Assange via Denmark," Journalisten, August 14, 2013.
13. Iceland Attorney General's Office, "Summary of the State Prosecutor and the National Commissioner of Police."
14. Marta Pacheco, "Jónasson: The Icelandic Minister Who Refused Cooperation with the FBI," *Katoikos*, December 7, 2016.
15. Gallagher, "WikiLeaks' Teenage Benedict Arnold."
16. Ibid.
17. Ibid.
18. Pall Hilmarsson, "From Iceland—Q," *Reykjavík Grapevine*, July 20, 2013.
19. Gallagher, "WikiLeaks' Teenage Benedict Arnold."
20. WikiLeaks, "Eight FBI Agents Conduct Interrogation in Iceland in Relation to Ongoing U.S. Investigation of WikiLeaks," Press Release, February 7, 2013.
21. Pall Hilmarsson, "From Iceland—Q."
22. Joel Gunter, "'There Was Never an Average Day': James Ball on Being WikiLeaks' In-house Journalist," journalism.co.uk, January 31, 2011.
23. Pall Hilmarsson, "From Iceland—Q."

24. Ed Pilkington, "Icelandic MP Who Released WikiLeaks Video Plans US Visit Despite Legal Threat," *The Guardian*, February 11, 2013.

25. Dana Liebelson, "Meet the WikiLeaks Guy Who Got His Gmail Seized by the Feds," *Mother Jones*, June 25, 2013.

26. *US v. Assange, Second Superseding Indictment*, Zachary Terwilliger, Tracy Doherty-McCormick, Kellen S. Dwyer, Thomas W. Traxler, Gordon Kromberg, Alexander P. Berrang, June 24, 2020.

27. Ibid.

28. Ibid.

29. Dell Cameron, "How an FBI Informant Orchestrated the Stratfor Hack," *Daily Dot*, May 31, 2021.

30. *US v. Jeremy Hammond, Sealed Complaint*, Milan Patel, June 24, 2020.

31. Gabriella Coleman, *Hacker, Hoaxer, Whistleblower, Spy: The Many Faces of Anonymous* (London: Verso, 2014), 345–46.

32. Ed Pilkington, "Jeremy Hammond: FBI Directed My Attacks on Foreign Government Sites," *The Guardian*, November 15, 2013.

33. "Targets Supplied by FBI to Jeremy Hammond," Guest, November 15, 2013, testimony published without Hammond's permission.

34. Ibid.

35. Ibid.

36. *Extradition Hearing, Before Westminster Magistrates' Court, Second Statement*, Gareth Peirce Lawyer, Birnberg Pierce & Partners, 2020.

37. Ibid.

38. Extradition Hearing, Before Westminster Magistrates' Court, Second Statement. (Peirce)

39. Ibid.

40. Bjartmar Oddur Þeyr Alexandersson and Gunnar Hrafn Jónsson, "Key Witness in Assange Case Admits to Lies in Indictment," *Stundin*, June 26, 2021.

41. Ibid.

42. Ibid.

43. Ibid.

44. Bjartmar Oddur Þeyr Alexandersson and Gunnar Hrafn Jónsson, "Key Witness in Assange Case Jailed in Iceland after Admitting to Lies and Ongoing Crime Spree," *Stundin*, October 6, 2021.

CHAPTER 8: THE ABUSIVE GRAND JURY

1. Charlie Savage, "Disclosing Subpoena for Testimony, Chelsea Manning Vows to Fight," *New York Times*, February 28, 2019.

2. Ibid.

3. Kevin Gosztola, "Chelsea Manning Risks Jail to Fight WikiLeaks Grand Jury," Shadowproof, March 7, 2019.

4. Kevin Gosztola, "Defying WikiLeaks Grand Jury, Chelsea Manning Carries On Tradition of Resistance and Goes to Jail," Shadowproof, March 8, 2019.

5. Mark Kadish, "Behind the Locked Door of an American Grand Jury: Its History, Its Secrecy, and Its Process," *Florida State University Law Review* 24, no. 1 (1996).
6. *Extradition Hearing, Before Westminster Magistrates' Court*, Robert Boyle, attorney, 2020.
7. Michael E. Deutsch, "The Improper Use of the Federal Grand Jury: An Instrument for the Internment of Political Activists," *Journal of Criminal Law & Criminology*, Winter 1984.
8. Ibid.
9. Extradition Hearing, Before Westminster Magistrates' Court, Boyle, 2020.
10. Kevin Gosztola, "Revisiting The FBI's 2010 Raids Against Political Activists," The Dissenter, October 24, 2019.
11. US Department of Justice, "Investment Fraud Operation," C-SPAN video, 22:00, December 6, 2010.
12. Charlie Savage, "U.S. Tries To Build Case for Conspiracy by WikiLeaks," *New York Times*, December 15, 2010.
13. Ryan Singel, "Key Lawmakers Up Pressure on WikiLeaks and Defend Visa and Mastercard," *Wired*, December 9, 2010.
14. Charles Arthur and Josh Halliday, "WikiLeaks Fights to Stay Online after US Company Withdraws Domain Name," *The Guardian,* December 3, 2010.
15. "PayPal Says It Stopped WikiLeaks Payments on US Letter," BBC, December 8, 2010.
16. WikiLeaks, "PayPal Freezes WikiLeaks Donations," Press Release, December 4, 2010.
17. Andy Greenberg, "Visa, MasterCard Move to Choke WikiLeaks," *Forbes*, December 7, 2010.
18. Darlene Storm, "Bank of America Using Three Intelligence Firms to Attack WikiLeaks," Computerworld, February 9, 2011.
19. "Apple Removes iPhone WikiLeaks App from iTunes," BBC, December 22, 2010.
20. "Twitter WikiLeaks Court Order," ACLU, January 25, 2013.
21. Michael Ratner and Margaret Ratner-Kunstler, "WikiLeaks: Letter to Google," Center for Constitutional Rights, January 26, 2015.
22. Ibid.
23. Ed Pilkington and Dominic Rushe, "WikiLeaks Demands Answers after Google Hands Staff Emails to US Government," *The Guardian*, January 25, 2015.
24. Eric Schmitt and David E. Sanger, "Gates Cites Peril in Leak of Afghan War Logs by WikiLeaks," *New York Times*, August 1, 2010.
25. Ibid.
26. Amy Goodman, interview with David House, "Exclusive: David House on Bradley Manning, Secret WikiLeaks Grand Jury, and U.S. Surveillance," *Democracy Now!*, July 11, 2011.

27. Kevin Gosztola, "Documents: Why Homeland Security Agents Seized Manning Support Network Co-Founder's Electronic Devices," Shadowproof, September 10, 2013.

28. *House v. Napolitano, Settlement Agreement*, May 20, 2013.

29. Goodman, "Exclusive: David House on Bradley Manning, Secret WikiLeaks Grand Jury, and U.S. Surveillance," *Democracy Now!*

30. Alexa O'Brien, "Witness Profile, David House," June 15, 2011.

31. Katie Benner and Scott Shane, "Justice Dept. Investigated WikiLeaks After Secretly Indicting Assange," *New York Times*, April 16, 2019.

32. Kim Zetter, "The Man Who Made the Mistake of Trying to Help WikiLeaks," Vice, May 23, 2017.

33. Ibid.

34. Sari Horowitz, "Julian Assange Unlikely to Face U.S. Charges over Publishing Classified Documents," *Washington Post*, November 25, 2013.

35. Seda Serdar and Ana Maria Roura, "Julian Assange Faces Extradition Hearing as Berlin Stays Quiet," *Deutsche Welle*, May 1, 2019.

36. Thomas Brewster, "Did a Copy and Paste Error Just Reveal U.S. Charges Against Julian Assange?" *Forbes*, November 16, 2018.

37. "Subpoena in Inquiry on Pentagon Papers Withdrawn by U.S.," *New York Times*, January 18, 1972.

38. Bill Kovach, "Harvard Professor Jailed in Pentagon Papers Case," *New York Times*, November 22, 1972.

39. Allison Trzop, "Beacon Press and the Pentagon Papers," Master's Project, Emerson College, May 2006, p. 41.

40. Trevor Timm, "Appeals Court Says that Nixon's Attempt to Prosecute Pentagon Papers Reporter Must Stay Secret—50 Years Later," Freedom of the Press Foundation, March 3, 2022.

41. Trzop, "Beacon Press and the Pentagon Papers," 31–32.

42. Camille Fassett, "Chelsea Manning Could Be Jailed Again Today," Freedom of the Press Foundation, May 16, 2019.

43. Chelsea Manning, *Letter to Judge Anthony Trenga*, May 28, 2019.

44. Kevin Gosztola, "Chelsea Manning Faces More Jail and Steep Fines to Force Compliance with Grand Jury Subpoena," Shadowproof, May 16, 2019.

45. Jeremy Hammond Support Committee, "Imprisoned Activist Jeremy Hammond Called Against His Will to Testify Before Federal Grand Jury in the EDVA," Press Release, Sparrow Media, September 3, 2019.

46. Free Jeremy Hammond Network, Twitter Post, November 17, 2020, 6:29 p.m.

47. Alexa O'Brien, "Bradley Manning's Personal Statement to Court-martial: Full Text," *The Guardian*, March 1, 2013.

CHAPTER 9: RETALIATION FOR EXPOSING TORTURE,
RENDITION, AND WAR CRIMES

1. WikiLeaks, "Julian Assange's Speech/Stop the War Coalition," YouTube video, October 10, 2011.
2. Idrees Ali, Jonathan Landay and Steve Holland, "America's Longest War: 20 Years of Missteps in Afghanistan," Reuters, August 16, 2021.
3. Barack Obama, "Remarks by the President at the Veterans of Foreign Wars Convention" transcript of speech delivered at Phoenix Convention Center, August 17, 2009.
4. Peter Baker, "Could Afghanistan Become Obama's Vietnam?" *New York Times*, August 22, 2009.
5. Eric Schmitt and Helene Cooper, "Leaks Add to Pressure on White House Over Strategy," *New York Times*, July 26, 2010.
6. Nick Davies and David Leigh, "Afghanistan War Logs: Massive Leak of Secret Files Exposes Truth of Occupation," *The Guardian*, July 25, 2010.
7. Ibid.
8. David Leigh, "Afghanistan War Logs: Secret CIA Paramilitaries' Role in Civilian Deaths," *The Guardian*, July 25, 2010.
9. Nick Davies, "Afghanistan War Logs: Task Force 373—Special Forces Hunting Top Taliban," *The Guardian*, July 25, 2010.
10. Ibid.
11. Ibid.
12. Margaret Besheer, "Humanitarians Fear Afghan Hunger Crisis Could Kill More Than War," *Voice of America News*, February 14, 2022.
13. Extradition Hearing, Before Westminster Magistrates' Court, Patrick Cockburn, The Independent, 2020.
14. Ibid.
15. Extradition Hearing, Before Westminster Magistrates' Court, John Sloboda, Iraq Body Count, July 17, 2020.
16. "BBC-Guardian Exposé Uses WikiLeaks to Link Iraq Torture Centers to U.S. Col. Steele & Gen. Petraeus," *Democracy Now!* March 22, 2013.
17. Nick Davies, "Iraq War Logs: Secret Order that Let US Ignore Abuse," *The Guardian*, October 22, 2010.
18. Ibid.
19. Ibid.
20. David Leigh and Maggie O'Kane, "Iraq War Logs: US Turned Over Captives to Iraqi Torture Squads," *The Guardian*, October 24, 2010.
21. "Allegations of Prisoner Abuse by US Troops After Abu Ghraib," Bureau of Investigative Journalism, May 23, 2011.
22. Kris Jepson, "Iraq's Secret War Logs: Iraqi Torture," Channel 4, October 22, 2010.
23. Mona Mahmood, Maggie O'Kane, Chavala Madlena, and Teresa Smith, "Revealed: Pentagon's Link to Iraqi Torture Centers," *The Guardian,* March 6, 2013.

24. Geoff Morrell, "The Defense Department's Response," *New York Times*, October 22, 2010.
25. Ibid.
26. "Establishing a New Normal: National Security, Civil Liberties, and Human Rights Under the Obama Administration," American Civil Liberties Union, July 2010.
27. Ibid.
28. US Embassy Madrid, Spain, "Spain: Prosecutor Weighs GTMO Criminal Case Vs. Former USG Officials," April 1, 2009.
29. Ibid.
30. US Embassy Madrid, Spain, "Garzon Opens Second Investigation into Alleged U.S. Torture of Terrorism Detainees," May 5, 2009.
31. International Commission of Jurists, "The ICJ Condemns the Conviction of Judge Baltasar Garzón to an 11-Year Ban from the Office," Press Release, February 10, 2012.
32. Giles Tremlett, "Julian Assange Defense to Be Led by Spanish Jurist Baltasar Garzón," *The Guardian*, July 25, 2012.
33. US Embassy Rome, Italy, "Followup: GOI Seeks USG Response on Legal Assistance Cases," February 22, 2006.
34. US Embassy Rome, Italy, "Italy: New Undersecretary to the PM Calls Relationship with US 'Essential;' Says Italy Will Be Supportive on Israel, Will Stick With EU on Iran," May 24, 2006.
35. US Embassy Rome, Italy "Italy: The Dogs Bark, and the Prodi Caravan Moves On," August 31, 2006.
36. US Embassy Rome, Italy, "SecDef Meeting with Italian Minister of Defense Ignacio La Russa on February 6, 2010," February 12, 2010.
37. *Extradition Hearing, Before Westminster Magistrates' Court*, Stefania Maurizi, Il Fatto Quotidiano, 2020.
38. *Extradition Hearing, Before Westminster Magistrates' Court*, Khaled el Masri, 2020.
39. Ibid.
40. *Extradition Hearing, Before Westminster Magistrates' Court*, John Goetz, Norddeutscher Rundfunk, 2020.
41. Matthias Gebauer and John Goetz, "Cables Show Germany Caved to Pressure from Washington," Spiegel International, December 9, 2010.
42. Ibid.
43. *Extradition Hearing, Before Westminster Magistrates' Court*, Andy Worthington, journalist, 2020.
44. Ian Cobain, "Guantánamo Bay Files: Al-Jazeera Cameraman Held for Six Years," *The Guardian*, April 25, 2011.
45. Department of Defense, Joint Task Force Guantánamo, Naqib Ullah, August 23, 2003.
46. Ibid.
47. Michael Busch, "WikiLeaks: Juveniles at Gitmo Didn't Come From 'A Little-League Team,'" *Foreign Policy in Focus*, May 1, 2011.

48. United Nations Geneva, Switzerland, "Communication From SRS On ESA Executions Regarding An MNF Raid In Iraq On March 15, 2006," April 3, 2006.
49. Ibid.
50. Ibid.
51. "Cable Ties U.S. to Iraq Atrocity," *Columbus Dispatch,* September 1, 2011.
52. Ibid.
53. "Obama: Iraq War Will Be Over by Year's End; Troops Coming Home," CNN, October 21, 2011.
54. *Extradition Hearing, Before Westminster Magistrates' Court*, Noam Chomsky, professor, September 30, 2020.

CHAPTER 10: US PRISONS AND TRUTH-TELLERS

1. *US v. Assange, Judgment*, District Judge Vanessa Baraitser, January 4, 2021.
2. *US v. Assange Judgment*, Chief Justice Ian Burnett, December 10, 2021.
3. Christie Thompson and Taylor Elizabeth Eldridge, "Treatment Denied: The Mental Health Crisis in Federal Prisons," The Marshall Project, November 21, 2018.
4. Richard Medhurst, "Classified Documents Invalidate United States' Appeal Against Assange," Richard Medhurst's Newsletter, November 28, 2021.
5. Kevin Gosztola, "US Justice Department Tries to Stifle Alleged WikiLeaks Source's Challenge to Cruel Confinement," Shadowproof, January 29, 2021.
6. "Controversial Manhattan Jail MCC Set to Close, U.S. Dept. of Justice Says," Associated Press, August 26, 2021.
7. Kevin Gosztola, "Drone Whistleblower Daniel Hale Imprisoned in Communications Management Unit Designed for Terrorists," The Dissenter, October 18, 2021.
8. *Extradition Hearing, Before Westminster Magistrates' Court*, Joel Sickler, Justice Advocacy Group, June 20, 2020.
9. "Disqualified Inmates and First Step Act Time Credits," Zoukis Consulting Group, undated [accessed on June 6, 2022].
10. Kevin Gosztola, "Appeals Court Agrees Reality Winner 'Hates' America—So She Will Remain in Pretrial Detention," Shadowproof, February 1, 2018.
11. "Episode #87: Reality Winner," *A Song Called Life* (podcast), August 25, 2022.
12. Ibid.
13. Kevin Gosztola, "Reality Winner's Sentence: The Culmination of an Effort to Break a Whistleblower's Spirit," Shadowproof, August 21, 2018.
14. Gosztola, "Appeals Court Agrees Reality Winner 'Hates' America."
15. Ibid.
16. "Reality's Reality (Part 2): Surviving the System," *This Is Reality* (podcast), February 9, 2022.
17. Kevin Gosztola, "Reality Winner Claims Bureau of Prisons Is Mishandling Classified Information by Sharing with Guards," Shadowproof, October 6, 2018.

18. Department of Justice, US Attorney's Office, Southern District of Georgia, "Statement from U.S. Attorney Bobby L. Christine Regarding Sentencing for Reality Winner," Press Release, August 23, 2018.
19. Kevin Gosztola, "CIA Whistleblower John Kiriakou Was Marked Dangerous after BOP Categorized His Crime as 'Espionage-Related,'" Shadowproof, August 7, 2014.
20. Ibid.
21. Kevin Gosztola, "Bureau of Prisons Considers CIA Whistleblower John Kiriakou's 'Letters from Loretto' on Firedoglake to Be Dangerous," Shadowproof, January 27, 2014.
22. Ibid.
23. Kevin Gosztola, "Bureau of Prisons Contends CIA Whistleblower Jeffrey Sterling Is Lying About Heart Problems," Shadowproof, September 28, 2016.
24. Ibid.
25. Kevin Gosztola, "Imprisoned CIA Whistleblower Jeffrey Sterling Put in Solitary After Officer Threatened Him," Shadowproof, April 29, 2017.
26. Ibid.
27. Stella Moris, "Julian Assange's Wife Stella Moris Reveals How They Raise Children Together While He Is in Jail Waiting an Extradition Decision," Australia Broadcasting Corporation News Online, June 7, 2022.
28. Ben Quinn, "Julian Assange Marries Stella Moris in London Prison Ceremony," *The Guardian*, March 24, 2022.
29. Moris, "Julian Assange's Wife Stella Moris Reveals How They Raise Children Together."
30. Kevin Gosztola, "'Essentially Dead': Doctor Who Visited Assange in Ecuador Embassy Testifies at Extradition Trial," The Dissenter, September 24, 2020.
31. Kevin Gosztola, "Doctor Diagnosed Julian Assange with Asperger's Syndrome," The Dissenter, September 23, 2020.
32. Kevin Gosztola, "Federal Judge Orders Chelsea Manning's Release from Jail," Shadowproof, March 12, 2020.
33. *US v. Assange, Judgment*, Baraitser.

CHAPTER 11: STANDARD NEWS-GATHERING PRACTICES

1. *Closing Submissions On Behalf of the United States of America*, James Lewis QC, Clair Dobbin, Joel Smith, November 20, 2020.
2. Sari Horowitz, "Julian Assange Unlikely to Face U.S. Charges over Publishing Classified Documents," *Washington Post*, November 25, 2013.
3. *Extradition Hearing, Before Westminster Magistrates' Court*, Trevor Timm, Freedom of the Press Foundation, 2020.
4. *Extradition Hearing, Before Westminster Magistrates' Court*, Stefania Maurizi, Il Fatto Quotidiano, 2020.
5. *Extradition Hearing, Before Westminster Magistrates' Court*, Mark Feldstein, University of Maryland, 2020.
6. Ibid.

7. Ibid.
8. Betty Medsger, Investigating Power, undated [accessed on June 6, 2022].
9. *Extradition Hearing, Before Westminster Magistrates' Court*, Jameel Jaffer, Knight First Amendment Institute, 2020.
10. *Extradition Hearing, Before Westminster Magistrates' Court*, Maurizi, 2020.
11. *Extradition Hearing, Before Westminster Magistrates' Court*, Nicky Hager, journalist, 2020.
12. Ibid.
13. *Extradition Hearing, Before Westminster Magistrates' Court*, John Goetz, Norddeutscher Rundfunk, 2020.
14. Ibid.
15. Ibid.
16. Ibid.
17. *Extradition Hearing, Westminster Magistrate's Court*, Carey Shenkman, Law Office of Carey Shenkman, 2020.
18. Ibid.
19. Ibid.
20. See Chapter 8, The Abusive Grand Jury, for more details.
21. Alison Frankel, "Newly Released Memos Show DOJ Weighed Prosecuting Newspapers in Pentagon Papers Case," Reuters, June 8, 2022.
22. Ibid.
23. Michael Isikoff, "Nixon Plot Against Newspaper Columnist Detailed," NBC News, September 13, 2010.
24. Mark Feldstein, *Poisoning the Press: Richard Nixon, Jack Anderson, and the Rise of Washington's Scandal Culture* (New York: Farrar, Straus and Giroux, 2010), 3-4.
25. Lowell Bergman and Marlena Telvick, "Dick Cheney's Memos from 30 Years Ago, PBS *Frontline*, February 13, 2007.
26. Emma North-Best, "NSA Wanted to Use the Espionage Act to Prosecute a Journalist for Using FOIA," Muckrock, October 24, 2017.
27. Philip Shenon, "Casey Said to Consider Prosecuting Publications," *New York Times*, May 7, 1986.
28. Kevin Gosztola, "Good Ellsberg, Bad Assange: At Extradition Trial, Pentagon Papers Whistleblower Dismantles False Narrative," The Dissenter, September 16, 2020.
29. Ibid.
30. Ibid.

CHAPTER 12: PRESTIGE MEDIA AID AND ABET THE PROSECUTION

1. David Leigh, "WikiLeaks 'Has Blood on Its Hands' over Afghan War Logs, Claim US Officials," *The Guardian*, July 30, 2010.
2. "Piecing Together the Reports, and Deciding What to Publish," *New York Times*, July 25, 2010.

3. Robert Mackey, "Taliban Study WikiLeaks to Hunt Informants," *New York Times*, July 30, 2010.

4. Robert Gates, Letter to Carl Levin, August 16, 2010, accessible online at Scribd.com.

5. Jonathan Miller, "Taliban Hunt WikiLeaks Outed Afghan Informers," Channel 4, July 30, 2010.

6. Bill Keller, "Dealing With Assange and the WikiLeaks Secrets," *New York Times Magazine*, January 26, 2011.

7. Gates, Letter to Carl Levin.

8. *Extradition Hearing Before Westminster Magistrates' Court*, John Goetz, Norddeutscher Rundfunk, 2020.

9. Ibid.

10. David Batty, "Pentagon Increases Pressure on WikiLeaks to Return Military Files," *The Guardian*, August 5, 2010.

11. James Ball, "WikiLeaks Publishes Full Cache of Unredacted Cables," *The Guardian*, September 2, 2011.

12. *US v. Assange, Judgment, District Judge Vanessa Baraitser*, January 4, 2021.

13. Ball, "WikiLeaks Publishes Full Cache of Unredacted Cables."

14. *Extradition Hearing, Before Westminster Magistrates' Court*, John Goetz.

15. *US v. Julian Assange, Defense Closing Submissions*, November 6, 2020.

16. WikiLeaks, "Guardian Journalist Negligently Disclosed Cablegate Passwords," Press Release, September 1, 2011.

17. Paul Marks, "Assange: Why WikiLeaks Was Right to Release Raw Cables," *New Scientist*, September 6, 2011.

18. Joel Gunter, "#cablegate: NYT Cut Out by WikiLeaks, Forced to Obtain Cables from the Guardian,'" Journalism.co.uk, November 29, 2010.

19. José María Irujo, "Spanish Security Company Spied on Julian Assange's Meetings with Lawyers," *El País*, July 9, 2019.

20. Marshall Cohen, Kay Guerrero, and Arturo Torres, "Exclusive: Security Reports Reveal How Assange Turned an Embassy into a Command for Election Meddling," CNN, July 15, 2019.

21. Irujo, "Spanish Security Company Spied on Julian Assange's Meetings with Lawyers."

22. Cohen, Guerrero, and Torres, "Exclusive: Security Reports Reveal How Assange Turned an Embassy into a Command for Election Meddling."

23. Martin Knobbe and Michael Sontheimer, "'Everything Was Done to Make Julian Assange's Life Miserable,'" Spiegel International, May 3, 2019.

24. Frida Ghitis, "Julian Assange Is an Activist, Not a Journalist," CNN, April 12, 2019.

CHAPTER 13: RUSSIAGATE AND WIKILEAKS

1. "About World Tomorrow," WikiLeaks, 2012.

2. Mark Mazzetti and Julian E. Barnes, "After Arrest of Assange, the Russian Mysteries Remain," *New York Times*, April 11, 2019.

3. Ibid.
4. Tessa Berenson, "Why the Charge Against Julian Assange Makes No Mention of Espionage or 2016 Russian Hacking," *Time*, April 11, 2019.
5. Tom Porter, "Democrats Accuse Assange of Being a Tool for Russian Intelligence, but It Remains Unclear If He'll Face Charges over Publishing Hacked DNC Emails," Business Insider, April 12, 2019.
6. Mark Warner, Twitter Post, April 11, 2019, 9:47 a.m.
7. Chuck Schumer, Twitter Post, April 11, 2019, 1:11 p.m.
8. Veronica Stracqualursi, "Democratic Sen. Joe Manchin on Assange's Arrest: 'He's Our Property,'" CNN, April 11, 2019.
9. Shimon Prokupecz, Samantha Vinograd, and Steve Vladeck, "Julian Assange Arrested in London," *At This Hour*, CNN, April 11, 2019.
10. Ibid.
11. Ibid.
12. Evan Perez and Isa Soares, "WikiLeaks Founder Julian Assange in Court after Arrest," CNN, April 11, 2019.
13. Susan Glasser, Jim Sciutto, and Jeffrey Toobin, "Julian Assange Expelled From Ecuadorian Embassy on Extradition Warrant from US," CNN, April 11, 2019.
14. Gerald Connolly, "CNN 'The Situation Room' Interview with Rep. Gerry Connolly (D-VA)," *The Situation Room* (CNN), April 11, 2019.
15. Ibid.
16. Ibid.
17. Kristinn Hrafnsson, "Current WikiLeaks Editor Discusses Assange's Arrest," CNN, April 11, 2019.
18. Ibid.
19. Ibid.
20. Ibid.
21. Jennifer Palmieri, Twitter Post, November 6, 2016, 7:59 a.m.
22. Kevin Gosztola, "Clinton Campaign Makes Wildly Inconsistent Claims About Emails Published by WikiLeaks," Shadowproof, October 20, 2016.
23. Lauren Carroll, "Are the Clinton WikiLeaks Emails Doctored, or Are They Authentic?" Politifact, October 23, 2016.
24. Kevin Gosztola, "The Podesta Emails Revelations: A Collection," Shadowproof, October 17, 2016 (updated November 6, 2016).
25. Kevin Gosztola, "Assange Criticizes U.S. Effort to Conflate WikiLeaks Publications with Russian Hacking," Shadowproof, January 9, 2017.
26. John Solomon, "How Comey Intervened to Kill WikiLeaks' Immunity Deal," The Hill, June 25, 2018.
27. Jason Leopold and Ken Bensinger, "New: Mueller Investigated Julian Assange, WikiLeaks, and Roger Stone for DNC Hacks," BuzzFeed News, November 2, 2020.
28. Ibid.
29. WikiLeaks, Twitter Post, February 15, 2019, 8:30 p.m.
30. MSNBC, Twitter Post, May 8, 2018, 11:56 a.m.

31. Neera Tanden, Twitter Post, July 13, 2018, 11:27 a.m.
32. Orion Rummler, "What They're Saying: Lawmakers, Press Activists React to Assange Arrest," Axios, April 11, 2019.
33. Dan Mangan, Kevin Breuninger, and Christina Wilkie, "Trump Offered Wikileaks' Julian Assange a Pardon if He Covered up Russian Hacking of Democrats, Lawyer Tells Court," CNBC, February 19, 2020.
34. Julian Borger and Owen Bowcott, "Donald Trump 'Offered Julian Assange a Pardon if He Denied Russia Link to Hack,'" *The Guardian*, February 19, 2020.
35. Michael Isikoff, "Rohrabacher Confirms He Offered Trump Pardon to Assange for Proof Russia Didn't Hack DNC Email," Yahoo News, February 20, 2020.
36. *Extradition Hearing, Westminster Magistrate's Court*, statement of Jennifer Robinson, Doughty Street Chambers, 2020.
37. Kaitlan Collins, Kevin Liptak and Pamela Brown, "Trump Talked Out of Pardoning Kids and Republican Lawmakers," CNN, January 19, 2021.
38. Kevin Gosztola, "In Rejecting DNC Lawsuit Against WikiLeaks, Judge Strongly Defended First Amendment Rights of Journalists," Shadowproof, August 1, 2019.
39. Ibid.
40. Ibid.
41. Ibid.
42. Kevin Gosztola, "The DNC May Have Paved the Way for Julian Assange's Acquittal," Shadowproof, February 23, 2020.

CONCLUSION

1. Parker Higgins, "Press Freedom Coalition Calls for End to Assange Prosecution, after Shocking Reporting on CIA Misconduct," Freedom of the Press Foundation, October 18, 2021.
2. "Free Assange Now!" International Federation of Journalists, undated [accessed August 11, 2022].
3. Ben Knight, "German MPs Demand Release of Julian Assange," *Deutsche Welle*, July 7, 2022.
4. International Peoples' Assembly, "Progressive Leaders Call on US President Biden to Drop the Charges Against Assange," Press Release, April 11, 2022.
5. Elías Camhaji, "López Obrador to Campaign to 'Tear Down the Statue of Liberty' If the US Convicts Julian Assange," *El País*, July 5, 2022.
6. Kevin Gosztola, "Patel Responsible for 'Slow-Motion Execution' If Extradited, Doctors Warn," The Dissenter, June 13, 2022.
7. *Secretary Antony J. Blinken at a Youth Moderated Discussion on Democracy and Human Rights*, State Department transcript, June 25, 2021.
8. "Press Freedoms: Criminalizing Journalistic Activity," *New York Times*, September 2019.
9. See Chapter 4, The Espionage Act, for further details.

10. Philip Taubman, "New Bills Set Rules on Classified Trials," *New York Times*, July 12, 1979.
11. Bill Richards, "Sen. Biden Says U.S. Lost an Entire Spy Network," *Washington Post*, January 13, 1978.
12. Ewen MacAskill, "WikiLeaks Website Pulled by Amazon after US Political Pressure," *The Guardian*, December 1, 2010.
13. Kathryn Watson, "How Did Wikileaks Become Associated with Russia?" CBS News, November 15, 2017.
14. Michael Barbaro, "The Moral Complexities of Working with Julian Assange," *The Daily* (podcast), April 15, 2019.
15. Jack Shafer, "The Art of Printing Secrets," Slate, August 3, 2010.
16. Dean Baquet and Bill Keller, "When Do We Publish a Secret?" *New York Times*, July 1, 2006.
17. Margaret Sullivan, "The Times Was Right to Report—at Last—on a Secret Drone Base," *New York Times*, February 6, 2013.
18. Dana Priest, "CIA Holds Terror Suspects in Secret Prisons," *Washington Post*, November 2, 2005.
19. Declan Walsh and Ewan MacAskill, "American Who Sparked Diplomatic Crisis over Lahore Shooting Was CIA Spy," *The Guardian*, February 20, 2011.
20. "From the Editors: The Times and Iraq," *New York Times*, May 26, 2004.
21. New York Times (Jo Becker), "Julian Assange Is Live with the New York Times," video, August 31, 2016.
22. Ibid.
23. Ibid.
24. Ibid.
25. Jo Becker, Steven Erlanger, and Eric Schmitt, "How Russia Often Benefits When Julian Assange Reveals the West's Secrets," *New York Times*, August 31, 2016.
26. Kevin Gosztola, "In Rejecting DNC Lawsuit Against WikiLeaks, Judge Strongly Defended First Amendment Rights of Journalists," Shadowproof, August 1, 2019.
27. "Dr. Kavita Patel Joins NewsGuard's Global Advisory Board," NewsGuard, October 1, 2020.
28. Joe Lauria, "'Mistaken' PayPal Email Means CN Is Permanently Banned," Consortium News, May 6, 2022.
29. US Senator for California Dianne Feinstein, "Senators Demand Briefing from Pompeo on Julian Assange's Presence in Ecuadorian Embassy," Press Release, December 12, 2018.
30. Kevin Gosztola, "Media Shield Law, Which Aims to Protect Only 'Real Reporters,' Moves Onward to the Senate," Shadowproof, September 12, 2013.
31. Ibid.
32. "A Statement from the Pulitzer Prize Board," Pulitzer Prize Board, July 17, 2022.

INDEX

Abu Zubaydah, 72, 161
ACIC. *See* Army Counterintelligence
    Center
ACLU. *See* American Civil Liberties
    Union
ADC. *See* Alexandria Detention Center
Addington, David, 156
Adelson, Sheldon, 98
Adkins, David, 38
Administrative Maximum Facility
    (ADX) Florence, 167–68
Afghanistan War Logs, xiii, 22
    civilian casualties in, 149–50
    documents in, 24
    files withheld from, 201
    Manning and, 36–37
    New York Times on, 205
    publication of, 204
    return request for, 55
    Taliban and, 24
    Task Force 373 in, 150
    US military massacres revealed by,
        148–51
AIPAC. *See* American Israel Public
    Affairs Committee
Albury, Terry, 79–80
Alexandersson, Bjartmar, 112–13, 115,
    126–27
Alexandria Detention Center (ADC),
    185
Alexis, Aaron, 76

Ali, Ben, 257
Alston, Philip, 163–64
Alter, Jonathan, 1–2
American Civil Liberties Union (ACLU)
    FBI investigation into, 72
    House lawsuit by, 138
    Speech, Privacy, and Technology
        Project by, 29
    against torture programs, 155
American Israel Public Affairs
    Committee (AIPAC), 65
Amnesty International, 15–16
Anderson, Jack, 199
Anderson, Pamela, 104
Anderson Papers, 199
Anonymous, xii, 30–31
Appelbaum, Jacob, 33, 120, 136–37
Apple, 85, 135
AQAP. *See* al Qaeda in the Arabian
    Peninsula
Army Counterintelligence Center
    (ACIC)
    report by, 56–58
    on undermining of WikiLeaks, 58
    on WikiLeaks as intelligence source,
        56–57
Assange, Julian. *See also specific topics*
    Anonymous and, 30–31
    as arbitrarily detained, 95
    arrest of, 107, 125
    assurances for, 15–16, 168–69, 173